THE

PIONEERS, PREACHERS AND PEOPLE

OF THE

MISSISSIPPI VALLEY.

BY

WILLIAM HENRY MILBURN,

AUTHOR OF "THE RIFLE, AXE AND SADDLE-BAGS," AND "TEN YEARS OF PREACHER LIFE."

NEW YORK:
DERBY & JACKSON.
1860.

W. H. TINSON, Stereotyper.

GEO. RUSSELL & Co., Printers.

THIS BOOK

IS DEDICATED TO

FLETCHER HARPER, ESQ.,

WHO HAS BEEN

A TRUE FRIEND TO ME AND MINE

FOR MANY YEARS.

PREFACE.

It is now nearly two and twenty years since my father pitched his tent in Prairie-land. I was then a lad. The broad savannas, clad with flowers; the emerald groves, that seemed like islands of the deep; the Father of Waters; the Mother of Floods; the Beautiful River; the fierce, ostrich-like Piasau, whose outline on the bluffs of the Mississippi above Alton commemorates the Indian's dread of the terrible being: these soon took a strong hold of my imagination. From that day to this, the West has been to me a land half of dream and half of reality. To read and hear everything connected with its history became a passion.

I have sought in this book to set in order the results of this reading and hearing. It would be almost impossible for me to say what parts came to me from tradition and what from the written page.

Only I must be allowed to mention two books which have been particularly serviceable. The one is the work of my friend, Francis G. Parkman, Esq., the "History of the Conspiracy of Pontiac," one of the most picturesque and vivid books of history that has ever fallen in my way; the second is the work of another of my friends, Albert J. Pickett, Esq., the "History of Alabama," naive as it is entertaining.

I have sought to follow the pilgrimage of the plumed cavaliers of De Soto in their quest of the Great River, and the gold which they fondly hoped was to be found upon its banks; I have floated with Marquette in his bark canoe as he went upon his gentle embassy to the Indians; I have wandered with La Salle as he vainly strove to found a French Empire in the West, and mourned by the Texan grave of one of the most unfortunate but heroic of men; I have sat down with the kindly French in their Paradise of Kaskaskia, and enjoyed the spell of their idyllic life; I have trudged with our own pioneers, as with stout hearts they crossed the Cumberland Gap and entered the Dark and Bloody Ground; I have stood with them at their guns in their blockhouses, have slept on their raw-hide beds, and shared their jerked meat and "dodger;" and I have sought to appreciate the development of Saxon sense under the tuition of the wilderness, and to trace the schooling of the mind under the auspices of social life, in application to the needs of self-government. I have travelled the circuit with the first preachers, sat in the congregation as they expounded the doctrines of eternal life, and welcomed them for their works' sake; and last, I have summed up in a few words what has been done, since the acquisition of Louisiana in 1803, in the way of exploration and development, on the other side of the Great River.

To me it has been a pleasant labor; I hope that the reading will be as pleasant.

BROOKLYN, *February*, 1860.

CONTENTS.

LECTURE VI.

LECTURE VII.

LECTURE VIII.

LECTURE IX.

LECTURE X.

Lecture I.

DE SOTO.

DE SOTO.

The contrast is most striking between the Spaniard of to-day, and the Spaniard of three hundred years ago. Now, he is indolent, often apathetic, grave, reserved, and whatever his inward capacity of passion or of exertion, an inefficient and idle man. But in those old days, the Spanish race was filled and inspired with a wild and tireless fourfold energy of avarice, religion, ambition and adventure, which swept them round and round the world in a long resistless bloody storm of conquest, conversion and slaughter, gained them their vast colonial realms and wealth, and brought to pass a panorama of achievements, miseries, cruelties and crimes whose very representations, in the antique wood-cuts of De Bry, are horrible to look upon. Governor Galvano quaintly says, speaking of the craze which fell upon Spain in consequence of the early American discoveries, that they "were ready to leap into the sea to swim, if it had been possible, into those new-found parts."

There is no stronger or stranger exemplification of the steady obstinacy with which this insane chase after riches and glory was pursued than the long chapter of disastrous Spanish inroads upon the territory of the southern half of the United States, then called Florida, which took place between 1512 and the foundation of St. Augustine in 1565.

The earliest European name associated with the southern coast of the United States is that of Juan Ponce de Leon, a brave old warrior, whose early manhood had been passed in hunting the Moors from Granada and in acquiring that inflexibility of purpose and hardiness of character, which enabled him to play his distinguished part as a conqueror in the New World. Sailing with Columbus on his second voyage, spending most of his remaining life in the West Indies, subjugating Porto Rico, where he ruled with an iron sway as governor, superseded in his command, thirsting ever for gold and glory, and yearning for a renewed life in which to enjoy the fruits of his valor, he turned his prow to the northward, in search of the land where the crystal waters of the fountain of youth washed those yellow sands of price, the discovery and possession of which would give the happy voyager the realization of the twin dream of Alchemy—gold and immortality. Fables were the faith of the time. Why not? Could credulity cherish a wilder phantasy than the Genoese mariner's? Yet this had been fulfilled. Might not De Leon's, too? So the stout old cavalier took his way to the north. Aged Indians had told him that in that direction lay the objects of his search. His many fights had left him full of wounds and scars; age was bending his manly form, weakness was creeping on apace. No matter, for the Fountain shall give him immortal youth, and with it, health and beauty.

Land was made Palm Sunday—Pascua Florida—1512, near St. Augustine. Beautiful enough for the shore of the Immortals was this which now rose before his eyes, covered with rich greensward, dappled with flowers of unnumbered dyes, overshadowed by giant trees clad with summer leaves, glorious with a rainbow garniture of tropic blossoms, over which hung long pendulous veils as if of silver tissue—spectral veils like Mokanna's, hiding the hideous face of the swamp miasma—veils which a sad experience has taught men now to call the "Curtains of Death." Softly came the land breeze freighted with the breath of flowers, upon that triumphal Sabbath morning, and it came—so thought the Spaniard—straight from that fabled spring, and with the fever of excitement in his veins, and the throb of rapture at his heart, "Florida," he cried, "is it not the land of flowers!" In honor of the festival, and in honor of the blossom-clad coast, he named a name which it bears to this day.

But alas for the hopes of Ponce de Leon! It was

no morning land of immortality to him, save as the name he bestowed preserves for us and after-times the dim shadow of his antique renown. Upon his second voyage, a poisonous arrow from an Indian's bow brought him his message of doom. Hastening to Cuba, he breathed his last, leaving his Flower-land a fatal legacy to Spain for many a sad year to come.

In those old days of Spanish rule, there was but one step from the Quixotic to the Satanic, and that step was taken by Vasquez De Ayllon, the next adventurer whose keels furrowed the waves of our coast. This monster came for slaves to work the mines of the West Indies, where the atrocities of the Spaniards had in less than thirty years well-nigh exterminated a numerous and happy people.

Reaching the coast of South Carolina, De Ayllon entered a river, called, in honor of the captain who discovered it, the Jordan; known to us by its Indian name, the Cumbahee. Landing on a pleasant shore, which the natives called Chicora—Mocking-bird—they were hospitably welcomed and entertained. But the Christian white man's return for the red heathen's courtesy was betrayal, outrage, and death. Having laid in his supplies, De Ayllon invited the Indians aboard his vessels; an invitation gladly accepted by the unsuspecting red men. While crowds of them were below, the hatches were closed, all sail made, and away over the blue waters sped the winged monsters with their prey. But did not that wild, despairing cry from ship and shore, of husbands and wives, parents and children, thus ruthlessly torn from each other, reach the ear of God? He heard and he avenged. One of the ships foundered, and all on board perished. The remaining Indians refused food, and thus died. The aborigines of this country could not be reduced to slavery.

Again De Ayllon came with three vessels and many men to conquer Chicora. The natives masked their purpose of revenge, received him kindly, lulled his suspicions into fatal security, and he dreamed the goodly land already his own. They made a great feast for their guests some leagues in the interior. Two hundred of De Ayllon's men attended—he with a small party remaining to guard the ships. Three days the banquet lasted. The third night the Indians arose and smote their treacherous invaders and slew them, so that not one of the two hundred was left to tell the terrible tale to his companions on the beach. But the Indians themselves bore the tidings, for they fell upon the guard, killed some, and wounded others, so that but a handful reached their ships and bore away for St. Domingo. De Ayllon himself seems to have died, either of his wounds, or shame, or both, at the port in Chicora.

A few years later Pamphilo de Narvaez, in com

mand of a splendid armament, undertook the subjugation of Florida. At an earlier date he had been sent by the governor of Cuba to arrest the victorious progress of Hernan Cortez in Mexico. Losing an eye, and failing in the attempt, he was conducted to the presence of Cortez, whom he complimented by informing that he must be a remarkable man, as he had succeeded in vanquishing him. "That," replied the redoubtable conqueror of the Montezumas, "is the least thing I have done in Mexico."

Landing at Tampa Bay, 12th April, 1528, with four hundred men and forty-five horses, Narvaez immediately dispatched his vessels to Cuba for fresh supplies, paying no regard to the prudent entreaties of the treasurer of the expedition, Alvar Nuñez. They soon roused the relentless hostility of the valiant Seminoles by their gratuitous barbarities, and every rood of their toilsome march, through tangled forests and endless quagmires, was rendered doubly difficult by ambuscades and attacks. Inspirited, however, by the stories of some captives, acting as guides, to the effect that in Appalache they would find a fertile province, abounding with gold, the object of their eager quest, they urged their way onward. On reaching the land of promise, Narvaez, who had pictured to himself another Mexico, was bitterly undeceived, finding only a rude village of two hundred and fifty cabins. They took possession unopposed, for the inhabitants had fled to the woods. Twenty-five days were passed here; but the army, now more clamorous for bread than for gold, learning that the sea lay nine days' march to the southward, bent its weary steps toward the village of Aute, where, it was said, were plenty of provisions and a harmless people. Their path, however, was beset by yet greater natural obstacles, and by the implacable fury of the savages. At length reaching Aute, not far from the present St. Marks, they found the village burned by the retreating inhabitants, but esteemed the discovery of a plentiful supply of maize, ample compensation.

What was to be done? Their hopes of conquest and treasure were gone; to remain in the land was impossible; to traverse the shore in search of their ships might be fruitless, and would needlessly expose them to the sleepless ferocity of the Indians. Many of their horses were slain; so were not a few of their bravest companions.

A day's march brought them to the banks of the river, which widened into a bay. Here they resolved to build them such boats as they might, and in them seek their ships or attempt a return to Cuba. Right vigorously did they ply their work; and at length five frail barks were launched, in each of which on the 20th of September, 1528, were crowded from forty to fifty miserable souls: crowded so that the gunwales were almost even with the water. Thus along that tropic shore did they hope to coast in the season of storms. Narvaez, remaining one day in one of his boats with a sailor and a sick page as a guard, while his crew went ashore to pillage for food, was driven out to sea by a tempest and never heard of more. The only survivors of this ill-starred expedition were Alvar Nuñez and four companions, who, after incredible wanderings along the northern shore of the Gulf of Mexico, westward through Texas to the Rocky Mountains, and thence to Mexico, exposed to every species of hardship and peril—after passing from tribe to tribe of Indians, sometimes starved as slaves, sometimes, we may believe, worshipped as demi-gods, in 1537—nearly ten years from the time of their sailing, finally reached Spain.

Such experiences and failures might have caused reflection. The adventurous Spaniards even might have questioned themselves what would be the probable best result even of success. Old Governor Galvano, in his history of the discoveries of the world, says, with rare good sense for that day, "I cannot tell how it commeth to passe, except it be by the iust judgement of God, that of so much gold and precious stones as haue been gotten in the Antiles by so manny Spaniards, little or none remaineth, but the most part is spent and consumed, and no good thing done." It seems as if these chivalrous aspirants for wealth and glory must have observed the same. And if not, still the sad fate of the pioneers in Florida, one would think, were enough to dishearten and deter any who might thereafter dream of its exploration and conquest. Not so.

A little before this time, in 1537, there had appeared at the court of Charles V. a renowned captain, adorned with laurels from the conquest of Peru, and enriched by 180,000 golden crowns, his share of the plundered treasure of Atahualpa. A gentleman by four descents, and therefore entitled to membership of the noble order of Santiago, he had nevertheless commenced life as a private soldier of fortune; his sword and target his only possessions. And thus far fortune and deeds of prowess had won him great success. His lance was said to have been equal to any ten in the army of Pizarro. In the saddle his match was not to be found. Prudent in counsel as he was brave in the field, he was no less knightly in denouncing what he esteemed the wrong—boldly withstanding his commander to the face, and charging home upon him the wickedness as well as bad policy of the Inca's murder.

He was proud, determined and reserved; as the Portuguese narrator describes him, "a sterne man and of few words; though he was glad to sift and know the opinion of all men, yet after hee had delivered his owne hee would not be contraried." A recently published fac-simile of his signature, a large and strong autograph, as by a powerful hand more used to wield sword and spear than the pen of the writer, corresponds well with his stately and haughty character. Although not naturally liberal, he was profuse and magnificent in his expenditure in this his first appearance at court, and was attended by a troop of gallant knights who had fought under him in Peru, and had brought back each a fortune from the treasure of the Incas. Luis de Moscoso de Alvarado, John Danusco, and a long list of others, with names equally claiming attention, did their histories come within our design, spent their wealth, acquired in soldierly wise, upon soldier's luxuries, mettled barbs and splendid armor; but Hernando de Soto surpassed in magnificence all the courtiers of the Emperor. Only five and thirty years of age, tall, handsome, commanding in presence and action, was it marvellous that Donna Isabella de Bobadilla, though the daughter of the very earl under whose banner he had first enlisted in the ranks, one of the fairest ladies of Spain, of one of the proudest and most powerful families, should yield her heart to the irresistible soldier? So fortune and his merit won him his best—alas, that it was also his latest boon!—a loving, prudent and faithful wife.

And now could he not rest in that pleasant palace at Seville, and buy him cornfields and vineyards and olive plantations, and become a great lord? With houses and lands and servants, friends and honor, great connections and a good and noble wife, had he not wherewith to be content? But when did the lust of fame or power or gold ever allow a man to be content? Here they united their spells, and De Soto must find new worlds to conquer. Find them he did —but finding and conquering are two things. So he sought for and obtained the magnificent appointment of captain-general for life of Cuba, Adelantado (civil and military governor) of Florida; and a marquisate of thirty leagues by fifteen, in any part of the to-be-conquered country. He is to undertake the conquest at his own expense, and to pay to the crown one fifth of the treasure found.

And now comes the wonderful story of Alvar Nuñez Cabeça de Vaca, like an additional demoniac spell, to tempt this goodly knight. To be sure, the treasurer of Narvaez brought home no treasure; but he threw out dark hints of the great wealth of the land he had explored, and had indeed intended to apply for the very adelantadoship which De Soto had obtained. In default of this, he asked and received the government of La Plata.

The imagination of De Soto, and of Spain, took new fire.

The triumphs and trophies of Cortez and Pizarro shall be as nothing to his; for what are Mexico and

Peru to Florida! Poor Ponce de Leon! thy fatal legacy hath fallen to another heir!

Florida at that day embraced all the country lying north of Mexico, extending upon its eastern coast from Key West to the banks of Newfoundland; so that it embraced what we know as the United States of America. Need we be sad that it was a woeful heritage to the sons of Spain? This land was held in reserve for the scions of a nobler stock than Charles V. governed, and for a sublimer civilization than Castile and Arragon were able to bestow upon the world.

In fourteen months the armament is ready to weigh anchor. Nine hundred and fifty men, the best blood and chivalry of Spain, gay young knights thirsting for distinction and wealth, well tried warriors from the fields of Africa and Peru, stout men at arms, halberdiers, cross-bow men and arquebusiers —more have come than the general can take. Men have sold their patrimonial acres to furnish themselves for the campaign. Shall not every such receive a hundred fold? One disposed of 60,000 reals * of rent; one of a town of vassals; Baltasar de Gallegos, of "houses, and vineyards, and rent corne, and ninetie rankes of Olive trees in the Xarafe of Siuil." The usual difficulty in fitting out an expedi-

* Real, the Spanish silver coin, worth an eighth of a dollar.

tion to well-known and rich countries was to find men. De Soto, bound to an unknown wilderness, was unable to find vessels for the multitude of volunteers, and many of those who had sold their estates for the sake of joining him, unable to find room on board the fleet, were forced to stay behind.

Amid the braying of trumpets and the roar of artillery, the *vivas* of the beholders and the shouts of the campaigners, the fleet of ten sail left the port of San Lucar de Barrameda, April 6th, 1538. They reached Cuba about the last of May, and here De Soto spent a year in organizing the government, and making preparations for his enterprise.

Cuba was noted for its noble breed of horses, wherewith our gay cavaliers supplied themselves amply; and by way of putting themselves in trim for the work before them, spent much time in tournaments and bull-fights. The inhabitants of the island, well-nigh crazed by excitement and the brave show, flocked in throngs to the standard of De Soto. At their head was Don Vasco Porcallo de Figueroa, a doughty old warrior who had seen much severe service in many parts of the world, and had now settled down as a wealthy proprietor in the Queen of the Antilles. As the horse smelleth the battle from afar, so did this veteran. To show him due honor, the Adelantado appointed him his lieutenant general.

The Portuguese narrator states that Don Vasco's

object was not glory, but Indians; whom he desired to obtain in order to supply the places of those whom toil and cruelty had slain in his mines and upon his estates in Cuba. This purpose seems, at least, consonant with the character of a Spanish Cuban proprietor; and that his treatment of his slaves was such as to require reinforcements to their numbers, may appear from a quaint old story of his steward. This steward, it seems, discovered that certain of the Indian slaves, as was the sad custom of their race, had agreed to meet at an appointed place and kill themselves, to escape from their tormenting taskmasters. So he repaired with a cudgel to the rendezvous, and when the miserable heathen had assembled, suddenly stepped among them and told them that they could neither plan nor do anything which he did not know before; and that he had now come to kill himself with them, in order that, in the next world, he might treat them worse than in this. The poor wretches believed him, and returned quietly to their labor.

All things were at last settled, and leaving his noble wife Donna Isabel to govern the island, De Soto sailed from Havana, with mirthful pomp, May 18th, 1539. Already Juan de Añasco had made two cruises, to discover an harbor in which to land. A point was selected, and thither the fleet sailed. It consisted of eight large vessels, a caravel, and two brigantines, and contained a thousand men, besides the sailors. Whitsunday, May 25th, they made a convenient bay on the western or Gulf coast of Florida, which, in honor of the day, was named Espiritu Santo: it is now called Tampa Bay. No sooner had they neared the shore than bale-fires were seen blazing, far as the eye could reach: vast columns of black smoke ascending, in token that the Indians were preparing to receive them. Eight days were taken to sound the bay, and then the debarkation commenced. A slight skirmish, in which the natives were soon dispersed, was all that occurred to impede them.

A march of two leagues brought them to the deserted village of a chief named Hirrihigua, where, on the capture of some of the natives, De Soto was made acquainted with the horrible atrocities practised by his predecessor, Narvaez. That worthy having entered into solemn covenant with the cacique, suddenly became enraged, at what no one could tell, ordered the dogs to be let loose on the mother of Hirrihigua, who was soon torn to pieces, and then commanded the nose of the chief to be cut off. This brutality had implanted in the breast of the Seminole an undying hatred toward the Spaniard. To all of De Soto's overtures he returned at first disdain and then evasion. At this village, the stores for the campaign were landed, and at the gathering of the forces a strange medley did the muster show. A thousand knights and soldiers, twelve priests, eight other ecclesiastics, and four monks; workers in wood and iron, miners and assayers; then three hundred and fifty thorough-bred horses, three hundred hogs to stock the country, and packs of bloodhounds to hunt the natives. There were matchlocks and cross-bows, pikes, lances, and swords; one piece of ordnance; manacles and iron collars for their prisoners; and a store of baubles, as presents for those whom they might wish to propitiate. Wine, bread, and flour for the mass, were there; and, lastly, cards for gambling—which, by the way, was carried to excess, men often losing the last article they possessed. Stately knights, clad *cap-à-pie* in burnished armor, bestrode their prancing steeds, while all the commonalty were well protected with breast-plates, bucklers, and helmets. There had been no stint of money to supply all that experience could suggest or that taste could hint as necessaries or luxuries in the enterprise of conquest and colonization.

Rumors having reached the camp that a Spaniard was living in a neighboring village, Baltazar Gallegos, a dauntless officer, was dispatched at the head of sixty horsemen to secure him for an interpreter and guide. As Baltazar and his troopers were rapidly pushing on, they espied a company of Indians on the verge of a plain. The Spaniards, anxious for a brush with the natives, manœuvred to attack them; but all save two fled to the forest. One of these two was wounded; the other, at whom Alvaro Nieto, one of the boldest troopers, was spurring, danced from side to side, seeking to parry Nieto's thrust with his bow, shouting the while, "Seville, Seville!" hearing which, the trooper cried, "Is your name Juan Ortiz?" "Yes," was the reply. Reining up his horse, Alvaro caught the other by the arm, raised him to the croup of his saddle, and hurried in triumph to Baltazar.

The story of Ortiz deserves a brief recital. Born at Seville, "of worshipful parentage," he had joined the expedition of Narvaez, had returned to Cuba with his vessels, and had accompanied the expedition which, ten years before, had put in at the bay of Espiritu Santo, in search of his commander. It was not long after the departure of that barbarian, and while Hirrihigua was in the agony of his recent wrongs, that, as the expedition was coasting along the shore, a few Indians appeared, pointing to a letter in a cleft reed, evidently left by Narvaez. The Spanirads invited them to bring it aboard. This they refused; but four of them, entering a canoe, came off as hostages for any of the crew who might go to fetch it. Four of the whites accordingly landed, and were instantly set upon by a crowd of savages who had been concealed in the thicket. The four hostages sprang into the sea, and swam ashore. The crew, anticipating the fate of their companions, and fearing the like for themselves, made sail with all speed. The captives were conveyed to the village, and condemned to be shot, one at a time. Three were thus dealt with, and the fourth, Juan Ortiz, was being led forth, when the wife and daughters of the cacique, touched with compassion at sight of his youth and comeliness, interceded with Hirrihigua, and gained a respite. His life was still a wretched one, softened only by the watchful kindness of the women, who once even rescued him after he had been half burnt alive by order of his implacable captor. At length, through their aid, he succeeded in escaping to the village of Mocoso, a neighboring chief, who treated him as if he had been a brother, and protected him from all danger. Here he had remained ever since, and was now residing; nearly naked, browned, painted, with a headdress of feathers, so that one might not know him from a savage, on an embassy from Mocoso to the camp of De Soto. Great was the joy of the camp at the recovery of Ortiz. The Adelantado received him as a son, gave him all that heart could wish, and thenceforth he became the interpreter of the expedition.

Meanwhile, Lieutenant-General Don Vasco Porcallo, whom we picked up in Cuba, testy and withal vain-glorious, yet longing to distinguish himself, entreats to be sent in pursuit of Hirrihigua, that he may ferret him out of his swampy fastness, and bring him, friend or prisoner, to camp. Despite monitions, he sets off, dashes forward, and is only arrested by a quagmire, where himself and horse are in imminent jeopardy of being smothered. Conquered by the mire, he returns crestfallen to headquarters, venting curses upon the country, natives and expedition. "May the devil fly away with the country where they have such names!" quoth he. "Let those fight in this accursed place for fame and wealth who will. As for me, I have enough of both to last me. So I will back to Cuba, and let the hot bloods see it out." Thus does Don Vasco Porcallo de Figueroa disappear from this story; for, at his request, De Soto sent him home. "The prudent man foreseeth the danger, and hideth himself."

A strong garrison was left to protect the stores, and the march commenced toward the northeast. As they left the coast, the country improved, and their way lay by pleasant cornfields, over grassy plains, and through forests where the eye detected many a tree familiar to them in the sunny groves of dear old Castile. The wild grapes, too, whose clambering vines festooned the branches, were grateful to men who had grown up among vineyards. Fifty leagues brought them, however, to the marge of a morass a league in width, and apparently impassable;

and hereabouts the natives, although not attacking, had concealed themselves, and were waiting opportunities for opening the war. A pass was at length discovered, and after immense trouble, the army was conveyed across. But here they were effectually checked by deep lagoons and bayous that seemed interminable.

Recrossing the swamp, in order to find a better line of march for the army, De Soto, who was ever in the van when difficulty pressed or danger threatened, at the head of a picked corps made an extensive tour of observation, and found what he sought. But himself and men were near starving; for three days and nights they had little rest and less food. Supplies must be had, and the army brought up. Calling to him Gonzalo Silvestre, a bold young soldier, "To you," he said, "belongs the best horse, therefore the harder work. Away, and hold not bridle until you have reached the camp. Bring us what we need and order the forces to join us. Be back by to-morrow night." Without a word Silvestre mounted and spurred away, calling to Juan Lopez, De Soto's page, to follow. Neither of these stout youths was one and twenty. Away over the twilight plain they sped. Fifteen leagues, tired as they and their steeds were, must be ridden that night. If morning found them in the swamp, almost certain death awaited them. Trusting more to the sagacity of their horses than to their own management to find the way on, through the thickening night rode our tired cavaliers; the silence broken by the moan of the cypress woods, the whir of a startled bird, the croaking of the monstrous frogs, and the plash of their horses' feet: and every now and then, as some camp-fire blazed on an island in the mire, revealing a party of savages engaged in feast or dance, a din as of an infernal orchestra broke upon their ears. The passage of a southern swamp is no easy feat at any time; but at night, by two youths, surrounded by hundreds of savage foes, it was an exploit worthy the hardiest. I mention it here to show the mettle of De Soto's troops.

Undismayed by sight or sound, they still pressed forward until Lopez, grown reckless through fatigue and want of sleep, threw himself upon the ground, swearing he would go not a rood further until he had slept. Silvestre had nothing for it but to submit. Falling asleep himself in the saddle, he awoke to find it broad day. Hastily rousing his companion they started, but there was yet a league before them, and the Indians were not long in descrying the two horsemen and sounding the alarm. Forthwith the woods swarmed with painted furies. Knowing there was no resource left them but resolution and their horses, they pushed on at a gallop, their mail defending them from the shafts of their enemies. The yells and war-cries of the savages at length reached the camp, and thirty troopers rushed to their aid. Thus did these brave youths reach their goal in safety.

Taking scarce an hour for rest, Silvestre was again in the saddle at the head of thirty lancers conveying two horseloads of supplies to the general; and not long after nightfall had reached the spot where he had left his commander the evening before. When the main body came up, they found the commandant encamped in the plain of Aguera, where maize was growing in abundance. Here they rested after their late privations.

The Seminoles had now commenced hostilities in good earnest; not indeed by pitched battle in the open field, but by ambuscades lurking in every thicket, picking off every little knot of Spaniards incautious enough to stray from the camp or line of march. Nevertheless they were all ardor to proceed, for some natives whom they had captured, in reply to their eager questions concerning the precious metals, assured them that in Ocali, a country to the northward, gold was so plenty that in war the people wore head-pieces of it.

But Ocali is reached, and no gold is found; only a poor small town, empty of people. The main body of the troops here came up with the commander, after a difficult and hungry march; making up for their failing provisions by boiling a few beets which they found here and there in the fields, and chewing the young stems of the growing Indian corn.

After brief delay, they press forward to the dominions of Vitachuco, a powerful chieftain, whose territories are fifty leagues across. After some days of amity the Spaniards discover a perfidious plot to destroy them. Vitachuco has ordered a grand review of his warriors, ten thousand strong. At a signal twelve of his braves are to seize De Soto and the massacre is to commence. Trusting to take the Spaniards unaware, they deem their destruction easy. But forewarned, forearmed. Vitachuco is seized and the Spaniards charge the hordes of natives with headlong valor, mowing hundreds of them down upon the plain, whilst masses fly to adjoining lakes to swim for their lives. One of these lakes, wherein is the flower of Vitachuco's army, is surrounded by the troops, and although they offer quarter, not a savage will submit. Night comes on; the lake shore is vigilantly patrolled. By daylight fifty have yielded; and at ten o'clock of the morning, after they had been in the water twenty-four hours, all the rest save seven come ashore. These hold out until three o'clock, when De Soto, unwilling that such steadfast valor should find a watery grave, sends twenty expert swimmers after them, who drag them to land more dead than alive. When questioned, after their recovery, by the Adelantado, why they held out so stubbornly, four of them replied that they were captains, and that such should never surrender. The other three, neither of whom was over eighteen years of age, replied that they were sons of neighboring caciques, and would be caciques themselves some day, and that it did not behoove such to be guilty of cowardice. This was the indomitable spirit of the men De Soto came to conquer.

The warriors of Vitachuco were reduced to slavery; still the untamed spirit of that chief revolved a plan for the extermination of the hated invaders. Communicating his scheme secretly, it was soon known to all his braves. On the third day, while the Indians were waiting on their masters at dinner, at the sound of his war-whoop they were to attack their oppressors with whatever they could lay hands on, and at once destroy them. At the appointed time, Vitachuco, who was seated near De Soto, sprang upon him and bore him to the earth, dealing him such a blow in the face as brought the blood in streams from nose, mouth, and eyes. Raising his arm for another blow, which would have been death to the Adelantado, he gave the whoop, which could be heard for a quarter of a league. At that critical moment a dozen swords and lances pierced him, and he fell lifeless to the earth. At the signal, his warriors fell upon their masters with pots, kettles, pestles and stools, and such arms as they could seize. But they were soon overpowered, for they fought in chains. Thus perished Vitachuco, and with him, in all, thirteen hundred of his brave warriors. Some of those slain performed extraordinary feats of valor. One, who was being led to the market-place to be murdered after the fight, first lifted up his master above his head and flung him down so that he was stunned, then seized his sword, and, in the words of the Portuguese narrative, though "inclosed between fifteen or twenty footmen, made way like a bull, with the sword in his hand, until certain halberdiers of the governor came, which killed him." Of the Indians who remained alive after the strife was over, about two hundred in number, some were given as slaves to those who had the best claim, and the rest were shot to death in cold blood, by the archers of De Soto's guard, or by the Indian allies.

And here it may be well to say a word, once for all, of the treatment of the Indians by De Soto and his men. This was such as excuses these high-spirited barbarians a thousand times over for their constant and unflinching enmity to the Spaniards, and for all the savage arts used to oppose the invaders. As De Soto went from nation to nation, he was accustomed to demand the services of large numbers of Indians as porters. Four thousand at one time were thus employed in transporting the baggage. This servile drudgery was sufficiently intolerable to the warriors of the woods. But the Christians were accustomed to make occasional expeditions for the express purpose of procuring, not friendly porters, but slaves to labor in chains. A hundred, including men and women, were thus taken in a single expedition, a little after the death of Vitachuco. These were led by irons about their necks, and were made to carry baggage, grind maize, and serve their Spanish masters in all things which a captive might do. Although the superior arms of the Spaniards enabled them to retain many of these captives, of whom some even accompanied the remains of the expedition to Mexico, yet their stubborn and revengeful spirit gave their captors constant annoyance. Sometimes, as one was led in chains to labor, he slew the Christian who led him and ran away with his gyves; others filed their fetters through by night with a stone, and thus escaped. They undoubtedly gave all the information in their power to their countrymen in the woods, which must have aided them materially in their desperate attacks upon the Spaniards.

De Soto, after the death of Vitachuco, bent his steps westward through the province of Osachile, where they still found their path infested by hostile savages, who stoutly contested every step of the way. At one broad morass, in particular, probably that at the head of the Estauhatchee River, in the middle of which was a lagoon half a league wide, the Indians made a resolute stand. The path downward through the tangled, swampy forest, would admit of but two abreast, and was cleared under water to the same breadth, until the lagoon was too deep to be forded. This deep centre was passed by a slender and perilous bridge of logs tied together, and on the other side the same narrow, dangerous path ascended through another tangled, swampy forest. Just beyond this morass, the Indians had impeded a large extent of woods by felling logs and tying and interlacing them among the standing trees, upon a piece of ground very near where, ten years before, they had defeated Narvaez. After three days of dangerous and most fatiguing fighting, up to their waists in water, and afterward in the barricaded forests filled with their yelling, invisible foes, the wearied Spaniards forced a way through into a region less beset, and at length reached the chief village in the fertile and populous province of Appalache, near Tallahassee, where they took up their winter quarters. A scouting party discovered the sea at no great distance, and found the bay of Aute, from which the unfortunate Narvaez had embarked. On the solitary coast were yet to be seen the coals of his forges, the skulls of his horses, and the troughs where he had fed them. The intrepid Juan de Añasco was now dispatched, with thirty troopers, to Pedro Calderon, who had been left in command at the village of Hirrihigua, to order him to join the general with his men and supplies. The enterprise was beset with difficulties from which the boldest might shrink. To traverse a country peopled by a warlike race, whose undying antipathy to the Spaniards had been aroused, to thread a maze which had well-nigh proved fatal to the main army, was a task which might well have made the stoutest quail. But, notwithstanding incredible hardships and peril, the dauntless Juan succeeded. Pedro Calderon joined the army, and the two brigantines were brought around from Espiritu Santo to the Bay of Aute. These, exploring the coast westward, discovered the bay of Achusi, now Pensacola. Appointing this as a rendezvous, De Soto ordered Maldinado to sail for Cuba, and to return with supplies.

At Appalache, or as it is also named, Anaica Appalache, not far from Tallahassee, De Soto went into quarters for the winter. The number of his men, his careful strengthening of his defences, and the precautions which he took, enabled him to repel the incessant attacks of the natives, who, however, kept him in constant watchfulness, and picked off every Spaniard who strayed from the camp. As a means of preventing these attacks, he succeeded in obtaining possession of Capafi, the chief of Appalache, a man so fat that he could not walk; but after a short time, the cunning old chief crawled away on his hands and knees from his guards while they were sleeping, and was never retaken. The hardy and fearless Spaniards, however, now well experienced in Indian warfare, kept watch and ward, repelled all attacks, and maintained themselves through the winter in comparative comfort.

And now the second year of the expedition opens upon them. The land is in the bloom of spring. The new-born leaves seem to clap their hands in joy, as they dally with the soft south breeze; the sward is tufted with flowers of every hue; the air is flooded with the mocking-bird's rich and ever changeful song; the tender blade cleaves the mold; and all the land is gay in the garments of the opening tropic year. Will not this man take her as a bride from God? Nay! unless she has yellow treasure on her breast. A yellow grave shalt thou have, Hernando de Soto! but no gold!

The captives tell them of Cofachiqui, a region to the northeast, where the precious earth can be had in plenty; their reports, doubtless, referring to the Georgia and South Carolina gold fields, which other authorities prove to have been early worked by the Indians.

Accompanied on part of their route by four thousand friendly Indians sent by the chief of Cofaqui to carry the baggage, and by as many more, under Patofa, the war-chief of Cofaqui, as escort; with various lot of hospitable welcome from friendly natives, and threatened starvation in immense pine barrens; now in lonely devouring bogs, and then in fertile and cultivated tracts; here feasting in the midst of plenty, there famishing in deserts of sand under the pine trees, that offer them nothing but a tomb—thus they cross the present State of Georgia diagonally from southwest to northeast, until they strike the Savannah River at Silver Bluff. On the opposite side was the town of Cofachiqui, where ruled a youthful queen of rare grace and beauty. Gliding across the river in a canoe, attended by her principal men, she gave the strangers a courteous welcome, presenting to De Soto a pearl necklace a yard and a half in length. Commanding her subjects to provide canoes and rafts, the army was transported across the river.

Here the host remained encamped for some weeks, in friendly intercourse with this peaceful and hospitable nation. In the tombs of their ancestors the Indians showed them vast treasures of pearls, computed to be not less than fourteen bushels, of which De Soto, though invited to take them all, preferred to select only a small number, leaving the remainder for a subsequent expedition. Here also, in a depository of Indian weapons annexed to a place of burial, they found a Spanish dagger and coat of mail, evidently the relics of the expedition of Lucas Vasquez

De Ayllon, which had come to an end so sorrowful and so well deserved, fifteen years before.

After a time, there came rumors of gold from the west; and bearing their specimen pearls, and inhospitably rewarding good with evil by seizing their beautiful and generous young hostess, in order that her authority might secure them good treatment and safety on the road, they march across the southern end of the Alleghany range to northwestern Georgia. On the road, the princess of Cofachiqui escaped, carrying a little treasure of valuable pearls. Travelling onward, they arrive at Chiaha, where they find a pot of honey, the first and last seen by the expedition, and the only honey mentioned, it is believed, as existing within the limits of the United States before its settlement by the whites, who are usually supposed to have introduced the bee.* Questioning the chief of Chiaha, if he "had notice of any rich countrie," the Indian said that at Chisca, toward the north, there was copper, and another finer and softer metal. De Soto sends two envoys with Indian guides to find the place; but they return with no gold, and with news of none, bearing a buffalo hide for their only prize. Next they travel through the great province of Cosa, supplied by the inhabitants with porters for the baggage, and with provisions. Resting in one

* Peter Martyr says that the Mexicans had both honey and wax. (Decades of the Ocean, Dec. 5, cap. 10.)

place twenty days, and twenty-five in another, they pass through this, the goodliest land they have yet seen, and bending southward, march by Tallise, through the territory now called Alabama, toward the capital of a great chief called Tuscaloosa, whom they meet upon the border of his dominions, near the present city of Montgomery. Tuscaloosa, or Black Warrior, a chieftain of a tribe probably the Choctaws, was the mightiest cacique in all this region; ruling apparently over a great part of the present States of Alabama and Mississippi. He was so tall that when mounted upon the largest horse in the army, his feet nearly touched the ground. He was eminently handsome, although grave, stern, haughty and repellant in demeanor. This magnificent chief, who was born to rule, received De Soto, sitting upon a simple wooden throne, and shaded by the broad round standard of painted deerskin which was his ensign in war. With a laconic welcome, he set out to guide the Spanish commander to his capital, Mauvila, or Maubila, situated ten days' march to the southward; a reminiscence of whose name exists in that of the city of Mobile. To insure good treatment from the natives, after his custom, De Soto surrounded the Black Warrior with a guard, professedly of honor, but really to hold him as a hostage. This the proud chief at once discovered; but betrayed no sign of displeasure. At length, within a day's march of

Maubila, De Soto with a hundred horse and a hundred foot, accompanied by Tuscaloosa, pushed forward to the capital, leaving the remainder of the force to be brought up by Luis de Moscoso, master of the camp. The Adelantado apprehended that danger threatened at Mauvila, and was in haste to resolve his doubt. Reaching the town early in the morning, he found it a walled place. A stockade of great tree trunks had been formed, transverse beams had been lashed to these by means of vines, and over all was a stucco of mud hardened in the sun. At every fifty paces were towers on the walls, capable of holding eight bowmen. Many of the trees in the stockade had survived transplanting, and were in full leaf, giving to the fortification a strange beauty. The houses were built on broad streets, and although but eighty in number were yet so large that each would hold a thousand persons. In the centre was a great public square. The town was built in the midst of a plain, finely situated upon a noble bluff of the Alabama River, whose peaceful current was seen in the distance gliding between beautiful banks. The other margin of the plain was skirted by a forest. Near the western wall was a beautiful limpid lake.

In obedience to the orders of Tuscaloosa, booths had been erected outside the walls for the accommodation of the army, while the chief house of the town had been set apart for De Soto and his officers.

Alighting, the proud chief moved haughtily off toward his people, to see, as he said, that all was in readiness for his guests. Not returning, and the houses seeming to be filled with warriors and young girls—many of whom were exceedingly beautiful—but no old people or children appearing, De Soto's apprehensions were quickened. Desirous of regaining the person of Tuscaloosa, he sent Juan Ortiz to announce that the Adelantado was waiting breakfast for the chief. Thrice was the message sent, but no chief appeared. At last a warrior, quitting one of the houses, shouted a threatening defiance to the Spaniards. Baltazar de Gallegos, who was near at hand, cut him down. The warrior's son attempting to avenge him, shared his fate. And now began the fight in frightful earnest. Indians swarmed from every lodge, and the earth seemed suddenly covered with them. De Soto and his men, fighting desperately, fell back outside the walls to where the horses were picketed. Gaining these, they flung themselves into the saddle and fiercely charged the foe. Backward and forward swept the tide of battle. Sometimes, driven by flights of deadly arrows, the Spaniards retreat to the edge of the forest. Then rallying, they come thundering down, with the war cry "Santiago and our Lady," upon the hordes of naked savages awaiting them. These, borne down by the terrible shock, retreat to the walls and close the ponderous gates, but send clouds of deadly missiles against their enemies. Hour after hour does the battle rage. The mail, the weapons and the discipline of the Spaniards give them a fearful advantage against the naked bodies and undrilled array of the savages; but the odds of numbers are overwhelming, two hundred against thousands—for Moscoso has not arrived. He and his men loiter in the shady glades, picking grapes and flowers, singing songs of dear old Castile, light of heart that they shall soon hear news from Cuba and receive abundant supplies—for it is now October, the month in which Maldinado is to be at Pensacola, and hence to that place is less than thirty leagues. As thus they loiter through the pleasant woods, the sunny river peeping every now and then between the branches, the land seemed as lovely as the valley of the Xenil, outspread beneath the towers of the Alhambra.

But suddenly the distant sound of trumpet-calls, and shouts and savage war-cries are faintly heard, far in front; and soon they discern a column of smoke slowly rising into the air in the distance. There is a battle!

The word is passed along the line; stragglers fall in, and at a rapid pace come up the reinforcements. The battle rages with redoubled fury; the Spaniards dash at the gates and force them. The streets and the square are filled with combatants and corpses.

The Christian's war-cry joins with the deafening shout of the Indians. They fall like grain before the mower's scythe under the swords and lances of their foemen; yet no one cries for quarter. The only targets which the steel clad Spaniards offer the Indian archers is mouth and eyes and the joints of the armor. The Indian women join their husbands and lovers in the fight, and are the fiercest of the throng. Everywhere De Soto is seen in the thickest of the mêlée. Rising in his stirrups to deal a fatal blow, an arrow strikes him in the thigh through the openings of his armor. Thenceforth he fights standing in his stirrups. But the Spaniards have fired the town, and the flames spread fearfully, enwrapping every dwelling. As their forked tongues lapped up Maubila and its brave people, the sun, hidden by clouds of smoke, was casting a sickly glare from behind the tree-tops. The tragedy is finished. Nine hours did the battle rage. At least five thousand Indians are slain. Nor is the plight of the Spaniards enviable. Eighty-two of their best warriors have fallen, while among the survivors seventeen hundred grievous wounds are distributed, and there is but one surgeon in the camp, and he unskilled. Forty-two horses, mourned as companions and friends, are slain. All the camp furniture, baggage and supplies, the pearls and trophies of savage wealth which had been placed in the houses or carelessly cast down about the walls, are consumed; and worst of all, the wheaten flour and wine, preserved with sedulous care for the Eucharist, are burned also.

A dismal night, indeed, was that after the battle of Maubila. Numbers of the wounded died before their hurts could be attended to. Eight days they remained, attending on the disabled, in wretched sheds within the town; and then, carrying them to huts constructed on the open ground without, they remained twenty days longer, ere the troops are in marching order, having recovered from the wounds of the battle, and measurably from a strange disease, occasioned by want of salt. This commenced with fever and speedily corrupted the whole body, ending, after three or four days, in a fatal mortification of the intestines. The use of the ashes of a certain plant was a preventive of this disorder; yet it destroyed, says Garcilasso de la Vega, as many as sixty of the Spaniards in one year.

But whither shall they go? Intelligence has reached the camp that Arias and Maldinado are arrived at Ochus, their appointed rendezvous, but seven days' march to the southeast, with provisions and supplies for founding a colony. At first, De Soto is filled with joy, for he sees at hand the means of establishing the settlement which he has always designed to make the headquarters for his further search after gold. But he is told that the army is full of murmurs at their endless and profitless hardships, and that his leaders and men are proposing to seize the opportunity, and sail for Mexico or Peru. *There* is gold for him who can win it; *here* are only toil, wounds, danger, disease, death. The Adelantado sees that, once at the seacoast, his army will desert him. No new troops will undertake an enterprise already branded with failure; and he has no second vast fortune to embark in the undertaking. He has staked his all on this one throw—fortune, fame, hope, honor, life. Shall he now slink back to Cuba, a hundred of his brave companions dead, poor in purse, vanquished by the poverty and the savageness of these wild forests and grassy savannas? These bitter reflections drive him to a desperate resolution, which he seems here deliberately to have formed, and silently to have adhered to until just before his death; namely, to send home no news of himself until he had found the rich regions which he had set out to seek. And, as if he had at the same time been hopeless of success, and acted merely in shame and desperation, his demeanor was thenceforth changed. Always stern and reserved, he grows now moody, silent, savage. The word of command is given, and the line of march resumed to the northwest, back into the wild forests, away from ships and home. And none dare demand a reason from the gloomy and severe commander

They resumed their march Sunday, Nov. 18, 1540. Crossing the Black Warrior and Tombigbee rivers, they at length reached the heart of the Chickasaw country, in the northwestern part of Mississippi, where it was determined to winter in a village called Chicasa. De Soto, on one occasion, treated the natives to hog meat, whereupon they acquired such a taste for it that his pig-pens were constantly invaded. He punished some of the hog-thieves severely, and this, together with the robberies and assaults committed upon the persons and property of the Chickasaws, kindled the wrath of that warlike people, and they determined upon summary revenge. They attacked the village at night, firing the houses, and succeeded for a time in throwing the Spaniards into confusion. Many of the latter were slain, together with a number of horses, which were more dreaded than the Spaniards themselves. But the natives were routed, with great loss, before daylight. It was, however, a victory dearly purchased, for the Spaniards lost forty men, fifty horses, and three hundred of their four hundred swine, besides nearly all their remaining clothes and effects; and were left in such evil plight, that, had the Indians attacked them again the next night, they must have won an easy victory. Attributing this damaging surprise to the negligence of the camp-master, Luis de Moscoso, who had already been so dilatory at the battle of

Maubila, De Soto deposed him, and appointed Baltasar de Gallegos in his stead. Removing to Chickasilla, a league distant, the Spaniards erected a forge, and re-tempered their swords which had been much injured by the fire, made saddles, horse-furniture, and lances, and wove mats of the long grass to shield them from the cold, which in March was still piercing. These mats, in their future wayfarings, served a valuable purpose, as bucklers, to protect them from the arrows of their enemies. At Chickasilla they wintered, amid cold and snow, and in great want of clothing.

As the spring of the third year of the expedition opened, the fierce Chickasaws renewed their attacks, but were repulsed; and on the 25th of April, the army set forward for a third summer of wandering after gold, marching northwestward. At the fortress of Alibamo, on one of the head branches of the Yazoo, the Indians made a resolute stand. But the invincible Spaniards took it by storm, and put to the sword all who fell into their hands. Hence to the northwestern corner of Mississippi, or the southwestern of Tennessee, they journeyed, through dark forests and deep swamps, until they struck a mighty river, which they named Rio Grande. Alvar Nuñez and the survivors of the expedition of Narvaez must have crossed it much lower down; but we are accustomed to name De Soto as the first European who set foot on the banks of the Mississippi—for this was their Rio Grande.

In April, 1541, they stood upon the bluffs which overlook that sublime stream, rushing from the icy regions of the north to a summer sea. This was the pioneer pilgrimage of European civilization to its banks, the advanced guard of that innumerable multitude which was here to be gathered together to make another attempt at solving the problem of man's relation to the earth, his neighbor and his God.

Building boats, they crossed the river, and after four days' march into the wilderness beyond, came to the village of Casqui, or Casquin, supposed to have been inhabited by the Kaskaskias Indians, afterward settled in Illinois. This village was in a province also called Casqui, and governed by a cacique of the same name. The chief inhabited a village about seven leagues further on, where he hospitably received the army, and provided it with provisions and quarters.

During the encampment here, the chief supplicated De Soto to pray to his God for rain, which was much needed. Hereupon the Spanish commander caused a vast cross to be erected, in a commanding situation, on a lofty hill near the river, and consecrated it by a solemn religious ceremony, in which both Spaniards and Indians joined. Then De Soto endeavored to make Casqui understand how prayers should be offered to the one invisible God, and related to him the life and sufferings of Christ.

As the intonations of the Litany, and the solemn strains of *Te Deum laudamus* rose upon the air, the children of the forest took up the strain, with plaintive voice and uplifted eyes, invoking the white man's God. Here, then, upon the shore of the Father of Waters, in the northeastern corner of Arkansas, was the symbol of our religion first planted, eighty years before a Puritan had touched the rock at Plymouth. And as if to substantiate the instructions of the Spanish commander, a plenteous shower of rain came down that very night.

De Soto delayed some days in the village of Casqui, and then set out northward, for the village of Pacaha or Capaha, who was at feud with Casqui, and whom the latter trusted to destroy by means of the Spaniards. He accompanied the latter, with his warriors, for that purpose; and did actually destroy numbers of his people, and laid waste his town. But De Soto, on his arrival, at once put a stop to these proceedings, and, after considerable difficulty, induced Pacaha to return home, and issued orders that none should do any injury to the inhabitants of the province or to their possessions. In this place he rested forty days, during which he sent two men to a hill country, forty leagues westward, where, the

Indians said, there was much salt, and much yellow metal. They returned, in eleven days, with a quantity of rock salt and some copper, but no gold. The Indians also said that northward, and beyond the line of their exploring trip, the country was cold, barren and overrun with buffaloes.

De Soto, therefore, resolved to return to the village of Casqui, and thence to strike southward for a country which the Indians called Quigaute, and represented as extensive and wealthy. Here he remained a little time, and then, turning westward, entered upon that long and dreary circuit in the regions of the Arkansas and Red Rivers, which at last brought him back to the shores of the Mississippi, to die. He passed through Coligoa, at the foot of a mountain, beyond which he fancied there might be gold; came to Palisema, in the country of Cayas; to Tunica, where were found salt lakes, from which the army furnished itself with a quantity of good salt; to Tula or Tulla, whose inhabitants, differing from all they had met before, were exceedingly ill-looking, having immense heads, artificially narrowed at the top, and faces horribly tattooed; whose ferocity was more brutal and untamable than that of any race they had met before, and who could not be terrified by threats and slaughter, nor cajoled by gifts. Thence they marched to Utiangue or Autiamque, where, fortifying part of a large village, the forlorn

Spanish host went into winter-quarters for the third time. The cold was severe, the snow deep, and the attacks of the savages incessant; but as food and fuel were plentiful, the condition of the troops was on the whole quite comfortable.

In Autiamque died Juan Ortiz, the interpreter—an irreparable loss to De Soto, who thenceforth found very great difficulties in maintaining even a circuitous and obscure intercourse with the natives.

When the spring returned, there remained, of the magnificent host of a thousand men, only three hundred soldiers, besides non-combatants; and of three hundred and fifty horses, only forty, and many of these lame and useless, and all unshod during the year past, for want of iron. Fatigue, sickness, privation, and the weapons of the fierce savages of the Mobilian and Muscogee races, had destroyed the rest. And even this scanty remainder were destitute and discouraged. The disastrous fires of Maubila and Chicasa had devoured clothing, arms, and wealth. They were now dressed in skins, and their weapons were, in many cases, such as they had wrought out themselves. His goodly armament thus worn out and wasted in endless hostilities with the savages, and thus rapidly diminishing, and his hopes of gold so long disappointed, even the obstinate and persevering courage and hopefulness of De Soto began to fail; and he at length decided to return to the Mississippi, fortify himself there, build vessels, and send to Cuba for supplies and men.

The troops accordingly set forward from Autiamque on Monday, March 6, 1542, being now the fourth year of their wanderings; and going through Ayas, or Ayays, and Tultelpina, reached Amilco, capital of the province of that name, and standing in the midst of a country more fertile and populous than any they had yet seen, except Cosa and Appalache. Hence they proceeded to Guachoya, on the Mississippi, apparently at the mouth of the Arkansas, where De Soto proposed to establish himself and build his vessels.

Setting the necessary preparations on foot, De Soto, having heard of a certain powerful chieftain called Quigalta, or Quigaltanqui, ruling a vast province on the opposite side of the Great River, sent an embassy to him, to say that he, De Soto, was the child of the sun; that all men along his road had hitherto obeyed and served him; and requiring Quigalta to accept his friendship and come to him, bringing something valuable in token of love and obedience. But the chief dryly and sourly answered, that if De Soto were the child of the sun, he might dry up the river, and he would believe him; and as to the rest of the message, that he was wont to visit nobody, but that all were wont to visit him, and pay tribute to him. That, therefore, if De Soto desired to see him, it was best that he should cross the river himself and come; that if he came in peace, he should be received with special good will; but if in war, he, Quigalta, would wait for him in the same place, and would not shrink one foot back for him or any other.

But when the messenger came back with this keen and haughty reply, the Adelantado was already on a sick-bed, confined with a slow fever. Ill as he was, he was irritated at the bold savage, and still more that he was unable to cross the river and seek him, to abate his pride. But the Indians were so numerous and so fierce, his own forces now so reduced, and the current of the vast river so furious and dangerous, that he was fain to think upon fair means, instead of foul.

And even while lying here, sick and discouraged, while the fever grew upon him, De Soto performed an action most characteristic of the deliberate, bloody-minded, brutal carelessness with which the Spaniards of that day regarded the Indians. Many reports came in of proposed attacks upon the camp, sometimes from one side of the river, sometimes from the other. In order, therefore, to intimidate the tribes about him, De Soto determined to devote one of them to destruction, and accordingly, sending a sufficient force, surprised the town of Amilco. The fierce troopers burst into this peaceful and unsuspecting village, with orders not to spare the life of any male;

and not only was this cruel order fulfilled, but sundry of the soldiers slew all who came in their way, though the surprise was so complete that not an arrow was shot at any Christian. This savage butchery was an astonishment even to the Indian allies who accompanied the troops, and served no good turn; and it was afterward noticed that those most active in it showed themselves cowards where true valor was needed, and that shameful deaths were visited on them in retribution.

But all the earthly projects of De Soto now drew to a close. Deeply feeling his fatal error in wandering so far from the sea, grieved at the losses and sufferings of his men, harassed with anxious forebodings as to the future, and his powerful frame at last undermined and shattered by the destructive climatic fever, he now sinks rapidly; and helpless and hopeless, one of the noblest cavaliers of the age lies dying in a rude Indian wigwam. Instead of gaining vast treasures, he has lost them, and found no more. Instead of founding an empire, he has exterminated a savage tribe or two, but has scarcely retained his authority over the relics of his small and shattered army. Instead of winning world-wide renown, he has disappeared from view in those vast western wildernesses, and for years has not even been heard of by Christian men. A sad and disastrous close for an expedition whose outset was so splendid and so hopeful!

And now his last hour draws nigh, and with the steady courage of a soldier and a Christian, for such he was to the best of his ability, whatever were his faults, Hernando de Soto calmly prepares to close up all worldly transactions, and to die. He makes his will; requests his officers to elect a captain to succeed him, and when they, in turn, desire him to choose, appoints Luis Moscoso de Alvarado, remembering only the virtues and ability of that captain, and no longer preserving anger for the errors for which he had removed him from his place of campmaster. He causes the officers and troops to swear obedience to their new leader, and then, calling them to him by twos and threes, and the soldiers by twenties and thirties, thanks them for their love and loyalty to him, expressing his regret at leaving them unremunerated for all their toils; charges them to remain at peace with each other, and asks pardon for any wrong or offence of which he may have been guilty toward them; and so, with tenderness, he bids them all farewell. Thus, resigning his soul to God, and confessing his sins, three years absent from Donna Isabella, and in the forty-third year of his age, on the 21st of May, 1542, perished in the wilderness, Hernando de Soto.

Anxious to conceal his death from the natives, and thus to preserve the spell of his name, his companions, with whispered prayers, and silent but fast-falling tears, buried him in the darkness in a pit, near the village of Guachoya, where they were encamped. But fearing lest the body should be discovered by the savages, and subjected to inhuman outrage, they disinterred it the following night, and, having prepared a coffin of evergreen oak, bore it to the middle of the Great River and sank it in a hundred feet of water. A sullen plunge, a murmured *Requiescat in pace!* from priest and cavalier, and the canoes return to land. The army mourned as if every man had lost a father.

Nevertheless, they resolved to abandon his plans and strike westward, thus hoping to reach Mexico; not seeming to know that their latitude was far north of that. Westward for months they wandered through swamp and canebrake, now in luxuriant meadows and again in waste howling wildernesses. Waylaid by savages, famishing, nearly naked, they kept on until the eye was filled with mountains towering to heaven. Back in haste; no Mexico is here. Returning, they are overtaken by fall rains, and winter rigors. Jaded, dispirited, miserable, their numbers reduced to three hundred and fifty, they reach Minoya, on the Mississippi, late in the year. Here they summon all their remaining energies and resources, and gird themselves for a last desperate struggle with fate. By spring they have built seven brigantines, of short and thin planks, insufficiently nailed together, undecked, and calked only with bark and grass. In these, on the second day of July, 1543, they depart, three hundred and twenty-two Spaniards all told, taking twenty-two of the horses alive, and the rest salted for provisions; and leaving the wretched inhabitants of Minoya starving to death for want of the maize which the Spaniards had used for subsistence and for provisioning their vessels. They also leave at their place of embarkation five hundred Indian slaves, retaining a number, including twenty or thirty women. Committing themselves to the current, they float down the river for nineteen days and nights, beset a great part of the way by a flotilla of canoes filled with hostile Indians who kept up incessant assaults upon them, by which they lost all their surviving horses and over fifty men; having now no weapons left except a few swords and shields, and being thus helpless against the arrows of the savages. This voyage down the river was subsequently computed at five hundred leagues.

They reach the Gulf, and here trusting themselves in their frail brigantines to the treacherous deep, after a painful and eventful voyage, they reach the river and village of Panuco in Mexico. They are kindly received, and Mendoza, the viceroy, causes them to be brought to Mexico, where they are treated with much attention and honor. Less than three hundred survivors of that gallant expedition which four years before had set out from Cuba with much music and rejoicing, now apppeared, haggard, blackened, with tangled hair, skins of wild beasts almost their only covering, a wretched band of wrecked, despairing men. And even now, the hearts of nearly all lust for Florida again. Each curses his fellow as the cause of his leaving that land, which they aver to be the goodliest on which the sun shines. Fierce words and fiercer blows are given, and thus amid execrations and contentions these worthies disappear from history.

A word of Donna Isabel, fair hapless lady. Faithfully had she sent Captains Maldinado and Gomez Arias with ships and plentiful supplies in the fall of 1540. Waiting for a long time, they then coasted east and west in search of intelligence concerning the Adelantado. The next spring they came again, and the next, and the next, spending each summer in searching for some traces of the ill-fated party. At length in 1543 the tireless captains touched at Vera Cruz, and heard the sad tidings. Hastening to Havana, they broke the news to the Donna Isabel. Having thus long borne up against racking suspense and torturing doubt, hoping against hope, she now yielded, and died in the prime of her glorious beauty, the victim of ill-fated love and man's wild ambition.

Oh, river of the future! thy discovery was made at heavy cost, of gallant lives and a broken heart!

Thy yellow waves are the enduring sepulchre of Hernando de Soto, and the murmur of thy floods the ever-chanted dirge of the lady Isabel, the noble and faithful wife!

Lecture II.

MARQUETTE & LA SALLE.

MARQUETTE AND LA SALLE.

Whatever else Jesuitism may have done, it has given to History one of the noblest of those armies of Heroes and Martyrs, with the record of whose deeds and sufferings its pages are glorified. Nowhere does the love of souls, the contempt of danger and death, patient endurance of hunger, cold, nakedness and bonds, serene self-possession under stripes, and the joyful welcome of martyrdom, stand out in more illustrious contrast to the ordinary sordid and selfish phases of our nature, than in the early mission story of one region of this continent.

In the first settlement of Canada the two classes which most enlist our interest are the missionaries and the voyageurs—the one giving themselves to the service of the Church, and man's salvation; the other, almost equally energetic and hardy, opening the resources of the Fur-trade, and thus connecting, by the ties of commerce, the kings and nobles of the old world with the hunting-grounds and wigwams of the Algonquins and Dacotahs, by the banks of Superior and on the headwaters of the Mississippi.

Trade carried its votaries far into the wilderness, over pathless snows, through interminable forests, up mighty rivers, over the bosom of lakes that seemed like seas. The spell of gold was mighty then, as now; but for once Traffic was outdone by Religion, and the Cross inspired men with a daring enterprise and lofty resolution, such as the world has seldom witnessed.

Father Dreuillettes penetrated the forest lying between the St. Lawrence and the Kennebec, down which he floated to the sea. Sojourning with the savages ten months, bearing them company in their hunts, suffering hardships like a good soldier, everywhere showing fortitude and courage, patience and strength equal to their own, he completely won their love and reverence. Youges, taken prisoner by the relentless Iroquois, was made to run the gauntlet three times, suffered torment of many kinds, saw his converts inhumanly butchered, cheered them by his ministrations of pitying love, although by so doing he exposed himself to their fate; and raising the chaunt in his captive journeyings, provoking the brutality of his persecutors by steadfastness, carving the cross on the trees near Albany, he showed himself faithful in all things. At length liberated by the Dutch of New York, he sailed for France, as the only way by which he could reach Canada again, returned thither, went upon an embassy of peace to his old tormentors the Mohawks, and there he met the death of which he had had presentiment.

Daniel fell beneath the remorseless blows of the same barbarians, as he knelt in pious ministry to the spiritual needs of his Huron converts. Brebœuf, a great strong man whose brawny courage knew no fear, whose ruling passion was a cupidity for martyrdom, could yet in humble patience bide his Master's time. Employing himself the while in uninterrupted missionary labors, he is taken with his associate L'Allemand, a man of delicate frame, but dauntless courage, by the Iroquois, in the midst of their neophytes. They refuse to save themselves by flight, lest the offices of the Church should thereby be lost to the dying around them. Brebœuf is tied to a stake, and exhorting his tormentors to repentance, and his converts to be faithful even until death, his brother priest is led before him robed in a garment of bark filled with rosin. As the torch is applied the unshrinking L'Allemand exclaims, "We are made a spectacle this day unto men and angels." Brebœuf's holy counsels are checked, as his upper lip is cut off, and hot irons thrust down his throat. He too is set on fire, and then boiling water is poured over both to extinguish the flames. Brebœuf entered through the gates into the City above, Jerusalem, the Mother of us all, in three hours. L'Allemand lingered seventeen; then he too joined that company which no man can number, that have come up out of great tribulation. When we hear of faith and love like theirs, can we say, contemptuously, "they were Jesuits," and forget that they were also Christians sealing their testimony with their blood?

As the ranks were thus thinned, they were filled by others, who pressed forward, coveting to wear the thorny crown, persuaded that in due time it would become a crown of glory. Among these was James Marquette, a young Frenchman. Born in the small but stately city of Laon, perched upon a hill-side in the provence of Aisne, his family name was a lustrous one in the annals of France before his time, and has been since. Our own land is indebted to others, bearing it, besides himself. Three Marquettes fell in the French army which aided in our Revolutionary struggle.

Born in 1637, our young Frenchman's early years were blessed by the care of a devout, godly mother, who infused into his mind a reverent simplicity and an ardent love which kept him pure unto the end. From our mothers we borrow our best treasures. They lend in gladness, not dreaming of return. But they receive a hundred fold in this world, and in the world to come life everlasting.

At seventeen Marquette renounced the world and became a Jesuit. Twelve years were spent in teaching, and then, burning with a holy zeal to do good to the heathen, his mind inflamed by the devotion of Francisco Xavier, the model he had chosen for imitation and emulation, he embarked for Canada in 1666. Buoyant with health and hopes of usefulness, the young missionary touched the shores of the new world. Behind him rolled the sea which separated him from home, friends and mother. Before him lay a wilderness continent, with its mighty lakes and rivers, its inaccessible forests and endless plains, now clad in tufted verdure and then garmented in snow and ice. The roving tribes that peopled the land were savages; but they had souls to be saved. True, their tomahawks had drank the blood of his brethren, and their scalping knives were yet red with the gore of martyrs. Still they had immortal souls which might be won for Christ. Was it not work for an angel? Surely it was for a Christian disciple. But he might perish? No matter. Would he not fall with his face toward Zion, die where he might? So he girded up his loins and betook him to his labor.

Not in haste are life's great achievements wrought; but slowly, and by sure degrees. So Marquette first patiently studied the Indian dialects, becoming a learner that he might fitly teach.

He was at first destined to a mission far to the northward, and we find him in 1667 at Three Rivers, preparing himself under Father Dreuillettes. But this design was abandoned and he was next appointed to the Ottawa Mission—as that of Lake Superior was then called—to labor with Father Allouez. Quebec had been founded by Champlain in 1608. Le Barron, a Recollet missionary who came with him, had ascended the Ottawa River, and reached Lake Huron. In 1629 Canada fell into the hands of the English, but in 1631 it was restored to France. In 1639 Nicolet, interpreter of the colony, had descended the Wisconsin to within three days' sail of the Mississippi, or *sea*, as he understood the Indian name "Great Water," to mean. Two years later Isaac Youges and Charles Rambout, Jesuits, stood upon Sault Ste. Marie, looking down upon the land of the Sioux and the basin of the Mississippi, with hearts longing to enter it. But an Iroquois war, the next year, frustrated their design. Thus, while the Dutch of New Netherlands were huddled around Fort Orange, five years before Eliot addressed his first Indian audience six miles from Boston, and while the country between Massachusetts Bay and Connecticut was almost a pathless wilderness, Jesuit Fathers stood upon the water-shed dividing the streams of the Atlantic from those of the Gulf. Honor to whom honor is due! "There is nothing new under the sun" is a well-worn adage which comes to us from a man of many experiences. And as our knowledge increases, the same cry is more than once forced from our lips. You will pardon me

I trust, for diverging from my narrative to furnish you another example of its truth. Two of the chief movements of our time were antedated on this Continent, nearly two centuries. I refer to the Know Nothing and the Maine Law parties. About 1670 it was made death, by a statute of New York, for a Jesuit to plant foot on soil of that colony; and about the same period there arose a formidable dispute in Canada between the civil and clerical authorities, as to whether the vending of ardent spirits to the Indians should be allowed. The question embroiled the colony, and was hotly contested for a long time. It even served to discolor the historic page of the time. At length the church side of the case was shown to be unconstitutional, or something of that sort, and the Indians were murdered the same as before, public opinion settling down into what is now the verdict of juries in railroad accidents—Nobody to blame.

But to return to our young missionary, whom we left in Canada, a little over thirty years of age, about to embark for his field of labor, the Ottawa Mission. His ultimate destination was the founding an establishment among the Illinois; but the novice must be tried in a vineyard already opened, before he attempts to plant one himself.

The south shore of Superior near Ste. Marie, and then La Pointe, are the centres of his operations. Allouez has gone to Green Bay, and so up Fox River, and he is alone with the savages. But not the less faithfully does he labor, that he has no superior to overlook him, nor brother to give him sympathy. On him, as on all, the Master's eye is fixed, always on us, never off us; and the exceeding great reward, does it not await the faithful workman's toils? And fellowship; has he not one ever near him, in his lonely lodge, who is touched with the feelings of his infirmities, who was tempted in all points even as he?

It is pleasant and helpful too, to read the unvarnished tale of this simple minded man's efforts to do good to the untutored children of the forest; how he taught the lessons of virtue and chastity, of forbearance and forgiveness of injuries; how he strove to win them from their idle superstitions to the worship of the living and true God; to go with him as he administers the holy rite of baptism to a dying child, or speaks kind words to sick and suffering men and women; to be near him as he devoutly performs the offices of the church or expounds the mysteries of the faith in his little thatched chapel of bark. He withstands the proud and willful to their face; the wayward he admonishes firmly but gently; he cheers the penitent and encourages the desponding; everywhere he seems striving to possess his soul in patience, to do the work of an evangelist, and make full proof of his ministry. Ever and anon news of the great river and the mighty tribes inhabiting its banks reaches him, and he longs to discover it and them. His heart yearns for the Illinois; for are they not his people? But the time has not come yet. The discoverer of the age must wait—as who must not? History were indeed a dead letter—were less serviceable by half than the debris of perished races, whereon the geologist reads the autograph of every separate cycle—did we not gather from it words and thoughts to inspire ourselves with strength. From the fields of the almost silent Past there comes a whisper which is yet mightier than thunder, a word for all the lowly and great, the striving and despairing, but most of all to the impetuous, easily discouraged young, who need it most: Haste not, Rest not! Time, Faith, Energy, these conquer the world. This lesson do I learn from Marquette's lodge in the wilderness. Therefore is his life, as that of all truly noble souls, of perennial interest to mankind.

Next year he will go to the Illinois. He has been studying their language from a young Indian of that tribe, and is already pretty well master of the tongue. But his hope is defeated, for a war breaks out between the Sioux and the people among whom he lives. With them he must voyage eastward, with his back upon the land of promise. But at length he is with his Hurons at Mackinaw, and his glance wanders over the lake to the west and southwest; it journeys whither his feet would go, his mouth filled with glad tidings to the people of the Illinois and the river Mississippi.

Long, as men count it, must he yet wait. Nevertheless, humbly but fervently does he pray that, if it be Heaven's will, he may go whither his heart leads. At last, on the eve of the festival of the Immaculate Conception, the feast of all the year to him, a canoe from Canada comes up the glassy plain. Its occupant is the Lieutenant Joliet, an old fur-trader, and he brings important letters to Father Marquette.

The minister of France has written to Talon, Intendant of Canada, to cause the South Sea to be discovered. This was the vision of the time, as the short route to China and the East is of ours. Then, they thought a river might bear them on its brimming flood to the South Sea; now, we opine the iron road will take us thither. M. de Talon, the retiring governor, suggests to Frontenac, the newly appointed, that Joliet is the best man for the purpose, and the ecclesiastical authorities appoint Father Marquette. Here are the letters. The winter is spent at Mackinaw in preparation. With crowds of Indians around them, the trader and the priest, kneeling on the ground, drew maps of such countries as the savages knew, lying toward the setting sun. After much study and prayer, with great hopes, yet lowly hearts, our friends set out for their long journey in the spring of 1673.

Across the lake to Green Bay; then to the head of Fox River, where is an Indian village, in the centre of which stands a great cross planted by the zeal of Allouez, and crowned by the Indians with wampum and peltries of the choicest kind. The Indians, with hearts warmed toward the French, throng around Marquette and Joliet with proffers of hospitality and kindness; but when told the object of their expedition, their faces express great solicitude, and their mouths are filled with dismal tales of the dangers of the way. The land of the Great River and the vast stream itself are filled with frightful monsters and terrible men. Every effort was made to dissuade the good father and his party from their mad enterprise. But they were not to be moved. A party of Indians helped them across the portage to the Wisconsin River, where, launching their canoe, they were quitted by their guides, commended their way to God, and committed themselves to the stream of the sky-colored water. Floating upon its tranquil bosom seven days, they passed through a country of marvellous beauty and fertility. It was the month of June, and Nature had donned her gayest colors. Vines clambered among the trees. Sometimes from a bold bank the grassy plain stretched as far as the eye could reach, without a mound or grove to obstruct the view—the green land at last melting into the blue-rimmed horizon. Then the bottom land meeting them with verdant freshness at the river's edge was terminated ere long in a noble bluff, whose sides and summit were crowned with stately trunks and branching foliage, casting lines of grateful shadow on the sward. The unflecked blue above them painted itself in the flood, seeming to create an azure vault beneath their birch pirogue. The breezy stillness was only broken by the river's lapse, the paddle's dip, or their own low murmurs of delight at the fairy-land scene around them. Thus for a week they floated, until, on June 17th, their placid stream swept them with its parting wave into the swifter current of the Great River, whose affluence makes glad a continent. Streams with broader openings to the sea there are, with grander historic associations, with more romantic memories thronging their banks; but what one of all earth's watercourses can vie with this in its majestic appeal to the imagination and the hope of mankind? Oh, James Marquette, can the rivers of thy goodly land of France, the Oise, by whose sedgy marge thy childish feet so often wandered, the Seine, traversing the great town of Paris, the Rhone, "the arrowy Rhone," the Rhine, burdened with its purple hills clad in vines and crowned with castles—can any bear comparison with this? They flow through the dreamy lands of the Past; its realms are the Future's. Like some great royal conqueror it leaps from its almost unnoted birth-place, Itasca

Lake, rushes forward to exact the tribute brought from far provinces, east and west, and after its triumphal procession of two thousand five hundred miles, freely receiving, freely giving in many a belting zone, hurls broad and far its accumulated treasure, that thereby a world may be enriched.

A great silent joy is in Marquette's heart, and as grateful tears wet his eyes, he offers a fervent thanksgiving that he has been permitted to look upon this wonder. The devout spirit thinks of the greatest birth of Time, and in commemoration of it he names the river "The Conception." This is the 17th June, 1673.

For eight days they glided over the crystal pavement between shores widening to the distance of a half league, and then approaching in rocky bluffs, as if they were the towers and battlements of hostile cities, to within a few hundred yards. In vernal pasture lands they beheld the moose and elk and deer cropping the herbage; and lower down vast herds of buffalo grazed in the meadows, and the woods were filled with flocks of wild turkeys. But for fifteen days they had not come in sight of trace or habitation of human beings. At length they discern a well-marked trail on the west bank of the river, and land to seek the men whose feet have left this trace. Silently, with minds moved alternately by hopes and fears, Marquette and Joliet proceed six miles, wher they descry three Indian villages. Uttering a loud cry, they rapidly approach them. A company of old men came forth to meet them, and when asked by Marquette who they are, replied, "we are Illinois." Great was the good father's joy. He explained who he and his companion were; whereupon they were joyfully welcomed with the peace-pipe. Then followed a six days' feast. Heartily did the simple natives urge the Frenchmen to tarry with them. But their task was not half performed, and they must up and away. Taking an affectionate leave of their kind hosts, they were escorted to their canoe and presented with a calumet magnificently adorned, than which no more valuable gift could have been made them.

Passing the mouth of the Illinois, our voyagers sighted the Piasau bluff, where frightful monsters were traced high up on stupendous rocks, and the relics of a rude limning are still to be seen. Soon after there arose upon the air a roar as from a distant cataract. As they drew nearer they found it to be the rush of the Pekitanonie (the muddy river, as the Algonquins had named the Missouri), which rushed like some untamed monster upon the peaceful Mississippi, hurling it with tremendous violence upon the opposite shore. In the boiling muddy tide, seething and tumultuous, were borne great trees which it had uprooted in its wild career. Already had the Father heard of a western river which flowed downward to the sea, and by this one, he hoped some day to reach it. Now his course was southward. Passing an eddy which the natives held to be a demon, they reached the Ohio, then called the Oubachi or river of the Shawnees. Still descending, they came to the warm lands of the cane, where the mosquitoes seemed to be holding a carnival. Wrapping themselves in their sails as a protection against the pestiferous insects, they were after a time hailed from the shore by a party of wild wanderers, who were armed with guns and knives, obtained they said by trading with Christians to the eastward. Further on they were threatened by a hostile demonstration from a large party of natives, who advanced with menaces and brandished arms to meet them. It was a trying moment. But Marquette was equal to it. Invoking the protection of the Virgin Mother, he calmly stood in the prow of his bark, holding aloft the calumet. It saved their lives. The warriors were pacified, received the strangers kindly, and entertained them with great courtesy. This was about the thirty-third parallel of latitude. Below this our little party only ventured ten leagues. They learned that the sea was ten days sail to the south; and that there were many tribes near it, who traded with Europeans and who were at war among themselves. Satisfying themselves that the river emptied between Florida and Tampico, and fearing to fall into the hands of the Spaniards, they determined to return. The main object of the enterprise was accomplished. Until this time it had been a vexed question whether the great river emptied into the sea near Virginia, into the Gulf of Mexico, or into that of California. Having discovered the river, learned the location of its mouth and above all else in the mind of the good Marquette, preached the religion of the Cross to the heathen, opening the way for other missionaries, they reascended to the mouth of the Illinois, to the head of which they went, passing through the most delectable land they had yet looked upon. Here they were met by the Kaskaskias, who hailed them with great joy, and conducted them in triumph across the portage to the Lake; for Marquette promised to return and preach to them.

Four months from the time of setting out, they reached the mission of St. Francis Xavier; and thus these seven men—five boatmen bore them company—performed one of the notable feats of history. The following spring Joliet embarked for Quebec, but as he was attempting to shoot a rapid in the St. Lawrence, not far from his destination, his canoe upset, causing the loss of his journal and maps and nearly of his life. We catch one more look at this worthy on the island of Anticosti, in the Gulf of St. Lawrence, which was granted him for his services; and then the shadow Joliet joins his fellow shades and vanishes forever.

Marquette, without thought of worldly fame or honors, or reward of any kind, studies only how he may recruit his health, which has been sadly shattered, and thereby be able to redeem his pledge to the Kaskaskias. This is his only earthly wish—to preach to his beloved Illinois. He shall not die until it be fulfilled.

Spending the winter of 1674–5 near Chicago, in great feebleness, suffering from cold and want, but cheered by a peaceful, loving heart, he is able to reach his Indians in the spring, and solemnize among them the Easter ceremonies. But his old malady returns. Nothing is left him now but to die. And with the mighty instinct of the human heart, longing to breathe his last among his brethren, he bids farewell to his sorrowing neophytes, and takes his way to Mackinaw. His three faithful boatmen accompany him, tending him with all gentle care, lifting him in and out of the canoe, for the wasted man is too weak to walk. As they reach the outlet of a small stream in Michigan, which now bears his name, he can go no further. A rude lodge is reared on the edge of the stream, with an altar before which the dying saint is laid. He calmly gives directions to his sobbing attendants concerning his burial. They take his crucifix from the breast, where it has lain through all these years of self renouncing toils, and hold it up before him. His face glows with a holy transport, as if it were an angel's; one word, "Jesus," is on his lips, and then—he is dead.

'Tis well. Nine years of untiring labor for the salvation of the heathen, a life of perfect self-abnegation, a discovery rivalling in magnificence any ever made, are thus terminated by a lonely death on a desolate shore. Thus died Xavier, his elected model, after living as he had lived. Two years after, in 1677, a flotilla of canoes from Mackinaw came to that dark wood at the mouth of the little river; the Indians among whom he had long and faithfully labored exhumed his remains and bore them to Mackinaw. A fleet advancing from the shore met them, with tearful eyes, and amid the slow solemn strains of "De Profundis," chanted by priests and Indians, the remains were borne to the shore and finally deposited beneath the church, on whose site he had so often led their worship.

For many a long year after, when the forest rangers abroad upon the stormy lake were endangered by sudden tempest or wild billows, their piteous cries were heard, and Marquette was the name they cried, asking his intercession, as of an all-powerful and undoubted saint.

Important as his discovery was, it is certain that it would have been of slight advantage to France, but for the exertions of a young adventurer, whose story we have next to trace.

When Joliet was on his way to Quebec, after quitting Marquette, he stopped at Fort Frontenac, on Lake Ontario, where the town of Kingston now stands. The commandant of this post drank in with greedy ears the trader's recital of his voyage. He was one of the few that ever saw the Journal and map of Joliet. The trader went his way and the young soldier of fortune remained to dream in the wilderness and work his way to renown.

Robert Cavelier de la Salle was born of an ancient and honorable family in Rouen. Renouncing his patrimony, or in some way deprived of it by unjust laws, he became a Jesuit, and received in a college of that order a thorough education. But finding the life of a priest incompatible with his tastes, he quitted the fraternity, receiving high testimonials of capacity and fidelity, and embarked as an adventurer for Canada, where he arrived between 1665 and 1670. Here the force of his character soon displayed itself by his successful prosecution of various difficult enterprises. In 1674 we find him commanding at the fort named in honor of Frontenac, governor of the province. The confidence of this functionary he seems to have completely gained. The next year he visited France with strong recommendations from the governor to the ministry. Colbert was then at the head of the cabinet of Louis XIV. This great statesman listened attentively to the plans of the young soldier, and induced his royal master to grant his request. To La Salle was accordingly given a title of nobility, a monopoly in the fur-trade around Lake Ontario, the command and ownership of Fort Frontenac, and the lands in its neighborhood, on condition of his erecting a stone fortress, and establishing a mission—for to overawe and convert the Iroquois, was the double object of the establishment. While engaged in this undertaking, he showed himself an able politician, by his skillful management of the tribes around him. On the completion of his task, he found himself ruined. To while away the long winter evenings in his frontier post, and to banish the demon of anxiety, he betook himself to the study of the Spanish accounts of America and its conquest. His mind now reverted to the narrative of Joliet, little heeded at the time, and he seems to have been the first to identify the river which De Soto had discovered, with that explored by Marquette. To the Mississippi and its valley, the heart of our adventurer now turned in his extremity. There his failure might be retrieved, and fortune be secured. If he can obtain a monopoly of the fur-trade in that vast region, extend a line of posts from Canada to the Gulf, found a colony at the mouth of the great river, and ship his peltries thence to

France, what easier? Gigantic enterprise, you will say. But what can not one strong will do?

Hastening again to France in 1677, he readily obtained, through the friendship of the great Colbert, and of his son, the Duke de Seignelai, minister of the marine, the sanction and authority he needed from the crown. His patent confirmed the previous one, empowered him to construct forts wherever necessary in the western part of New France, and gave him a vast monopoly of the fur-trade, including, with some exceptions, the whole Mississippi valley. Recruiting a company of mechanics and mariners, he starts a a third time for Canada, and September of the next year, 1678, found him once more at his seigniory of Fort Frontenac, on Lake Ontario, with sixty men, prepared and resolved to carry out his great scheme of discovery, trade and settlement. He brought with him one Henry de Tonty as his lieutenant. This Tonty, said to have been the son of the inventor of those life insurance schemes called Tontines, was an Italian, who had been highly recommended to La Salle by a great noble of the French court; and he thenceforth ever proved himself an unswerving ally, a faithful and able officer, and a trusty friend. He had been a soldier seven years in the French wars, and having lost a hand by a grenade in Sicily, had supplied its place with a rude claw of iron.

With his vast plans revolving in his mind, shaping

out the conception of that belt of forts and missions and settlements twelve hundred miles long, which was at once to secure the great continent for the Grand Monarch, to gird in and overawe the English and Spanish seaboards, to gather the Indians into the Catholic church, and to give himself unbounded riches and a mighty lordship—with all these magnificent dreams in his soul, La Salle nevertheless applied himself diligently to the details and drudgery of their small mercantile beginnings, sending forward traders to gather furs, and organizing matters at and about the Fort.

His design was to build a vessel above Niagara, to sail in it as far on his way as the upper lakes would admit, and then to cross by land to the Mississippi, and proceed down the great river in another vessel. He therefore sent Tonty in a small craft of ten tons which had been built at Fort Frontenac the year before, with workmen, tools, materials, and provisions, to select a proper spot for building his brigantine, and also for erecting a fort.

They arrived at the mouth of the Niagara River in the beginning of January, 1679, and leaving their vessel and going round the falls, chose their dockyard; but finding the Indians dissatisfied with the plan of erecting a fort, they pacified them, not without difficulty, and confined themselves to palisading the cabins in which they passed the winter.

La Salle embarked from Fort Frontenac, a short time after their departure, in another small vessel with merchandise, provisions, and rigging for the new ship, delaying, as he came, to conciliate the Senecas. He reached Niagara on the 20th of January; and already there began to lower over him the dark clouds of that long series of misfortunes against which he bore up for so many years, with such heroic but unsuccessful strength and resolution. All at once he was assaulted with all the evils which afterward pursued him; timidity or dislike or senseless obstinacy in his men, bitter and unscrupulous enmity from the traders with whom his monopoly interfered, and rapacious severity from his creditors. The two pilots of his vessel quarrelled about the route, and wrecked her on the south shore of Lake Ontario. The anchors and the rigging were secured with great difficulty; but the goods and provisions were lost. The Indian traders too, with whom his monopoly interfered, and those connected with them in business, had begun to poison the minds of the Indians, by representing that his forts and ships were intended, not for trade, but to subdue the tribes.

But La Salle, with the able diplomacy of the French, conciliated the Senecas in his one short visit. Deferring his fort at Niagara to please them, and urging on his main expedition to the West, he at once chose, from among the sites which had been explored for a dock-yard, a locality about six miles above the falls, on the English side, at the mouth of a creek, and himself drove the first bolt in the frame of his intended vessel, a week after his arrival. Then, leaving Tonty in charge of the ship-building, he hastened back again to Fort Frontenac by land, almost three hundred miles through snowy forests, with a bag of parched corn to eat, and with two men and a boy as guides and baggage-train. His errand now was to complete his arrangements for raising money, and for the management of his property during his absence. For nearly six months he was thus industriously at work in preparation, and struggling against the busy and unscrupulous intrigues of his enemies. His creditors too, in Montreal and Quebec, frightened at the stories which they heard of his wild schemes and monstrous expenses, seized and sold at ruinous sacrifice whatever of his property they could lay hands on.

But he could not stop to set these things right—that would have been precisely what his enemies designed; so letting his peltries and merchandise go, and making a farewell grant out of his estate at Fort Frontenac to the Franciscans, of a hundred and eighteen acres of land—he had already erected for them dwellings and a chapel—he set off again for Niagara, hearing that his new ship was launched and ready. Coasting the southern shore of the lake in a canoe, he renewed his friendship with the Indians by the way. He found his vessel already launched, and towed up the river to within a mile or two of Lake Erie. She was named the Griffin, was of sixty tons burden, armed with two brass guns and three arquebuses, and adorned with a wooden griffin for a figure-head.

After some delay the expedition, of thirty-four souls, including three Franciscan missionaries, embarked on the 7th of August, 1679, amid shouts and salvoes of artillery, upon the untried waters of Lake Erie, westward bound. They steered boldly into the unknown depths of the lake, confident in their compasses and in the skill of their pilot; crossed the lake in less than three days; threaded the shallows of the straits of Detroit and St. Clair, and the lake between them, to which they gave its present name in honor of the day; then entered the broad expanse of Lake Huron. In crossing this, they encountered a tempest so terrible that they gave themselves up for lost, La Salle himself even crying out that they were undone, and offering fervent vows to the great St. Anthony of Padua, in case they should escape alive. Only the tough old sea-dog of a pilot would neither fear nor pray, but, Hennepin says, "did nothing all that while but curse and swear against M. de la Salle, who had brought him thither to make him perish in a nasty lake, and lose the glory he had acquired by his long and happy navigation on the ocean." They escaped, however, and arrived safe at Mackinaw.

Here La Salle found that the influence of his enemies, the traders, had gone before him. They had made the Indians believe that he intended both to restrict to himself all trade in skins, and also to subject them to the crown of France; and they received him coldly and suspiciously, though with ceremonious politeness. They had also tampered with his advanced guard, most of whom had been indolent and unfaithful in their task of gatheriug furs and provisions. Still, the energetic leader was not to be diverted from his purpose. He left his faithful lieutenant, Tonty, to collect some of the deserters, and himself pushed on again in the Griffin for Green Bay. At the entrance of this arm of Lake Michigan, on a small island occupied by Pottawatomie Indians, he found some of his missing fur-traders, with great store of peltries, the proceeds of their barter with the Indians.

La Salle here takes a sudden and singular resolution; and one not pleasing to his men. But he is not wont to ask counsel at their hands, or indeed at the hands of any. Of few words, and of reserved and even harsh manners, he evolves his plans in silence and alone within his own soul, and sets himself to accomplish them with a will seemingly incapable of diversion or discouragement; but he asks no man's advice, "talks things over" with no one; only resolves, and then orders. Strange character for a Frenchman—and not only strange, but unfortunate, at least so far as popularity was important to him. For a chief impediment to his plans, and the cause of his own untimely end, was the insubordination and enmity of his own men. In truth, there seems to have been not one faithful and thoroughgoing helper among them all, except Henry de Tonty the iron-handed Italian, and one poor Indian of some distant eastern tribe, called Nika, a hunter of exquisite skill, who followed his fortune hither and thither as closely and steadily as a dog, often the sole support of La Salle himself and all his party for days and days together, and finally murdered with his master, for his faithfulness to him. Peace to the poor forgotten shade of that brave and faithful red man!

This strange resolution was, to send the Griffin, laden with the furs at Green Bay and what others could be gathered on the road, back again to Niagara, that her cargo might pay his debts. All the rest would much prefer the stanch and hitherto fortunate brigantine, for the remainder of the perilous navigation through Lake Michigan, to the frail slender canoes, exposed to furious tempests and thievish or hostile savages. But none thinks it best to remonstrate; and with a prosperous westerly wind, the Griffin sets sail on the 18th of July, manned with five men and the swearing unterrified pilot, firing a farewell gun as she departs.

She was never heard of more. Somewhere in the

depths of the north end of Lake Michigan, between Green Bay and Mackinaw, her decayed timbers, and the rusty relics of the "two brass guns and three arquebuses," her vaunted armament, yet repose. All else must long since have disappeared. Father Hennepin, with unclerical, careless disregard for the six unfortunate souls, her ship's company, dismisses the subject by saying, "This was a great loss for M. de la Salle and other adventurers, for that ship with its cargo cost above sixty thousand livres,"—twelve thousand dollars.

But La Salle, hopeful and cheery, as trusting in speedy freedom from debts behind, and speedy glory of great discoveries before, now pushes on southward in four canoes, burdened disproportionately with weighty property, even including a blacksmith's forge, and with a party now reduced by detachment and desertion, to fourteen. After a most toilsome and dangerous journey along the western side of the lake, sometimes entertained generously by friendly Indians, once embroiled with a roving squad of Outagamies or Foxes on a thieving expedition, on the first of November they safely entered the Miami River, now called the St. Josephs, the appointed rendezvous for Tonty and for the Griffin.

All that winter was spent in waiting for the expected comers. The men, weary of living by the uncertain fruits of the chase, dreading the winter and its famine, dreading the dangers of this vast unknown region into which they were to be led, murmured and complained, and desired to proceed into the Illinois country, where there was corn. But La Salle refused, gave them good reasons, and kept them busy in building Fort Miamis on a hill at the mouth of the river, while he sounded and staked out the channel, and sent two men to Mackinaw to hasten the coming of his ship.

After long delay, Tonty appeared, gladdening the hearts of the party by the reinforcement and the two canoe-loads of venison he brought, but also bringing to his commander the heavy tidings that the Griffin had not been heard from. La Salle had already become apprehensive respecting her, since nearly twice the time had elapsed which should have brought her to the Miamis. And thus disappeared a large part of his means, and his hopes of promptly paying his debts. But the strong-hearted man wasted no useless grief over misfortunes now past. Delaying yet a little longer, until it became necessary to depart to escape from the winter, the expedition left Fort Miamis on the 3d of December, in eight canoes, leaving instructions for the captain of the Griffin, in letters conspicuously fixed on branches of trees. Ascending the Miami about seventy miles, they make a portage across to the head of the Kankakee, follow that slow and crooked stream through a hundred miles of desolate frozen marsh, then emerge into a prairie country, and after two hundred miles more of voyaging, enter the river Illinois.

Thus they navigate southward, descending the two rivers, during the whole of December, supplying themselves with corn from the *caches* of a large Indian town whose inhabitants had departed to the hunt, leaving their cabins empty. Floating onward through Lake Peoria, they come suddenly, at its southern end, into the midst of a great camp of the Illinois tribe, occupying both sides of the river. But, putting on a bold face, and forming in order of battle, the brave commander of the little band meets the Indians as their superior in force, and only holds out the calumet of peace in answer to their signals; satisfies them for the abstraction of their supplies of corn, explains his designs, and concludes a solemn alliance.

That same night came an emissary of his busy foes the private traders, a Mascouten chief named Monso, and poisoned the minds of all the Illinois—a fickle, cowardly, suspicious, thievish and lascivious race—with the same old story that his plan was to exterminate their nation, and that an army of the terrible Iroquois would soon be upon them. This he industriously told to one and another all night long, confirmed the tale by valuable presents of knives and hatchets and such coveted goods, and fled away before morning, that the unsuspecting Frenchman might be ruined without knowing whence came the blow. La Salle saw at once, when next day he went among his savage hosts, that their yesterday's jovial friendship was quite changed into suspicion and fears. But discovering the trick by means of an Illinois chief who had imbibed a strong liking for him, his frank and judicious explanations soon dispersed this threatening cloud, in appearance at least. Yet the minds of the Illinois were not entirely at rest, and an eminent chief, one Nikanape, took occasion, at a great feast which he gave the French, in a long speech filled with flaming descriptions of terrible savages on the land, and vast monsters and hideous whirlpools in the great river, to dissuade them from going further. It may easily be supposed that the steadfast leader of the French was not moved by this savage rhetoric, whose plain meaning he saw clearly to be, "We do not want you travelling about our country at all; so please go straight back by the way you came." He calmly rebuked the oratorical Indian for the veiled unfriendliness of his purpose, and the feast proceeded. Yet the infection worked among his men, as usual, and six of them, including two sawyers upon whom he depended to build the vessel in which to descend the Mississippi, ran away, like faint hearts as they were. It is even said that they basely planned a cruel death for their bold commander, and that he only escaped the effect of the poison they gave him, by a strong dose of *treacle*, a sovereign antidote in that day, and which, as well as *orvietan*, another ancient antidote, La Salle seems always to have had in his medicine chest.

To prevent the rest from further dwelling upon future dangers, he explained to them the peril of leaving him in the winter, promised that those who desired it should be permitted and aided to depart in the spring, showed them how unsafe was their undefended condition, and proposed to build another fort. To this they agreed, and he at once laid out the ground, and employed part of them in erecting a stout stockade, and the rest in building the vessel in which he proposed to descend the Great River. When the fort was completed, and it only remained to give it a name, La Salle for once took counsel of his sorrows. He remembered the virulent pursuit of the revengeful traders; the disappearance of the Griffin, with its rich freight of furs, and its richer freight of human souls; the wasteful seizure of his goods by the creditors at Montreal and Quebec; the long, weary journeys to and fro across stormy lakes and wintry forests; the base desertions, and vile, murderous schemes of coward followers; and named his little stockade *Crèvecœur*, "The Fort of the Broken Heart."

But this first and last access of discouragement was soon repelled, and the clear, strong mind of the great discoverer regained its steady balance. Having completed the bark on the stocks so far as was possible without the rigging and other materials in the Griffin, and having given up hopes of seeing her, he recognizes the fact that his means for proceeding are exhausted, and quickly and quietly prepares for another winter's trip to Fort Frontenac, to refit, recruit, and return. He sends Father Hennepin, one of his Franciscans, with two stout French canoe-men, to explore the upper Mississippi during his own absence; takes with him three Frenchmen and his faithful Indian hunter, and departing, passes over the twelve hundred miles between Forts Crèvecœur and Frontenac, taking the route along the south shore of lakes Ontario and Erie, either near their coasts or upon the highlands dividing their affluents from those of the Ohio, deterred now no more than before, by the deep melting snow of the forests, or the floods and floating ice of so many rivers. Sending word back to Tonty to build another fort on the strong site afterward occupied by the French, Fort St. Louis, and even now called Rock Fort, on a bluff two hundred feet above the Illinois River, he disappeared in the pathless woods; and neither of his adventures nor of his solitary thoughts during the weeks of that long, toilsome way, have we any record. But experienced woodcraft, a hardy frame, and a strong will, brought him safely through.

Of course, misfortune and his enemies have played into each other's hands and against him all the time of his absence. Besides the loss of the Griffin, he has been heavily swindled by his agents in trade on Ontario; has lost a whole cargo of merchandise in the lower St. Lawrence; several valuable canoe-loads in the rapids above Montreal; a quantity more by other employees, who stole them and ran away to the Dutch at "Nouvelle Jorck;" and still another large quantity by forced sales at the instance of creditors, who had heard (or wished they had) that he and all his party were drowned.

Penniless, deeply in debt, all Canada full of his enemies, all his plans crushed, is he helpless, too, and will he succumb and disappear from Canada and from history? Never! He has still one powerful and trusty friend—Count de Frontenac, the governor; and one more, yet more powerful and more trusty—himself. With the aid of these two he bestirs him with such energy and success, that he again secures men and means, and only varying his scheme by giving up the idea of navigating the Mississippi in a large boat or brigantine, and trusting to canoes instead, he departs again, July 23d, 1680. After a long journey, delayed by contrary winds on the lakes, he arrives, by way of Fort Miamis, at the chief village of the Illinois. It is burned and empty. In surprise, he proceeds to the site where he had directed Tonty to build his second fort. There is not a vestige left of human labor or human presence. He turns about, without going further down the river, and returns to the Miamis, where he remains during that winter, occupied in negotiating peace among the Indians. In the course of this season he learns, from some wandering Illinois, a sad story of the disasters of their nation, but gains no news of Tonty or his men.

But without them, his party is not large enough to proceed down the Great River. In the end of May, 1681, therefore, he returns again toward Canada for further reinforcements, and at Mackinaw, to their mutual surprise and joy, finds Tonty and his men. They exchange the stories of their separate experience. Tonty related how mutiny had obliged him to give up both Fort St. Louis and Fort Crèvecœur, and had driven him to take shelter with the Illinois; how an Iroquois army had invaded and scattered that tribe, and destroyed the villages; and how, after long endeavors to avert the destructive purposes of the savage Iroquois, he and his few men had been forced to flee for their lives to Green Bay, some scouting Kickapoos murdering Father Gabriel de la Ribourde on the road. If he had taken the south road at Lake Dauphin, instead of that to the north, Tonty would have met his commander, on his last outward expedition, with a well furnished little fleet of canoes.

Then La Salle, with a steady countenance, as indifferently as if they had been the mishaps of another, in turn related a still longer and heavier catalogue of misfortunes and disappointments. Father Membré says, in admiration, that though any one but he would have renounced the enterprise, he was "more resolute than ever to continue his work and complete his discovery."

We must here advert for a moment to the liar Hennepin, who had, during La Salle's absence, made an exploring voyage on the upper Mississippi, and endured a short captivity among the Indians. From this he had escaped, and a few weeks after La Salle's meeting with Tonty at Mackinaw, he passed that post, made the best of his way to Canada, and thence to Europe, where he afterward published an account of a pretended voyage down the Great River, in which he endeavored to rob La Salle of the glory of discovering its outlet.

Nothing could be done at Mackinaw for the great object of the persevering La Salle, so he and his party soon returned to Fort Frontenac. Here he rearranged all his finances, selected a strong body of Frenchmen and of New England Indians, Abenakis or Mohegans, with these returned to Niagara, and in August, 1681, embarked thence once more for the mysterious mouth of the "Hidden River," as the Spaniards named it; at last, after undaunted and indescribable exertions, this third time destined to succeed.

With fifty-four souls in all, including ten Indian women to cook, and three children, the expedition passed from the Miamis to the Chicago River, up this on the ice to the portage, down the Illinois to Lake Peoria, and thence by water, the river being open, toward the Mississippi. They swept past the Fort of the Broken Heart, barely delaying to look in upon the garrison now reëstablished there, and pressing forward with happier auguries, glided down a deserted river—the Indians being at their distant winter hunting-grounds—and on the 6th of February, 1682, floated upon the long-desired stream, which La Salle now named the Colbert, after his staunch patron, the great French statesman.

They swept downward, with various adventure; fishing or hunting; holding peaceful intercourse with many a savage tribe; erecting a splendid cross, bearing the arms of France, near the mouth of the Arkansas River, in token of the proprietorship of the French king, and amid the ignorant rejoicing of the savages, who took the ceremony to be a show for their amusement, instead of a formal theft of their land, and after their departure carefully inclosed with palisades the ornamented cross.

Onward still; past the sun-worshipping Tensas, whose ceremonies, large canoes, and profound reverence for their chiefs, seemed to indicate that they were of kin to the brave and interesting tribe of the Natchez. Onward still, past the Natchez themselves; past the Koroas and the Quinipissas, and sundry other tribes; past a village just plundered, and tenanted by the corpses of the slain; and now, all at once, the vast stream divides before them into three mighty channels. The brave commander's heart beats high, for he must be near the southern sea; and sending detachments down the eastern and middle channels, under Tonty and Dautray, he himself pursues the western, the largest. The muddy waves of the broad flood are gradually found to become brackish, and then quite salt; and now the measureless expanse of the Gulf of Mexico lies wide before them. The mouth of the Great River, the Hidden River, is found.

Of the emotions of the stern and lofty-minded La Salle, as he thus floated out toward the goal of his vast and long-pursued enterprise, no record exists. Whatever they were, his high and resolved features gave small trace of them; and speedily returning to the prosaic duties of the mere discoverer, he spends one day in exploring and sounding the river's mouths and the neighboring shores, and another in finding a spot dry and firm enough, amidst those dreary expanses of fat alluvium, all overgrown with rank sedge and reeds, to afford a site for a memorial column and its attendant cross, tokens of the empire of Christ, and of the great French king. "Henceforth," saith La Salle, "my God and my king are supreme forever over the innumerable souls and the immeasurable lands of this great continent."

Having selected a suitable place, on the 9th of April, 1682, La Salle draws up his whole party under arms; they sing the *Te Deum*, the *Exaudiat*, and the *Domine salvum fac Regem*—thanking God, imploring his continued help for themselves, and then loyally asking it for their king, by the three sonorous old Latin chants. They fire a formal salute of musketry, and shout *Vive le Roi!* Then the column is erected, and with a long enumeration of nations, and rivers, and lands, he formally proclaims that all the lands and waters of Louisiana, "along the River Colbert or Mississippi, and rivers which discharge themselves therein, from its source beyond the country of the Kious or Nadouessions, and this with their consent, and with the consent of the Motantees, Illinois, Mesigameas, Natchez, and Koroas, as far as its mouth at the sea," are henceforth part of the realms of the king of France. And he demands of Jacques de la Metairie, the notary, his official certificate of the transaction. The scribe draws up the instrument, and it is signed by the notary himself, and by La Salle, Father Zenobius Membré, the missionary, Henry de Tonty, and the other Frenchmen of the party, and delivered to the commander.

Then they erect a cross, bury at the foot of the tree to which it is attached a leaden plate, with an inscription commemorating their discovery and their claim; chant more Latin hymns, shout again *Vive le Roi;* and thus the Mississippi valley is made French for almost a century—until the peace of 1763.

But they are hard pressed for food; and barely delaying to finish the ceremony, must push rapidly up the river. This they do; and after a combat with the Quinipissas—the first into which La Salle had ever been driven with the Indians, so wise and skillful had been all his actions toward them—and after some suffering from hunger, the party proceeds safely on its return. At Fort Prudhomme, however, the intrepid chief is stricken down by a wasting fever. He sends his faithful lieutenant, Tonty, with an account of his voyage and discovery, to Count de Frontenac, with orders to return at once; and himself remains forty days on his sick-bed, under the care of the good priest Father Zenobius Membré, and was even then so worn down by illness that it was almost the end of September before he reached his establishment at the Miamis.

La Salle now purposes to return down the Mississippi during the next spring, and to establish a strong colony near its mouth. He sends Father Zenobius to

France with full accounts of his doings hitherto; but for nearly a year he is occupied—probably, for he has left no record of his deeds—in trading, travelling, and keeping up his influence and connections with the Indians, the plan of the colony being postponed or modified by circumstances, or, more probably, by his own thoughts.

For during the long months of that sojourn in the wilderness, the scheme of his Mississippi colony has grown and expanded within his mind. Twice has he proved his influence upon the rich and magnificent government of Louis the Fourteenth. Why should he not a third time look to a mighty empire for the assistance he needs, rather than to his small individual resources; and cross the ocean with a strong company in great ships, instead of boating obscurely down the vast wilderness river in frail canoes?

He resolves to try; and leaving the Chevalier de Tonty his financial agent and lieutenant commanding, he departs down the St. Lawrence, takes ship at Quebec, and lands at Rochelle, December 13th, 1683.

As usual, he find that his enemies have been active, and that fortune has aided them. His munificent patron, Colbert, is dead. De la Barre, now governor of Canada, has written to the home government that La Salle stirs up Indian wars; that all his tales of discoveries are lies; that he has acted the part of a petty tyrant among those far-off wildernesses, with a small band of vagabond followers, stealing and fighting. But it was not such an attack as this which could obstruct La Salle. Aided by his friends, Father Zenobius Membré, and Count Frontenac, now returned to France, by the inherited prepossessions of Colbert's son, the Duke de Seignelai, now high in office, and by his own inexhaustible energy and strange power over the court, he goes straight on with his plans. The absurd slanders of the spiteful De la Barre die in silence; and the authority and means now confided to him were far greater than before.

The king gives him a free gift of a ship of six guns, and the use of three more, a thirty-six gun frigate, a transport of three hundred tons, and a ketch; and furnishes supplies, sea and land forces, colonists: in short, the whole personal and material constituents of a colony. And not only has La Salle the supreme command of this great expedition, but territorial jurisdiction over all the great valley whither he is bound, and over all colonies established therein.

The reputation of the enterprise and its leader draw to him a number of volunteers, all respectable, and including several families, a brother of La Salle's, who was a priest, two of his nephews, and another relative, also a priest.

And even now, at this very moment, when the impregnable, steady energies and inexhaustible wise perseverance of this man seem at last to have brought him to a point promising the full reward of so many years of labor and incessant wanderings—even now opens the longest and saddest of all the long sad chapters of his fateful life. On the very point of embarking, the careful chief, who had been forced to enlist his soldiers, mechanics, and laborers by means of others, found that these faithless hirelings had raked together the very scum of the sea-ports; giving him for soldiers beggars, vagabonds, and cripples so deformed that they could not handle a musket; for skilled artisans, men perfectly ignorant of their pretended trades. In urgent haste, he partly remedies the evil, but, as usual, must let much of it pass; trusting, not without reason, to the calm and ready strength which has made head against so many troubles before. But another evil he cannot remedy. The generous king has appointed to the naval command a Norman, M. de Beaujeu; and it would be ungracious, and is now too late to endeavor to displace him: a little-minded, obstinate, quarrelsome, pompous man, ridiculously vain of his rank of captain, snappish and irritable, of all men on earth the very one to be vexed at the silent, self-reliant, haughty reserve of La Salle. Even before sailing, this unhappy captain writes peevish and dissatisfied letters to the marine department. How fatally and bitterly the fool vented his spite afterward, will quickly appear.

Let us hasten; the narrative is painful; who would protract the sorrowful story? They had to return one hundred and fifty miles to replace a broken bowsprit; then sailing again, La Salle, with wise and cautious speed, refused to stop uselessly at Madeira, and the wretched Norman, Beaujeu, and all the lazy ships' companies, murmured and were enraged. Then he positively forbade the sailors to subject his followers to the brutal abuses usual at crossing the tropic line, and they grumbled and complained still more. As the fleet approached St. Domingo, a storm scattered it; and eagerly seizing the opportunity of making trouble, the mean Beaujeu, instead of entering Port de Paix, the rendezvous agreed upon, and where were the royal officers whom La Salle was to meet and who were ordered to aid and promote his designs, passed round the island and landed at Petit Goave, far to the southwest. And now, also, the inscrutable purposes of God add to fierce tempests and hatefully perverse unfriends aboard, two other enemies. The Spaniards, now at war with France, surprise and seize his ketch, the St. Francis, with thirty tons of merchandise and military stores—a grievous loss, which would not have happened had Beaujeu put in at Port de Paix, as he should have done. But La Salle calmly adds the item to that long list of shipwrecks in Canada, and dismisses it from his mind. A wasting disease, however, is the second and worst of these added foes; and under the furious assault of a tropical fever, his life even is despaired of. But he is not yet to die; we may even suppose that that powerful will urges him through this peril of disease: that he *will* not die—unless God so decree. And in three weeks, though yet feeble, he consults with the governor and intendant, who came to Petit Goave to meet him; takes on board provisions and domestic animals; obtains sailing directions, and hastens away; for his miserable band of vagabond soldiers, living in licentious disorder, are diseased and dying, or desert the jangling and ill-omened fleet for the luxurious ease of St. Domingo.

Embarking in the slowest sailer, and taking the lead in her, he sets sail again; coasts the southern shore of Cuba; stops three days at the Isle of Pines; weathers Cape Corientes, and then Cape San Antonio, and after being once driven back, steers north west into the great Gulf of Mexico, straight for the mouth of the Mississippi. They sail eight days, and now the soundings tell of land not far off. In two days more they discern it. Where are they? Consulting and hesitating, they conclude that they are in the great Bay of Appalache; for the pilots at St. Domingo told them of strong currents, which they accordingly believe have carried them eastward. Fatal error! They were, doubtless, already far west of that strangely-hidden river, in one of the bays of the coast of Texas.

But thus they judge; and coasting further west to find the Mississippi, they leave it yet further behind them. Sailing a whole week, they still imagine themselves in the Bay of Appalache. Sailing two weeks more, they become convinced of their error; the coast trends southward; they are approaching Mexico. They turn about, and it is proposed to find the Mississippi by coasting eastward again. But Beaujeu flatly refuses, without a supply of provisions, which La Salle will not give, lest the wicked captain should sail away to France.

Returning, however, a little way up the coast, they enter Matagorda Bay, which La Salle names the Bay of St. Louis, and which he vainly hopes to find one of the mouths of the Mississippi. It is decided to disembark, and all the emigrants go ashore, leaving the crews only on board the ships. The neighborhood is explored, the harbor sounded, and the Aimable, the transport, ordered in. Her captain, a brute or a villain, or more probably both, refuses a pilot, and running his vessel ashore, she bilges; some one takes pains to destroy her boat; and the greater part of her cargo—the very sustenance of the colony—is lost. The Indians take some goods which float ashore; and a party of Frenchmen, sent to reclaim them, seizing some canoes and skins in reprisal, the enraged savages make a night attack upon them, kill two and wound two more.

The demoniac cunning and ferocity of the red men thus coöperates with these devouring shipwrecks. And the colonists already begin to lament, to murmur, and to talk of returning to France. But their leader, though cruelly grieved, is not discouraged nor moved; his fearless resolution is a tower of strength to all the band, and the enterprise proceeds.

Beaujeu departs, still angry and venomous, carrying away all the cannon balls for the eight great guns of the colony, because, forsooth, he would have had to move part of his cargo to get at them; leaving on that wild and distant shore about two hundred souls, the small vessel, La Belle, and that portion of provisions and goods saved from the Spaniards and the sea.

This is in the middle of March, 1685. The commander orders a temporary fort to be constructed, and then explores the coast. Finding a pleasant site some distance west, he moves his colony thither, and in the course of July they are all there, their only misfortunes by the way, one death from the bite of a rattlesnake, and a conspiracy among the soldiers to murder their officers and run away, this last detected in time to crush it. On this new site are erected, with terrific labor, even fatal to some of the colonists, dwellings and a fort, named Fort St. Louis; and La

Salle, having thus provided for the security of his colony, prepares to make a journey by land for the hidden fateful river. In October, having been delayed by his brother's sickness, he sets out, the Belle accompanying him part of the way by sea. On the first night six men, detached to take soundings, keeping careless watch, are murdered by the savages. The commander marches on eastward, discovers the Colorado, examines the eastern part of Matagorda Bay, and returns, after an absence of more than four months, with but eight of the twenty men who set out with him. Six are dead; one, a quarrelsome, vindictive villain, named Duhaut, deserted, and has returned alone some time before; and the others are searching for the Belle, of which no news has been received. They came in next day; nothing could be seen of her; she was doubtless lost, and with her disappeared their last means of communicating with civilized men, unless by journeys scarcely less than sure to be fatal.

But such communication must be had. The necessity of it being recognized, the strong and calm commander quietly and quickly prepares for it, as coolly as if he were only intending to step across the fort; gathering resolution—if, indeed, that indomitable will ever looked for encouragement at all—from the evident alternative of swift destruction. His journey shall be to the Illinois, where, in his strong hill fort, the valiant and faithful Tonty is sure to be at his post, waiting orders as directed—unless orders which cannot be disobeyed have summoned him away from all earthly obligations. Once in Illinois, he can obtain assistance there, and can send or go to Quebec or to France. Taking twenty men again, he sets out by land, in the end of April, 1686, leaving M. Joutel, as before, in command of the fort.

He returns in August, having travelled far up into the interior, and having there been delayed for two months and more by a violent fever. Their ammunition becoming exhausted, during this time, and being entirely dependent on hunting for provisions, they had no alternative but to turn back. Of this second company of twenty, but eight returned; four had deserted to the Indians, one was lost, one devoured by an alligator, and the rest, being unable to endure the fatigue of the journey, had set out to return and were never heard of.

These failures cast a deep gloom over the little company in the fort, now reduced, by death and desertion, from about two hundred to forty; but, says Joutel in his journal, "the even temper of our chief made all men easy, and he found, by his great vivacity of spirit, expedients which revived the lowest ebb of hope." He had given up the Belle for lost, and therefore rejoiced exceedingly to find that his kinsman, M. Chefdeville, and some others of her crew, had escaped, and had saved his own clothes and part of his papers, although the little vessel herself, as he had concluded, had perished.

La Salle at once set about building a storehouse, to keep his men employed; and still retaining his intention of proceeding to the Illinois, they talked daily about the journey. Being taken ill, however, his stout-hearted lieutenant, Joutel, offered to go instead, if he might take fifteen men and the faithful Indian hunter, who had followed his chief to France and back to Mexico. But the commander recovers his health, and again—as he would have done a hundredth time, had he failed ninety-nine—makes his arrangements and sets out, taking with him a third twenty men, and leaving thirteen men and seven women in the fort, with a considerable stock of provisions and arms.

Thus, on the 12th of January, 1687, departs Robert de la Salle, for the third time, from his little colony, as resolute and cool as ever; but the parting was saddened as if by presentiments of evil. "We took our leaves," says the veteran man of war, Joutel, "with so much tenderness and sorrow, as if we had all presaged that we should never see each other more."

And now the long, brave struggle with fate and with enemies, draws to its melancholy close. The little party, with their five horse-loads of provisions, disappears from the eyes of the Sieur Barbier, left commander of the scanty colony in the fort; and plunging into the woods, marches northeastward, across the pleasant prairies and through the open woods of Texas. They ford rivers and pass through swamps, often easing their progress by following buffalo paths; negotiate, as they go, with the Indians, always friendly, but always on their guard; and Nika, the hunter, ever purveys for them abundance of game.

On the 15th of March, La Salle sends Duhaut, the mutinous wretch before mentioned, Hiens, a German buccaneer, Liotot the surgeon, Nika the Indian, and his own footman, Saget, to bring in some provisions which he had concealed a few miles away, on his last journey. These they found spoiled by wet, and as they returned, Nika killed two buffalo, and they sent the footman on to advise their commander to have the meat dried, and send horses for it. He does so, sending his nephew, Moranget, a violent and reckless young man, with several more of the party.

Moranget comes, and finds that Duhaut and the rest are smoking the buffalo meat, and that, by the common right of hunters, they have laid by some marrow-bones and choice bits for themselves. In a sudden burst of unreasonable and inexplicable passion, he reproves and threatens them, and seizes not only all the smoked meat, but all the tidbits which they had saved according to custom. This last offence filled up the cup of their anger, even to running over; for these three, the surgeon Liotot, Hiens, and Duhaut, fancied they had—and most probably had—other causes of complaint against the unhappy young man. With black looks, their hearts all boiling with hot wrath, but still withheld for the moment by lack of concert from wreaking the revenge for which they all thirst, they silently draw off, and consult apart upon the matter. Seared and hardened by crime, the inhuman wretches easily agree upon their measures. They will murder Moranget in his sleep, and so square their account with him. But, one of them suggests, the Indian and the footman are faithful—they will avenge the deed, or inform upon us. The answer is easy—they, too, will be asleep; we have only to kill them too. Accordingly, taking into their plot Teissier and Larchevêque, two more of the party, they wait, revelling in the devilish satisfaction of anticipated revenge, until their unsuspecting victims have eaten, and are peacefully asleep, dreaming, doubtless, of distant homes and loving hearts in sunny France. Liotot, the surgeon, arises, takes an axe, and strikes Moranget many blows on the head; then leaving him, dispatches the Indian and the footman, who never stirred. But such was the vitality of the young officer, that, though mangled and speechless, he sat up, alive, a horrible spectacle of misery. The murderers oblige his fellow, De Marle, though not a conspirator, to put him out of his pain.

Crimes are seldom single. It needs not long reflection to show them that they must do yet another murder, or suffer for those already done. They must kill La Salle too. And they will the more readily do this, because they have some harshness of his to punish. They would at once have set out to attack him, had not the river between them risen too high. But he comes to them, as if impelled upon his fate. Uneasy at the delay of his nephew, and, as if under some presage of misfortune, or consciousness of fault in his own or his nephew's conduct, he asks his men if Liotot, Hiens, and Duhaut have not expressed some discontent. No one seems to know of it, and, his apprehensions increasing, he sets out on the third day to find his nephew.

Approaching the tragic scene, he sees some eagles, and thinking carrion near, he fires a shot, as a signal to his friends, in case they have killed game and are within hearing. Silent in death, they are beyond all human summons. The doomed commander's signal serves only to insure and hasten his own fate. The conspirators hear it; Duhaut and Larchevêque cross the river; Duhaut hides in the reeds, and Larchevêque shows himself at a little distance. La Salle calls out to him, asking after Moranget. The man answers, vaguely, rudely, and omitting the usual gesture of respect, that he is along the river. The punctilious and severe chief advances, as if to reprove or chastise the impertinent manner of his follower; Duhaut takes fatal aim from his lair, and fires. His ball passes through the head of La Salle, and he falls without speaking a word.

Father Anastasius Douay, who was with his leader, prepares to share his fate, but on their telling him that he is safe, endeavors to do the last priestly offices for him. But the dying man can only feebly press the hand of the good father, in token that he understands him, and his spirit quickly passes. The death shot brings up the other conspirators; and they strip and insult the poor corpse. The surgeon, Liotot, laughs and mocks at it, and, in the excess of his brutal glee, cries out over and over again, "There thou liest, grand bashaw—there thou liest!" And they fling the naked body aside among the bushes, a prey to wild beasts; though they do not prevent the sorrowing priest from burying it afterward, and erecting a rude cross over it.

Thus died Robert Cavelier de la Salle, at a time when a fairer prospect than ever of some permanent success was opening before him. His faithful follower, Joutel, who was one of the party, but not present at his death, thus delivers his funeral oration, with terse military frankness, mingled of praise and blame: "His constancy and courage, and his extraordinary knowledge in arts and sciences, which rendered him fit for anything, together with an indefatigable body, which made him surmount all difficulties, would have procured a glorious issue to his undertaking, had not all those excellent qualities been counterbalanced by too haughty a behavior, which sometimes made him insupportable, and by a severity toward those under his command, which at last drew on him implacable hatred, and was the occasion of his death."

Few words may close this sad story. A swift retribution overtook Liotot and Duhaut, who were a little after slain in a quarrel, by Hiens, who remained among the Indians. Six of the party, all the conspirators having left them, reached, in July, a post established by Tonty at the mouth of the Arkansas, and proceeding onward, reached Fort St. Louis, thence went to Quebec, and thence to France; hiding, with difficulty and equivocation, their heavy burden of sad news, until they first revealed it to the French king.

La Salle's little colony vanished away. The Indians assaulted and took it, slaying all but four youths and a young girl, who were afterward rescued by a Spanish force from Mexico, sent to observe the French establishment.

Tonty had descended the Mississippi while La Salle

was in Texas, but not finding him, left a letter for him with the Indians, who delivered it safe to Iberville, fourteen years after, when he entered the river. Then returning, he resumed the duties of his lieutenancy in Illinois; and spent the remainder of his life, as far as is known, in military services in various parts of North America: a stout and faithful soldier to the last.

Not one written word from La Salle's pen has reached us. His papers perished in the lonely fort on Matagorda Bay. Nor have we even reports of his statements as to his views or motives; for it was not his custom to speak of what he intended, but only to order what he desired, and thus it happens that our estimate of him must be based upon our scanty information of his actual achievements, preserved either by ill-informed or unappreciative friends, or unscrupulous and cunning enemies.

We need not elaborate a description of his character; our story has sufficiently exhibited it. The lessons of his life are easily read. It is true, that that haughty silence, that harsh, peremptory manner, were faults; but how manifold the excuses—how terribly complete the expiation! Tenderly we would touch upon those errors, and would rather enlarge upon the unspotted honor, the far-seeing plans, the wise practical sense, the tact and skill in governing and negotiating, and organizing, the stainless, impregnable courage, and, above all, that calm, colossal power of will which impelled him so resistlessly through and over the opposition of so many foes, so many misfortunes, with an inscrutable, gigantic momentum, like that by which the vast icebergs of the Arctic ride crashing through the thick fields of ironbound ice, with a force beyond human admeasurement, but calmly and steadily, as if floating in a summer sea. No grander model of superiority to the vicissitudes of human life is to be found in history.

Farewell, strong and brave man! From thee may we well learn a lesson of courage, of perseverance, of patient endurance and undying hope; and if the perplexing question should arise within us, How can it be just that such heroic struggles should at last so utterly fail—why could not this noble life at last be crowned with peace and honor and happiness? let Faith answer, from behind the mysterious veil of death—Ye shall know all, when ye come hither!

Lecture III.

THE

FRENCH IN ILLINOIS.

THE FRENCH IN ILLINOIS.

THE IDYL OF AMERICA.

IN the history of the exploration and settlement of the great valley of the Mississippi, as far as we have hitherto examined it, the four predominant influences may be named as Romance, Religion, Ambition, and Greed, each conjoined with the others in varying proportions.

The early history of New England is a manifestation of a stalwart courage that dared to face cold, hunger, peril, nakedness, and barbarism, solely for the maintenance of a faith dearer than life itself. But this unrelaxing sinewy exertion, this undaunted courage, this determined and irreversible resolve to live out the principles of religious belief, in things political and social as well as in things ecclesiastical —all these powerful and noble and lofty characteristics are combined with and colored by a certain degree of severity. The Puritan social life was rugged to hardness—stern, uninviting. None of its features were refined, delicate, genial. Sentiment was unknown to the majority, and ruled out for all. The temporal exigencies of the place and the time were too terrible and too pressing—the requisitions of the current Calvinism were too serious—too gloomy —to encourage or even to permit the expansion and development and cultivation of the more beautiful social faculties.

Nor did the origin, the process and the progress of the settlement of other parts of the continent, afford more space for the growth or exercise of these faculties. Further south, on the Atlantic coast, we see the workings of the European mercantile system, as modified by the colonial monopolies of the respective governments who sent or protected the settlers. New York was a depot and agency for the traffic of the Dutch West India Company. The spirit of the early lords of Virginia is well illustrated by the brutal exhortation of that nobleman who replied to the colonial representations of the wants of their souls, and their need of mental and spiritual improvement, by saying, "Damn your 'souls;' make tobacco!" Carolina was an endeavor to realize the fantastic political dream of the philosopher Locke. In Florida and Louisiana, the predominating influences were the prominent traits of the rulers and people of the parent nations, reproduced with bad fidelity in the American settlements which sprang up under their colonial monopolies: greed of gold, lust of landed property, pride of conquest, fanatical zeal. The transatlantic plantations were primarily to serve as distant gardens to the royal palaces of Europe, and secondarily, to spread the dominion of the Roman Catholic faith.

But we are, at this point, brought to the consideration of one beautiful exception to the remainder of all the broad continent. Not to a perfect Paradise—not to a true and ideal Eden; but yet to such a peaceful sunny spot, such a benign and kindly social life, such a scene of universal heartfelt instinctive courtesy, of patriarchal subordination, of mild and blessed neighborly virtue and forbearance, of harmless, simple, sufficing pleasure, of perfect health, blooming, happy youth, unambitious, industrious manhood, quiet old age, as is nowhere else to be found throughout all the broad page of American history.

The conduct of the French toward the aborigines of this continent was far more humane and generous, wise and successful, than the policy of any other European nation. The Spaniards treated the Indians like slaves and beasts of burden, and with a cold-blooded, selfish, blind brutality, which, by exterminating the unhappy race, exhausted its own materials and disappointed its own objects. The Anglo-Saxon, a man of higher grade, but not less self-contained, self-satisfied, exclusive, and resolute than the Spaniard, did not prove himself brutally bigoted and avaricious like him, in his intercourse with the red men, but only unconciliating, severe, exacting, and strangely inconsiderate of the defects and misfortunes of savage nature and savage education. Planting himself in the wilderness with all his institutions, his common law and statutory code, with the Mosaic intensifications which obscurity and distance allowed, he did what was fair, just, lawful and right, by his laws and according to his principles. And if the Indians transgressed these, instead of inquiring under what code, or upon what violation of savage principles it was done, he stolidly inflicted a statutory English penalty; and if this roused retaliation, the united colony, with the same stolid ignorance, retorted by judicial and military devastations and murders that might, it is true, temporarily quell opposition by the death of their enemies or the intimidation of the survivors, but which always left alive the smoldering embers which kept up the constant and fiendish border warfare, and ever and anon blazed out into one of the frightful and perilous Indian wars.

The French were no whit less zealous for their religion than the Spaniards; beyond all comparison more so, as missionaries, than the English. Nor were they less eager than either for gain, for adventure, or for empire. But the genial social qualities, the inborn national adaptability and courtesy, even the less stringent sense of moral obligation, their greater habitude to feudal law, and their patient subjection to seignorial rights, which may be called faults or defects, gave them incalculable advantages in founding, maintaining, and cementing the public and individual intercourse which they so long maintained with the Indians. In truth, had it depended alone on the success of alliances and coöperation with Indian tribes, instead of the fortunes of civilized war and the exigencies of European politics, it is well-nigh certain that the vast French belt of fortresses and settlements which so perilously girded in the Atlantic seaboard, would have fulfilled its purpose; that the English settlers would have been driven into the sea, exterminated, or reduced under the French power; and that the lilies of France, instead of the lion of England, would have waved over the whole vast domain of central North America during the latter half of the eighteenth century.

There is no more striking exemplification of the advantages in point of personal character thus ascribed to the French, than the history of those settlements founded in Illinois by the successors of La Salle, during the period from about 1680 until the removal of so many of the French at the transfer of authority to British hands in 1765.

The way to the prairie land, it will be remembered, was pioneered by the saintly Marquette. Next came the indefatigable and far-seeing La Salle, and his faithful and no less indefatigable lieutenant, Henry de Tonty. These able leaders and skillful negotiators, and many more of like character and less renown, diffused among all the numerous tribes from the St. Lawrence to the upper waters of the distant Missouri, where the stout sieur Juchereau maintained his lonely trading-post, a spirit of friendly regard for the French, and of deep reverence for the great French king. And in the footsteps of trappers and traders there followed Jesuit missionaries of zeal as fervent and character as beautiful as the holy Marquette himself: Allouez, his predecessor on Lake Superior, his successor on the alluvial lands that border the rivers of Illinois, and good Father Gravier, who founded the oldest permanent settlement in the great Mississippi Valley, the Village of the Immaculate Conception of Our Lady, afterward named Kaskaskia. The time of the foundation of this ancient town is not positively ascertained; but such data as have been determined seem to justify the belief that Philadelphia, Detroit, Mobile, and Kaskaskia, were all founded in about the same year. Then came Father Pinet and Father Marest, preaching in like manner to the unsophisticated but most discouragingly vicious denizens of the woods, the doctrines of Jesus and of the Resurrection. These holy fathers built them little unpretending chapels of bark, and their humble sanctuaries were crowded with such numbers of natives that many were obliged to stand without the threshold.

Then, enticed by the stories that reached them, under the inclement sky and the strict feudal system of Lower Canada, of the good livers of this distant land, the mildness of its climate, the richness of its soil, the fruitfulness of its pastures and its groves, one straggler after another descended from those rigorous regions, navigating the vast circuit of the great lakes, and passing by Lake Michigan, across the portage from the Miamis to the Kankakee, or from the Chicago to the Illinois, and erected a humble home within that great expanse of low-lying, fertile soil now called the American Bottom. This region, beginning on the eastern bank of the Mississippi River, nearly opposite to where its mild and placid stream is joined by the turbid waters of the Missouri, extending from this point sixty miles southward, and in width, from the river's bank to the bluff beyond, from five to eight miles—formed a tract of such fertility as is scarcely elsewhere to be found on earth. Here, surrounded by the exuberant products of nature, the French raised their half-wigwams, half-cabins, by driving corner posts into the ground, and then transverse laths—for they scarce deserved the name of beams—from one to another of these posts; plastering over these with the hand, a coating of "cat-and-clay," as the American settlers called it: soft clay worked up with prairie grass and Spanish moss. With this stucco upon the outside and the inside of the latticed walls, and neatly whitewashed, with roofs thatched with long grass carefully woven and matted together, and lasting, it is said, longer than shingles—with spacious piazzas all around the house—there presently arose picturesque villages, bordering a single street, so narrow that the settler might sit, smoking his pipe, beneath the shade of his piazza, and talk to his neighbor across the street in his ordinary tone of voice.

But let us orderly describe this simple and happy community in its prime—perhaps about the year 1750—their laws, their religion, their social organization, their manners, their occupations, their characters. For the whole texture and character—the gross and the detail—are so utterly and diametrically opposed to the ideas and conceptions of the descendants of English settlers, that the amplest delineation which the occasion admits may well fail to communicate a full comprehension of them.

The laws of the French settlements in Illinois were based upon the same great Roman code which underlay the jurisprudence of all the south of Europe. But some considerations, either of expediency or liberality, caused the substitution of allodial titles to land for the feudal tenures of Canada; that is, the settlers were permitted to own land very much as a New

England farmer owns it, instead of being obliged to hold it at the pleasure of the feudal lord, in whom was vested the real ownership. Thus the villagers of Kaskaskia, and the other neighboring settlements of our "terrestrial paradise," as La Salle aptly termed these regions, possessed, at the time to which we refer, each his parcel of land, granted by government to all the village in common; one great tract for tillage, and one for pasture, separated by a fence, and stretching back from the river bank to the limestone bluff. In this each family had a portion set apart for itself, and sacred from all intrusion. The village authorities, the senate of the settlement, enacted regulations requiring every family to commence planting, cultivating and harvesting on certain fixed days. The consent of this same body, as representing the whole settlement, was required for the admission of any new settler to a share in the common field.

Of statute and common law, courts and attorneys, fees and pleadings, these fortunate people knew nothing. Quarrels were as rare among them as in an affectionate family. No courts of law were established there until after the country passed into the possession of the British; and after they were established, no actions were brought before them until after the Anglo-Americans possessed the land. The sour, pugnacious litigations, as well as that much vaunted but very doubtful institution, the trial by jury, of the English, were an evil and a remedy equally foreign and terrible to the kindly disposition of the French. If any differences arose which the parties could not settle, they were referred to the arbitration of the priest, or, in the last resort, to that of the commandant at Fort Chartres, a mighty potentate, ruling, in name at least, territories. vaster than most kingdoms, representing all the power and wisdom of the French king, and looked up to by the simple settlers as the perfection of all human strength and judgment.

The religion of this far-off prairie settlement was Catholic. A reverend Jesuit father, head of the college established in Kaskaskia, and superior of all the missions in the valley, and the curate of the village, who received a small salary from the government, eked out by marriage and burial fees, and the gifts of his parishioners, were the highest ecclesiastical dignitaries in Illinois. Pomp and pride they had none; devoted, poor and humble, it was the purity and goodness of their lives which gave them their powerful influence among their little flock. The people were sincerely religious after their kind; and with the characteristic laxity of practice so abhorred by the stricter followers of Calvin, after the services of the Sabbath were over, they devoted to quiet amusements and pleasures the remainder of the holy day.

They were ignorant of letters, and happy in their

ignorance. The Jesuits established a few little schools, where were taught the elements of reading and writing; and this was learning enough for the Frenchman of Illinois. The great world and its weighty affairs troubled him not. He supposed that the Pope managed all spiritual concerns, and Louis of France all temporal concerns. With their wisdom and power at the helm, represented by those two reverend and awful dignitaries, the curate and *monsieur le commandant*, he, the French settler in Illinois, was perfectly certain that all would go well; he let the world wag on, and made himself happy with the trivial enjoyments brought by each peaceful day. He could read enough, and write enough, to draw, understand, and sign the simple instruments, which were all he needed, and to spell out the stories of the saints, or a tale of the crusaders; and more he needed not.

Each family held from one to three acres of land in the central part of the village. This was the property of the first settler of the name. Here the patriarch built his lowly cabin; and as son or daughter married, another mud-walled and grass-roofed cabin arose near his own, and within the same inclosure. With each new marriage appeared a new home. These peaceful, easy lives, the pure, sweet air, the healthful out-door manners, and plain nutritious forest food, prolonged life to a remarkable degree; and thus around the house of the patriarch there gathered a dozen or a score, nay, forty or fifty dwellings of children and grandchildren and great-grandchildren, even to the fourth and fifth generations.

These communities were, perhaps, chiefly agricultural. Each family carefully tilled its separate allowance of the common field, and that wealthy soil repaid their neat though homely husbandry with plenteous and more than sufficient crops. Six hundred barrels of flour were shipped to New Orleans from the Wabash country alone, in 1746, besides hides, furs, tallow, wax, and honey.

But the first settlers had been the daring *coureurs de bois*, the runners of the woods, who had found their wild pleasures and their perilous profits in vanquishing the hardships and dangers of the pathless forest, the roaring rapid, the toilsome portage; in the skillful but laborious occupation of the hunt; and in trading with the fickle, treacherous and savage Indians of those remote regions, from the Abenakis of New England and the Outaouacs, or Ottawas, of the St. Lawrence and Lake Huron, to the distant Sioux, or, as they were then termed, Nadouessions. And however quietly and easily the sons and grandsons of these roving men lived in the shaded cabin or the narrow, sunny street of Kaskaskia, or among the luxuriant fields without; however gaily their hours might pass amid the light labors of the day and the jovial dances of the evening; there was scarce a young man in whom the wild longing for the forest and rivers did not at some time wake up. Then, in his frail canoe, he passed far up into the region of lakes at the head of the Mississippi, or the rugged, desolate plains upon the upper waters of the Missouri; traversing the distant Sioux country, or even the rugged ranges of the Rocky Mountains. Hunting and trading, he returned with a canoe-load of furs; floated afar off down to that great capital, New Orleans, or round by the bayous and creeks of the coast, to the distant city of Mobile; exchanged his wild commodities for whatever civilized merchandise seemed good unto him, and returned up the rapid river to his quiet prairie home, perhaps to refit and depart upon another expedition to the Indian country; perhaps to trade away the goods from below for produce, and return again to barter at the southern cities; or perhaps to bury a bag of French livres and louis-d'ors, or Spanish doubloons or dollars, beneath the floor of his home, and resume his labors in the fields.

Whether the young wanderer returned richer or poorer in purse, he brought home one certain and lasting treasure—a great store of wild tales of incidents by flood and field, his own strange and varied experiences, and many more, told him by the trappers of the mountains, the canoe-men of the river, and the various men he met in the cities of the south.

The return of these travellers, after their long voyage of twelve or twenty months, was—like every festive occasion—celebrated by a ball; for here, as everywhere, dancing was a peculiar and prominent amusement of the light-hearted, social and active French. Word passed through all the settlement, of the return of the wanderers, and at once the place of entertainment was fitted up, and the arrangements made. Young and old, grandfather and grandchild, negro slave and fair maiden, all came to join in the festive scene. The entertainment was regulated with the same quaint municipal orderliness that controlled the operations of tillage and pasturage. Provosts were appointed, male and female; usually some well-respected grandsire and grandam had charge of the ceremonial, saw that every lady was danced with and that every gentleman had his partner, that the negro slaves enjoyed their rightful equal share of liberty within the room, that even the little children had opportunity to frisk through their share of the dance among the rest; and thus all passed innocently and gaily. At a given hour the company separated, and, joyous and satisfied, all went home. The ball-room was often graced by the reverend presence of the priest of the village—for his simple parishioners had no social amusements which he could not approve and witness—and in these rustic gaieties there was a degree of propriety and dignity—I might almost say of decency—which it would be hard to match, I fancy, in the ball-room of our own more intelligently Christian and more elaborately civilized society.

Other balls they had, with somewhat more of ceremonious observance. On New Year's Eve, the young men of the village patrolled the town in the costume of beggars, and entering the cottages in which dwelt the fairest maidens, petitioned for bread. Being well feasted and entertained, they then extended an invitation to each hospitable damsel for the dance to-morrow evening. This was the inauguration of the festival of the coming year. About the 8th of that month, great cakes were baked, and in these were carefully deposited four beans. The cakes were cut, and the gentlemen to whose share fell the pieces with beans in them, were called kings. These four bean-kings selected four queens, and the queens then selected the kings of the next ball that was to be given. At its close, the lady queens of the occasion selected four other gentlemen, whom they elected to the honor of this shadowy kingship, inaugurating them with all due solemnity, by the granting of a kiss. These gentlemen inaugurated other ladies by the same interesting process, and they became the regulators and governors of the following ball. And this, the "King-Ball," as it has been called, has been kept up, and still is, through all these years; and if you ever travel in the State of Indiana, and stop at the ancient town of Vincennes, and there have a friend or acquaintance who can introduce you to the French society of the place, you may, on a given evening of almost any week in the calendar year, have an opportunity of attending the king ball; for it has never been allowed to pass out of fashion from the early settlement of Illinois down to the present writing.

These people, with their kind and simple habits, easily fraternized with the Indians, and although there was great difference between them and those original owners of the soil, by reason of physical, mental, and moral condition, their differences seemed to relate and ally them more intimately to each other than white and red men were ever allied on this continent before. To the honor of both parties let it be said, there was scarce ever a fraud, a quarrel, or a murder between the French and Indians upon the soil of Illinois; and it constitutes, in this particular, the one only grand exception, saving the enterprise of Friend William Penn in the establishment of his City of Brotherly Love. And there, even, as soon as the good Penn himself had passed away, and the equally good, if not better, James Logan, who after him came into the dignity of Secretary of the Colony of Pennsylvania—so soon as their official sway and authoritative influence was gone, the Quakers were found to the full as overbearing, unjust, avaricious, careless, and regardless of the good of the natives, as the Puritan Fathers of New England. But these Frenchmen of Illinois, singularly enough it seems to the student of American history, in all their intercourse with the Indians treated them like human beings and equals in every respect, and received the kind and faithful treatment which was the natural result, in turn. The friendly and trustful reciprocity of benefits, the intimate neighborly communion, between these forest Frenchmen and forest Indians, constitutes one of the few beautiful pages in the record of American colonization, usually so dry and barren, or so blood-stained and full of miseries.

And thus, in that pleasant untroubled far-off land, and except for their happy family relation and the wise separate ownership of their lands, holding their property in common, sheltered almost like children under the mild influence of the good priests to whom, as to a father, they told all their sweet confidences of love, or their little sorrows and troubles, resting in sunshine, and far from wars and disturbance, beneath the broad banner with the lilies that streamed from the battlements of the old fort: thus was enacted this brief poem of the ages, this Idyl of America. This atmosphere of rural freshness, of delightful confidence, of unrestrained liberty, free from the sordid, troubled, eager haste of trade, the hardening touch of avarice, the gnawing tooth of care—

passed so far backward toward that lovely dream, the Golden Age, that in truth and reality it began to reproduce the lengthening of days, always a feature in the limning of that ancient legend. These people, it seemed, would have come to live forever, if forever were a possible term on earth.

And why should they grow old? It is care that wears us all out. We struggle beneath burdens inexpressible. Anxiety, with terrific plough, scars dreadful furrows over brow and cheek; worn out and weary, the springs of life exhausted, and desire even all but dead, we tremble on the verge of the grave at the age of fifty or sixty. Yet the French in Illinois retained good spirits, physical elasticity, and exceeding animation, to the age of ninety, one hundred, one hundred and ten, and one hundred and twenty; and such cases you may find even now in Attakapas, Opelousas, or Bayou Lafourche, the French Creole regions of Louisiana.

Thus went their lives kindly and cheerily by, though with no impulse, little enterprise, no inspirations; and though it was perhaps but a droning life—no contribution to the accumulated treasures of the ages, no exemplification of a stern struggle for principle, nor of a mighty aspiration and effort for the ideals of the race—yet it was such a sunny, peaceful life, so quietly, brightly joyous with the genial play of benign feelings, of the kindly social faculties of our nature, as gladdens us to look upon. We must long, sometimes, to escape out of the mighty rushing current of our civilized life, and to rest awhile upon some green island like this, where God's heaven hath not a cloud, where storm and tempest are unknown, where the still waters around us have not a ripple on their surface.

Thus were they living, missionaries, fur-traders, voyageurs, farmers, simply and innocently, in honest labor and harmless enjoyments, in the year 1719 or 1720. A sort of border war was then carried on between the French in Louisiana under their great leader, Bienville, and the Spanish viceroyalty of Mexico. Offended at the rapid daring with which the French were pushing their explorations and planting their outposts west of the Mississippi, and toward the great Santa Fe trail, which had even then been opened by traders, they secretly organized a great expedition at Santa Fe, for the purpose of exterminating such of the French settlements on the upper Mississippi as they could reach, and substituting Spanish colonies instead; to which end were sent priests, artificers and women, property and domestic animals, all the materials for a new establishment. Their plan of operations was to join forces with the Osage Indians, and in concert with them, first to exterminate their enemies the Missouries, the allies of the French, and then to quench the light of the flourishing settlements in a storm of blood and fire, and plant instead the standard of Spain.

After a long desert march of nine hundred miles across the plains which have of late years become so familiar to us, they reached that recent battle-ground of politics, the upland prairie country of Kansas, the supposed abode of their expected allies, the Osages. By a strange fortune, they fell in with their intended victims, the Missouries, instead, who spoke the same language with the Osages; and confident of their men, at once revealed to them the plan for the total destruction of their tribe. The imperturbable savages received the startling news with no sign of surprise, signified their approbation of the scheme, requested two days to assemble their warriors, and took their measures in savage secrecy. They drew from the Spaniards full details of the plan, and in character of the Osages received the ample supplies of ammunition and more than a hundred guns, destined for their own slaughter.

And now the next morning was to witness the setting forth of the joint expedition. But to the treacherous and self-deluded Spaniards that morning never came. In the night the Missouries rose up and smote their invaders and slew them, until but one living soul was left—a Jesuit priest, whom they sent back to Santa Fe with the doleful tidings.

Though thus providentially preserved, this nine hundred miles' march awakened the apprehensions of the French for their distant settlements in Illinois and on the upper Mississippi; and they promptly erected Fort Orleans, on an island in the Missouri above the mouth of the Osage River; and for the immediate defence of the Illinois settlements, that dignified and famous stronghold already mentioned, Fort Chartres. This fortress was completed during the year 1720. It was placed about a mile and a half from the Mississippi River, within the great American Bottom which we have already described, near the five chief villages of the Illinois country—Kaskaskia, Cahokia, Prairie de Rocher, St. Philip, and St. Geneviève, which last alone was west of the Great River. To these was soon added the village of Fort Chartres, which grew up under the walls of the fort.

This redoubted fortress, long the strongest garrison on the North American continent, occupied an irregular square of about three hundred and fifty feet to the side. Its walls were of solid masonry, three feet thick and fifteen feet high. Its ramparts were defended by twenty great guns; and such was its strength and armament, that it was impregnable to any force then available against it. Here, for forty years, was the centre of the French power in Illinois, the key of all the land, an important link of the great chain of fortresses between Quebec and New Orleans; the residence of the French commandant; the metropolis of the gaiety and fashion of all the country round: as an old Illinois chronicler, with pardonable local enthusiasm, calls it, "the Paris of America." But, alas for the brief duration of human prosperity! In 1765, the last French commandant of the Illinois, M. St. Ange de Bellerive, formally gave up the fort and his authority into the hands of the British captain, Sterling. And all this time, the capricious, mighty flood of the Mississippi was silently marching across from the westward, arraying against its strong walls powers not to be opposed by great guns nor by regiments of armed men. Steadily the eating flood swept nearer and nearer, and presently—in 1772—two bastions were undermined. The English dismantled and deserted the old fort. Fifty years ago, part of its site had been swept away by the devouring river, and it was a venerable ruin, solitary and overgrown with wild vines and with trees, some a foot in diameter.

The Spanish invasion had long passed by; and under the kindly despotic patriarchate of the commandant in Fort Chartres, and of the little village senates of old men, in the beauteous prairie land—where the land lies rolling like the billows of the sea, heaved in gentle undulations beneath the summer sun, studded with groves like islands far out on the deep, carpeted with flowers that lend their rich fragrance to the air until for sweetness you seem to be walking in Paradise, where all that is around gladdens the senses and rejoices the heart—the French colonists lie down and rise up without fear or guile, thinking no evil against any, and themselves without apprehension of incursion of savage, attack from hostile army, or any robbery or theft or fraud. Here life is serene as if man were never driven out of Eden, and the flaming cherubim stationed at the gate with his terrific sword.

But far away beyond the mountains is gathering the storm of war, which is to transfer all this vast valley from French to English hands, and to substitute for the bright, peaceful happiness which I have striven to depict, the rough and passionate cupidity of the Anglo-American backwoodsman—the violent sway of arms. The English settlers, eager after the magnificent lands beyond the Alleghanies, are slowly stealing over the ridge; and military detachments, and families, and single hunters, push westward into the great valley. The French have long been steadfastly advancing the design conceived by La Salle almost a hundred years before; and from Quebec to New Orleans the vast girdle of fortresses and confederate nations, at once held together and made accessible by the wondrous highway of the Great Lakes and the Great River, is almost complete, keyed by the great metropolitan stronghold of Fort Chartres, and lacking but one or two more fortresses between that and New Orleans.

That mighty and terrible confederation, the Six Nations, has long resisted the furious attacks of Onondio, the great French captain, and governor of Canada; has kept the valley of the Ohio unknown and inaccessible to their missionaries, their traders, and their settlers; and has, for the most part, negatively or positively, been ranged on the side of the English. Some of their young men, on distant scouting parties, have seen large bodies of French troops moving up the rapids of the St. Lawrence. They bring the news home; and in the great confederate senate-house at Onondaga a council of the Six Nations is held, to consider the important information. It is resolved to send the tidings to the Governors of Massachusetts, New York, and Virginia, and it is done. But these great men are little inclined to bestir themselves; they are busied in squabbling with the provincial assemblies, or they are at ease, and would fain be left "in their lazy dignities"—all but Governor Dinwiddie, of Virginia, an able, shrewd, stirring Scotchman, who sees at once the importance of the juncture. The troops now pushing up the St. Lawrence, are destined to occupy and hold for the French king the valley of the Ohio—for notwithstanding the Mississippi had been explored a hundred years before, and routes had long been open between

Quebec and New Orleans, by way of the Illinois and Wabash, it was not until about 1740 that the Ohio, above the Wabash, had been even explored by the French. The present scheme is to move by way of Niagara across to the headwaters of the Alleghany, to occupy thence downward all the valley of the Ohio, and in course of time to secure the whole land close west of the Alleghanies, and confine the growing English settlements to the narrow belt between the Alleghanies and the sea.

The Six Nations send the French commander a message of entreaty, remonstrance, and threats. But these are treated with contempt, and the standard of France moves forward. Governor Dinwiddie sends a messenger to ask the French what is their design in thus entering the valley of the Ohio—of the Beautiful River, as the French boatmen call it. "For," say the English, "all the land is ours, from the stormy Atlantic across to the peaceful sea on the west; because"—admirable logic!—"our countrymen first settled the eastern shore. We deny the claim of the French to the Mississippi valley, founded on the descent of its chief water-course, the river," by "one La Salle," as Washington called him.

Yet the title by which the English held the Atlantic slope was no better, if even as good, as that of the French to the great inland valley. The only Englishman who had entered that valley before 1740 was

Captain Barré, the agent of Dr. Daniel Coxe, proprietor of New Jersey, who entered the Mississippi River from its mouth in a corvette of twelve guns. Stemming the deep and muddy current, all at once the English captain is hailed from a small boat that meets him in one of the reaches of the river. A lad of twenty-one, in command of the skiff—it is Bienville, then and long after the Governor of Louisiana for the French king—stands up and addresses Captain Barré. The truth is, that his army is with him in that little boat, and he has scarce a better weapon than his naked hand, for he is on an exploring expedition, not a conquering one. Yet he hails as sternly as if the commander of regiments and embattled forts. "Turn about," he orders, "and go down the river! I am loth to harm you, but if you go beyond the next bend, I have guns enough in position there to blow you out of the water, and I will do it!" The daunted Englishman, believing every word, obeys, and escapes with his sloop-of-war, as fast as he can, from the boy and his boat's crew; and to this day the point in the river where he retreated is called the English Turn. This was the only entrance of the English into the Mississippi Valley until Dr. Walker's first exploring expedition over the Cumberland Mountains, about 1748.

What right had either nation to these lands? Said an old Delaware to an English partisan, "The king of France claims all the lands one side of the Ohio, and the king of England all on the other side. Now, *where are the Indian's lands?*" And the confounded backwoodsman was speechless. The red men owned the lands. Neither Onondio nor Corlear—neither Englishman nor Frenchman, had the shadow of any claim to a foot of land in the valley of the Mississippi.

But of all this the shrewd Scotch governor of Virginia neither thinks nor cares. He rests satisfied upon the usual claim by discovery, and is the more certain of the justice of his country's pretensions because his own estates in forest lands depend thereon. So he inquires by the mouth of his messenger, one Major Washington of the Virginia provincial forces, what does the king of France mean, and what do his servants of Canada mean, by thus presuming to intrude upon undoubted English territory in the Ohio valley? The young major of course receives a curt though courteous reply, and carries it back to those who sent him.

Not, however, to let the affair rest; for their glowing zeal for the pretensions of his Britannic majesty is intensified and made practical by their own. For the Ohio Company of Virginia has received a gift—no matter though the king who gave it did not own it—of six hundred thousand acres of the best land west of the mountains; and in this company, two elder brothers of our youthful provincial major, and Governor Dinwiddie, are principal shareholders. If the French hold the Ohio valley, these present broad domains on earth, and still fairer future castles in the air, will alike disappear, and great prospective gains will be lost. This, I hasten to add, is said without meaning to impute any sinister motives to George Washington. He sincerely believed in the English claim, and in his own and his friends' property; and he would have been more than human if these pecuniary interests had not reinforced the alacrity which he would, no doubt, have shown in the cause if he had never owned a foot of Ohio land, nor expected to.

He returns, at any rate, in 1754, now promoted to the rank of lieutenant-colonel, and in command of a small body of troops, to arrest the progress of the French, who have commenced actual hostilities by taking from the English (in April, 1754) a small stockade fort in the forks of the Alleghany and Monongahela Rivers, and by beginning a stronger and more serviceable fortress in its place, which they call Fort Duquesne, in honor of the governor-general of Canada. Washington crosses Laurel Ridge, and gains the Great Meadows, a pleasant open spot some fifty miles southeast of the new French stronghold. Here he learns from an old friend and companion in forest journeys, one Christopher Gist, settled near by, and from the half-king of the Delawares, Tanacharison, that a party of French are in his neighborhood, with warlike intentions. His Indian allies search them out, and about sunrise he discovers them encamped in a retired and secret place among the rocks. Discerning the tall form of the Virginian advancing from among the trees, and the troops behind him, they spring to arms, and at once commence a vigorous fire upon the English. But being surrounded and outnumbered, ten of them, including their commander, M. de Jumonville, are killed, and the remainder made prisoners.

That brief command, "Fire!" echoed all over the earth. That scattering blaze of musketry among an obscure pile of wild rocks beneath the western Alleghanies, kindled a conflagration that spread throughout the continent of Europe, as fire runs through the dry prairie-grass in autumn time; and burned even on the far shores of Asia. It was the beginning of the Seven Years' War, a struggle which called forth the genius of Pitt as a minister and parliamentarian, and of Frederic the Great as a warrior; which crushed the doctrine of legitimacy in France; and which, under the over-ruling of Him who sees the end from the beginning, not as man ordereth, but who maketh the wrath of man to praise Him, did more to elevate the masses of the population of Europe, and to prepare the way for the freedom and independence of our own country, than all other causes together.

The war thus fairly commenced, Jumonville's brother, De Villiers, commandant at Fort Chartres, hastens eastward to revenge his brother's death, and finds Lieutenant-Colonel Washington still in the neighborhood, opening a military road for troops expected from Virginia. The Frenchman came upon him with double his forces, but declining the battle which the bold young commander offered in the open ground before the fort which he had constructed, he laid siege to the small and ill-provisioned stockade, which, with a judgment giving little promise of his after wisdom, Washington had planted in low ground, where it was commanded and almost thoroughly raked from the secure covert of the wooded ridges on either side. An attack was soon commenced, and after nine hours of sharp firing, during which thirty of the garrison were killed and three wounded, the French commander, afraid that his ammunition would fail, allowed Washington to capitulate and retire east of the mountains with all the honors of war; the articles of capitulation, which were in French, by means of the ignorance or treachery of the interpreter, admitting the death of Jumonville to be an "assassination," and promising that no further establishments should be attempted west of the mountains for the term of one year. This obligation was not taken to be binding.

Then comes the expedition of General Edward

Braddock, whose hot-headed valor, absurd routinism, and arrogant conceit, we all know; as well as the inconceivable obstinate folly with which he persisted in trying to dress ranks, and form by platoons, there among the forests, "as if manœuvring his troops upon the plains of Flanders;" and the genuine English pride and stubbornness with which he refused to take advice from the provincials, experienced in bush-ranging and Indian fighting; and how the hard-headed fool thus threw away his own life, and the lives of three hundred better men, great treasures wasted to no purpose, with the certain prospect of taking Fort Duquesne; for nothing was further from the minds of the French and Indians than a victory, and they were on the point of evacuating the fort.

And now, in good season, the Great Commoner, William Pitt, takes the helm of English affairs. "What are we to do?" cries Chesterfield; "abroad reverses and disgrace; at home, poverty and bankruptcy—what are we to do?" In America, the French line of midland forts was steadily and rapidly closing in behind the belt of English settlements along the sea. In India, the other side of the world, Dupleix had laid at Pondicherry the foundations of a power which promised quicky to exterminate the timid traders of the East India Company, and to bring the oriental wealth and the swarming millions of Hindostan beneath the power of France. In the Mediterranean, Minorca was taken by the French forces under the Duke de Richelieu. On the continent of Europe, the single ally of England, of any power, Frederic of Prussia, was attacked at once by the three vast empires of Austria, France, and Russia, and that in a quarrel where he was flagrantly in the wrong; and the English king's own hereditary dominions of Hanover were overrun by French troops. The tremendous energy, the pride, the rapid decision and daring of the great minister, inspired fleets, armies, the whole nation. From being sullen, gloomy, discouraged, fearful, they became, in a year or two, daring, high-spirited, fearless, and enterprising, almost beyond the bounds of human belief or human capacity. Under his strong, haughty, and energetic direction, the stout Prussian king is brought safely through his terrific war; Hanover is cleared of the French; the coalition between Russia, Austria, and France is shattered; the victories of Clive and Lawrence eradicate the very foundations of the French empire in Hindostan, and lay the corner stone of the vast dominion of British India. In America, the brave New England hosts take the stronghold of Louisbourg, and the gallant Wolfe, scaling the heights of Abraham, as it were buys with his heart's blood the victory over Montcalm and the surrender of the great French citadel of Quebec. An irresistible flood of British conquest sweeps round and round the world; and the humbled monarch of France, making peace in the year 1763, yields up to Great Britain all Canada, and all Louisiana east of the Mississippi, excepting only the district and city of New Orleans, which, with all the rest of Louisiana, is given to the Spaniards, by a private treaty made with Spain the year before.

Thus this great garden land, this granary for the nations, this home for that better time coming, to which we all look forward with such longings and such love, passes from the grasp of hereditary monarchy, of the ancient French divine-right rulers, from under the heavy shadow of dead mediæval law and dying feudal tenures, into the hands of England and of Spain. Not, however, into their hands as in fee; not in permanent proprietorship; but in trust, for the future use and behoof of a people whose career, as we hope, shall fulfill in the near future the dreams of the long past, and realize that golden time of the world's history which the prophets saw in shadow, which the poets have told in broken words and vain aspirations after adequate expression, which all good men pray for and look for; the period when the trustworthiness of the people shall be vindicated by their righteousness; when the true equality of the nation shall be found, not in levelling those above, but in the rising of those below, by a celestial gravitation, to the level of the highest; when humanity, free, educated, justified, the Bible in its hand and the love of

God in its heart, and led by His Holy Spirit, shall stand as upon a lofty mountain summit of attainment, not upon a ghastly peak of cold sterility and eternal ice, but where the smile of God makes summer sunshine, and God's love makes all the air benign; where all humanity is bound up together in the bundle of God, in bonds of brotherly love and kindness.

Lecture IV.

THE RED MEN;

AND THE

WAR OF PONTIAC.

THE RED MEN, AND WAR OF PONTIAC.

At the commencement of Europe's acquaintance with the Indians this side the Mississippi, so far as we can calculate, from 180,000 to 300,000 of the red men occupied that tract of country now included within the limits of our republic, and lying between the Atlantic and the Father of Waters. These aboriginal tribes were divided into three families—the Algonquins, the Iroquois, and the Mobilian races. The Mobilians occupied the region of country lying south of the Ohio River and east of the Mississippi, including the States of Kentucky, Tennessee, western Georgia, western South Carolina, Florida, Alabama, Mississippi, and Louisiana. The Iroquois, or Five Nations, subsequently increased to six by the addition of the Tuscaroras, who migrated from western Carolina, dwelt in the western part of New York. The remainder of the country was occupied by the tribes of that great family known as the Algonquins. Whilst there were certain tribal peculiarities, certain distinctive features, marking and separating these tribes, they yet shared traits and features in common, showing them to belong, all of them, to one great parent stock. Their manners and customs, their views and opinions, modes of action and forms of speech, afford us perfectly reliable evidences of this.

The Indian is the child of the wilderness, born amidst its rugged grandeurs, cradled amidst its storms, surrounded with its vastness, schooled by it from his earliest infancy in the development of his perceptive faculties, almost to the exclusion of his reasoning powers; employed in those occupations which develop athletic strength of body, the chase, war, predatory incursions upon his neighbors; seeking his food from boundless hunting-grounds. Nurtured in a school like this, the delicacy of his senses has passed into a proverb; and he acquired such fineness of eye, such exquisiteness of ear, as is scarce paralleled or approximated in the records of history.

The relation between the parent and the child among the Indians constitutes, it seems to me, a peculiar feature, and one marking them among the nations of the earth, distinct from all others. What is called parental authority, was hardly known among them. The child was brought up in the wigwam of its parents; but they never expected, so it seems, to impose on it their authority, their will, their command. The child grew up his own master, basking and sporting around the door of the bark lodge, enjoying the care of the mother, the notice of the father, until, attaining nearly our own age of majority, he was pre pared by vigil, fast, seclusion among rugged rocks in the depths of inaccessible forests—tried by visions and dreams, and communings with what he thought the Great Spirit—for his future career of heroism and conquest. American children, carried in their early years, as captives, to the homes of the Indians, nurtured and trained by their adopted red fathers and mothers, asseverate, and their evidence is conclusive, that they have never seen a hand raised by a parent against a child—and yet, so far as the conditions of their iron nature would permit, such tractableness, such docility, such loyalty, such glad and willing obedience from children to parents, is rarely to be found even in the highest stages of civilized society. That opposite beliefs are current in the popular mind, I well know; and that there are examples of barbarous desertion, of inhuman cruelty from children toward their aged parents, when the latter have grown to be an incumbrance, this I know; but these are the exceptions—the other is the rule.

One of the primal elements of the Indian character is hero worship, and if Mr. Carlyle is intent upon consolidating and organizing his Utopian society upon this basis, I know of no realm or clime to which he may resort with such hopes of success as to the Rocky Mountains of our own continent, where, among the Blackfeet, the Sioux, the Apaches, and all those wandering tribes, he will find this element in the full grandeur of its supremacy. The child is taught it from his earliest infancy. When first he can interpret the words spoken around the watch-fire, in the sombre lodge of his people; when the grey-haired fathers of the tribe, in the long evenings of the winter time, when the chase is no longer open to them, and the war-path ceases to invite them, over the blaze of their household fires, relate the deeds of the forefathers of the tribe, and tell the traditions of the olden time—then the children are wont to listen with eager interest to all these recitals, to cherish in their memories and in their hearts the admiration of this older time, and to resolve to emulate their ancestors, and to surpass, if possible, their deeds of prowess and hardihood.

And these old chief and sachems, wise men, held in universal reverence, to whom is paid a sort of homage, not only of the intellect, but of the heart—these old men, by this kindly and genial influence upon the juvenile character, while that character is yet plastic in their hands, do much to determine its strength and scope. Hence the reverent loyalty to which I have referred, from the younger members of the tribe to the older, first in the relation of child to parent, and then, more generally, in that of junior to senior. And I fancy that in these times of ours, of excitement and turmoil, of self-conceit, arrogance and presumption, when the young exaggerate their powers and capabilities, when juvenility is set in, or usurps, every high place, when the young man takes grey hairs for the tokens of a dotard, and a wrinkled face for the sign of a driveller—feels that he is the great object on whom the gaze of the world, and in whom the hope of the future, is concentrated—in these wild times of ours, with their rash enterprises, their fury and folly, filibustering, factions and seditions—I fancy that in this age of Young America, many good lessons might be learned from the Indian ancestors of the soil, the red aborigines; who, whatever of the noblest manhood they lacked, had, at least, respect for the aged, and reverence for those wiser than themselves.

In that wild, unfettered, disjointed democracy, where the will of the people—but even that completely subordinate to the will of the minority or the individual, for itself or himself—was the prominent source of power, men were exalted for their wisdom. The aged were the repositories of tradition, the repertories of good counsel, the vehicles of instruction; they could not only tell of times long past, of ancestors long departed, but they could tell the pathways of the woods, the old feuds of the tribes, the manner of leading the young men to combat and to triumph; and this attribute of abstract and practical wisdom exalted men to chieftainship. Their sachems or wise men were their leaders in all matters of counsel and debate, and the young men deferentially listened, standing around, their swarthy figures leaning against the door-posts of their cabins, or against some noble tree. While the father spoke, the sons listened in silence, and the words of the aged fell upon their ears and their hearts like the dew from the brow of the evening.

There was another kind of chieftainship, however; another sort of authority besides this of wisdom in matters of counsel and debate. Those who were enterprising and dauntless, who burned to lead their brethren to war, could nominate themselves to a sort of temporary chieftainship—a war chieftainship. These, if they had any quarrel to settle, any wrong to avenge, any hope of success in some foray, were accustomed, after vigil, fast, incantation—after dwelling apart until their features were harsh, their bodies shrunken, and they were reduced halfway to inanition,—coming back to the wigwams of the nation, to send invitations through the tribe, to all the young men to meet them at a festival. Here abundant provision was spread before the guests, the chief dainty being commonly dog's meat; and all must be dispatched before they were allowed to depart. He who had summoned them, meanwhile, sat in silence, abstaining from all gratification of appetite, albeit nearly famished. When the festival was ended, his body painted black, he springs into a ring prepared for the purpose, in the centre of which stands a blackened post; around this he marches, singing a sort of recitative, a monotonous cadence, in which he recounts the deeds of his forefathers and his own heroic achievements, every now and then brandishing his tomahawk and furiously striking it into the post in the centre. Thus he inflames the passions and imagination of his audience, till warrior after warrior springs into the ring like himself, and in like manner chants, recites, raves and strikes. Then rises a fierce tumultuous clamor of voices from all, and when they have aroused themselves to the highest pitch of frenzy, the war-path is prepared. Decorated with fanciful paints, and with all the ornaments they can command, and marching, in single file, one, two, or three miles from the village, if there be a convenient camping ground near a brook, here they pause, and discharge their guns slowly, one at a time. Here they encamp, and now the ornaments and trinkets are gathered and sent back to the squaws at the village, to be kept till their return. Then, in silence, in single file, under the lead of this self-nominated chieftain, they proceed upon their errand of destruction and blood. Whatever the result, when they return great rejoicings are had in the village, or in the wigwams of the nation; and if any have fallen, their manes are appeased by the sacrifice of such victims as have been captured, their torture being considered a lawful and even obligatory offering, that shall satisfy the spirits of the dead.

But this portraiture of Indian character, intended as a sort of introduction to the theme of the occasion, is drawing me on too far. I must hasten to complete the rough outline, though with the omission of many interesting points. The leading and most remarkable peculiarities of the Indians are, indomitable resolution and endurance, haughty pride, daring and arrogance toward an enemy, a calm and unmoved exterior, that hides impenetrably all secrets of thought and feeling, as a mantle of ice and snow the blazing fires of the volcano beneath; and a natural wild independence, nourished and confirmed by their solitary perilous lives; which, although they may act voluntarily under the guidance of these self-appointed chieftains, preserves them unconstrained by any law, subject to no authority, bound to none by fealty, and subordinating themselves only to the heroic virtues and preëminent abilities of their few great statesmen and warriors. Such salient peculiarities, exemplified, too, in such endless displays of savage heroism and skill and strength, cannot but open to the student of human nature a chapter of absorbing interest.

All three of the great families, Mobilians, Iroquois, and Algonquins, though the innumerable battles between and among themselves sprinkled the whole continent with blood, were united by one singular and wide-extended bond of friendship, which well deserves a short consideration. This was that sort of free-masonry, or association into fraternities, which may be called the Totemic, as depending upon the signs or emblems of these families, called their *Totems.* Such emblems were the Hawk, the Eagle, the Tortoise, the Bear, the Wolf, the Snake. And as these associations were limited neither to one nation nor set of nations, so we find, for instance, a family of the Wind, among both Mobilians and Iroquois; a family of the Tortoise, both among the Iroquois and the Algonquins.

The brotherhood of the totem bound its members, whether in peace or war, to aid and comfort each other in whatever need. The lonely wanderer, weary and starving after a long and unsuccessful chase, could never ask in vain for relief and admitance at the cabin of one of his brethren of the totem, however far removed his language, tribe, or blood. This singular association a little alleviated the many horrors of the constant warfare of the hunters of the woods. Another of its rules was, that members of one family or clan should not intermarry with each other; but that the young man of the totem of the Tortoise must choose his wife from the family of the Bear or the Hawk, or of any totem but the Tortoise. This provision, in strict conformity with physiological truth, was well calculated to perpetuate the physical vigor and hardihood, the integrity and individuality of the race.

Hereditary distinctions, so far as they existed among the Indians, descended not directly, in the male line, but collaterally, through the female. Thus, it was not the son of the chief who inherited his chieftainship after him, but the son of the sister, or some female relative of the chief. Nor was even this inheritance sure or necessary. No mantle fell by any law of succession upon unworthy shoulders. The candidate for the autnority of his uncle received and retained his power, if he did receive it, because he also was preëminently wise in council, powerful in debate, sagacious in planning, and heroic in strife. Wanting these merits, he fell unresistingly into a private station, and the poorest and obscurest youth of the tribe, if his abilities entitled him, assumed the power of sachem. Insignia the office had none.

Having thus hastily sketched out some prominent traits of Indian character, I now come to the more immediate subject of this lecture: the great conspiracy organized against the encroaching whites, by one of the greatest, if not the very first of Indian statesmen and warriors; and to the life and character of its leader—the War of Pontiac, the Ottawa.

In 1760, near the close of the old French war,

when the three victorious armies of England had met, converging at Montreal; when Canada had been subjugated, and the French empire was about to cease over the new continent, Sir Jeffrey Amherst, commander-in-chief of the English forces in this country, dispatched a New Hampshire ranger, Major Robert Rogers, with a party of his men, to take possession of the French forts west of the lakes. This Major Rogers was a companion in arms of old Israel Putnam; an experienced and successful Indian fighter, of desperate courage, yet of the coolest and most sly and cautious prudence. A tall, strong man, of a somewhat evil countenance, he was little troubled with conscience, was strongly suspected of treachery during the Revolutionary war, and, indeed, became a colonel in the British service; and last—an odd feature in the character of a backwoodsman—he possessed no inconsiderable tincture of good literature, having published a well-written journal of his adventures as a ranger, and even—it is believed—all or part of "The Tragedy of Ponteach," a drama of the fortunes of the very chieftain of whom I am about to speak.

This hardy adventurer, at the head of two hundred men, in a fleet of whaleboats, proceeded as far as to the site of the present city of Cleveland, which he reached in November, 1760. Here his advance was arrested by a party of Indians, who met him, saying that they were the envoys of one Pontiac, the monarch of all that realm, and who bade him halt there until a conference should be had with him.

Thus steps forth, for the first time within the light of history, from the obscurity of his small tribe—the Ottawas, fugitives among the great Algonquin nation, the Ojibwas of Lake Superior, from the destroying fury of the terrible Iroquois—the great chief, Pontiac, sometimes even called the Emperor of the Ottawa Indians, so extensive was his sway, and so vast his power.

Before nightfall, the great chief made his appearance, and proudly demanded wherefore the English were in his country? Rogers made answer, that the English, having conquered the French, were now taking possession of the forts of the vanquished, and that this was his errand to Detroit. Taking until the next day to answer, the Indian chieftain concluded with prompt decisive wisdom that the English power was, in truth, becoming uppermost, and that he would worship the rising sun. He returned and made a corresponding reply; and on the journey, which the English party completed successfully, averted at least one intended attack by the Detroit Indians.

While with Rogers, Pontiac was very inquisitive to learn how the English manufactured such guns of the black rock called iron; how cloth was woven, and powder made; how they drilled and disciplined their troops; and asked a thousand other questions about European matters. This man was the head chief of all the Ottawas, and high in the esteem of all the neighboring tribes on the peninsula which projects from the main base of the continent, and is surrounded by lakes Michigan, Huron, St. Clair and Erie. The Ojibwas, Wyandots, Pottawatomies, and other neighboring tribes entertained for him a sort of reverence, similar in kind, and even greater in degree, than that afterward commanded by Tecumseh, himself—as were King Philip and Pontiac—of Algonquin blood.

A year or two passed away, and British troops and British influences had replaced those of France through all the vast belt of inland possessions which had for nearly a century owned the power of the French king. It is not necessary here to describe the difference, so often enlarged upon, between the light-hearted, social and plastic French, and the haughty, gruff, and arrogant English, in their intercourse with the punctilious and irritable sons of the forest. Instead of the generous and easy hospitality, the careful, courteous, and indulgent observance, with which the French officers and traders had so judiciously and successfully treated the Indians, they were suddenly everywhere used with rude overbearing insolence, neglected, driven off with curses, and even with blows—the last indignity to which an Indian could be subjected.

And while this unhappy, invariable course on the part of the English, together with the brutal swindling of their traders, the rapid advance of their settlements, the ruin of their hunting-grounds, and the swift and steady circumscription of their territories, kindled all along the vast extent of the Indian frontier the smoldering exasperation and bitter enmity that ever and anon flamed out into murders and devastating inroads by individuals and war-parties of the young men of one and another tribe; the chiefs themselves, long accustomed to the special distinctions and valuable presents which formed so agreeable a part of the French system of colonial administration, were still more bitterly mortified and enraged at the neglects and insults which they received from the coarse and proud men with whom the British forces were almost always officered.

Pontiac felt all this, and felt it the more profoundly, by as much as the depth of his intellect and the strength of his passions and his pride surpassed those of his savage contemporaries. But his wrath, and sorrow, and mortification, were yet a thousandfold more inflamed by disappointments of a character which very few of the tribesmen under his command could even comprehend, much less sympathize with.

The dream and desire of his life was, the progress and improvement of his people, and their advance in power and in happiness. And so just and far-reaching were the views of this wild Ottawa sachem, that he comprehended the necessity of the manufactures of civilized races, and would fain have rendered the tribes independent of both English and French, in this respect, by enabling them to supply all their own wants. He neither loved nor feared the English or the French; and his alliance with each, and his preference of either, was decided singly by the advantage which he hoped thus to secure to his race. So long as the French held much territory and many fortresses in America, he remained in alliance with them. When they were conquered, and the places of their troops filled by the red-coated soldiery of England, he as promptly made friends with the English.

But the hopes of elevating and bettering his race, which, though delusive, had been long maintained by the fair professions and careful external observances of the Frenchmen, were quickly quenched by the more honest rudeness, neglects and insults, which the British officers inflicted upon the Indians; and Pontiac soon perceived that the Ottawa nation, and all the Indian tribes, would perish, unless their white invaders should be destroyed, or their progress arrested. This design he at once set about accomplishing; and forthwith he organized a conspiracy, far the most gigantic ever originated by an Indian on this continent, and which, for extent, secrecy, and ability of conception and execution, will vie with any plot in history.

His own personal qualifications, and the circumstances of the time, made the opportunity a perfect one. In the prime of a leader's life—being about fifty years old—despotic ruler of the confederated tribes of the Ottawas, Pottawatomies, and their third ally, the great tribe of the Ojibwas—long possessed of a paramount influence over all the Indians of Illinois, and known and honored throughout all the wide territories of the Algonquin race—no other chieftain could have aroused such hosts as he, or could have sustained or controlled their wrath so long; nor were the Indians at any other time ever so extensively and fiercely hostile to their white aggressors. From the distant trading-stations in the cold regions beyond Lake Superior, to the far southern tribes back of the settlements in Carolina and Georgia, the savages were all yet hot with their anger of the recent strife in which they had fought for the French; and this wrath was still more vehemently enkindled by the insulting treatment of which I have spoken, by the brutal conduct and enormous impositions of the English fur-traders, and still more by the ominous rapidity with which the white frontier marched westward, destroying one hunting-ground after another, covering the lands, and annihilating or expelling the tribes.

In the latter portion of the year 1762, therefore, there went out from the Ottawa village, which stood just below Lake St. Clair and above Fort Detroit, on the Canada side of the river, many messengers. They sped into the distant forests of the northern Algonquins beyond the great lakes; to the banded nations of the Iroquois; to the pacific Delawares in Pennsylvania; to the savage Tuscaroras, and the warlike Mobilians, west of Carolina and along the Gulf coast; to the various tribes all along the Mississippi; and to the nations of the Illinois country. Everywhere they carried the great red war-belt and the words of the great Pontiac; and everywhere, in response to the wild call of the savage envoys, the young men rose up and prepared for war. To all was appointed a certain time in the next May, when every tribe was to exterminate the garrison nearest it, and the whole wild host were then to break in upon the settlements. And all the savage confederates, and Pontiac himself—who was in this deluded with all the rest—expected decisive succor from the armies of the French king, which they believed to be on the march to recover their great Canadian possessions. This expectation was kept up by the reports of the Canadian French, and even by forged letters, giving advice of the march of French troops up the St. Lawrence.

The spring arrives; and in all the long range of

English forts, from Michilimackinac and Sault Ste. Marie, to the northwestward, to Fort Niagara, and all along the line of lake forts, Detroit, Sandusky and Presqu' Isle, and south by Venango and Fort Pitt to the frontier posts in the west of Virginia, all is safe and secure. Here and there have been heard or seen indistinct signs of irritation or disturbance among the savages; and in one instance—at Fort Miami—the commander had even heard of the war-belt, held a council with the Indians about it, reproved them, and sent the news, and their cunning disclaimers, to Major Gladwyn, at Detroit, and he to Sir Jeffrey Amherst, at New York. But none dreams of anything worse than a temporary state of uneasiness among the tribes; and the English forces in his majesty's colonies in North America remain dispersed and feeble, and all the royal posts careless and almost unrestrainedly open to the Indians.

Pontiac himself determined to commence the war by attacking Fort Detroit, the strongest of all the English posts in the Indian country, except Fort Pitt. After the Indian fashion, he at first tried stratagem. Having unsuspectedly made a satisfactory reconnoissance of the interior of the post, he entered it some days afterward, on pretence of a council, with three hundred chosen warriors, all armed for war, and with their guns cut short and hidden under their blankets. But Major Gladwyn, the English commander, a cool and brave man, had been put on his guard only the night before by his Indian favorite, a beautiful Ojibwa girl named Catharine. Making all the necessary preparations, therefore, he deliberately admitted this savage host. They saw with dismay the military array of the garrison, and only after uneasy delay would they seat themselves and go through the deceitful ceremonies under cover of which they had intended to murder the commandant and his force, and to throw open the gates to the Indian army without. Pontiac made a speech, as usual on such occasions, professing friendship and peaceful intentions as if he had as heretofore come only for rum or for presents. He even raised his hand with the peace-belt of wampum, the giving of which was to have signalled the onset of his braves, but paused in speechless amazement when, at that very moment, in obedience to Gladwyn's command, the rattle and clash of weapons and the roll of the drum sounded from without the room. After a short and somewhat stern reply from Gladwyn, the Indians departed in disappointment and anger, but yet quite sure that the English were either utterly ignorant of their scheme, or arrant cowards if not, for letting them escape alive. And accordingly, Pontiac visited Gladwyn with a few companions next day, to endeavor to confirm him in a belief in their peaceful intentions, and one day afterward, tried to obtain admis sion into the fort with a large number of his warriors. Being now briefly and sternly refused, the savages, bursting at once into all the fiendish rage of Indian warfare, murdered two English families who lived at a short distance, and the next day closely invested the fort; a mixed and numerous swarm of four nations, Ottawas, Pottawatomies, Wyandots and Ojibwas, all under the command of the great Ottawa war-chief Pontiac.

And now all along the far-stretching frontier, the dark forests swarm with war-parties. All the English posts west of the mountains were attacked. Traders, travellers and emigrants, the forlorn hope of the advancing invasion of the white settlements, were killed. Every secluded farm or lonely hamlet, of all those that fringed the interval between hunting-grounds and farms, was burned. Hundreds and hundreds of families were exterminated, or driven back within the area of the denser settlements scared and penniless, and too often with the loss of some of the beloved circle.

Such was the perfection of this gigantic project, and the secrecy of its thousands of confidants for months together, that the savage outbreak was nowhere expected except for those few hours of warning at Detroit—and even there it was many days before Gladwyn would believe it to be more than a temporary outbreak of anger, or that all the posts were assaulted so nearly together that none could assist any other. One after another, in rapid succession, eight of them fell. On the 16th of May, Fort Sandusky was surprised by a body of Indians, who gained admittance as friends, and murdered all but the commander and two or three of the garrison. On the 25th, St. Joseph's, at the south end of Lake Michigan, was seized in a similar manner, eleven men of the little garrison having been killed, the other four made prisoners, and the fort plundered; all within less than two minutes after the signal yell was given. Two days afterward, Fort Miami, on the Maumee, was surrendered to the savages, Ensign Holmes, the commander, having been enticed out and shot dead, and the sergeant taken prisoner. On the 1st of June, a similar stratagem made the Indians masters of Fort Ouatanon on the Wabash, the garrison, however, being all preserved alive, and sent prisoners to the Illinois country. On the 4th, the Ojibwas, by means of a game of ball called *baggatiway*, surprised Fort Michilimackinac, massacred nearly all of the garrison, made prisoners of the rest, and seized the large quantities of liquor, stores and merchandise, public and private, accumulated in that important depot of the Indian trade. On the 15th, after a siege of twenty-four hours, eighteen of them of incessant furious attacks, with the aid of intrenchments and mines, and of desperate hardihood in defence, Fort Presqu' Isle was surrendered, and the garrison, despite a capitulation providing that they might retire to the nearest post, were sent prisoners to the camp of Pontiac at Detroit. On the 18th, Fort Le Bœuf, a few miles south of Presqu' Isle, on a branch of the Alleghany, was attacked toward nightfall by a large body of Indians, and set on fire by fire-arrows; but the commander and his little squad of thirteen men, desperate with their horrible peril, cut a way out through the rear of the blockhouse while the Indians were waiting to see them driven out through the door by the flames, and fled away to Fort Pitt; six of them, utterly exhausted, being left behind in the woods. And lastly, Fort Venango, still further south, at the junction of the same stream with the Alleghany, was about the same time surprised by a large force of Senecas, who, admitted as friends, murdered all the garrison except the commander, tortured him for several nights over a slow fire until he died, burnt down the works, and departed. Fort Pitt, Fort Ligonier, some distance southwest of it, and Fort Augusta, on the Susquehanna, were also attacked, but the Indians were repulsed.

And now the English held not one fortified post west of Fort Pitt, save Detroit alone, where the undismayed Gladwyn still maintained himself, though closely beleaguered by the great confederate host under Pontiac. The vigor and constancy of this siege are without precedent or parallel in Indian history. From the beginning of May until the end of October did the power and influence of their indomitable leader hold the savage host in watchful array against the fort; wearying the scanty garrison with a fire of musketry that left them no rest day or night; contriving plan after plan to destroy the two small vessels which remained under the protection of the works, and served to guard the water-front; to rake the north and south sides of the walls, and to make an occasional attack upon the enemy's camp.

No other Indian chieftain—at least none of pure blood, for an exception must be made in favor of General Alexander McGillivray, the chief of the Creeks—ever showed such breadth and quickness of mind in comprehending and practising the arts of civilized life, a characteristic not less indicative of the lofty rank of his intellect, than was that vast magnetic power which enabled him so long to concentrate and wield the forces of those flitting and unstable warriors of the woods. Unable to read or write, he employed one secretary to write letters and another to interpret those received, and with diplomatic shrewdness, kept each ignorant of the business of the other. To satisfy until he could pay them, the French Canadians from whose live stock he was forced to support his army, he issued securities, of the nature of notes of hand, drawn on birch bark and signed with his totem, the otter, which were all punctually redeemed. He organized a regular commissariat department, gathering into one stock the provisions thus collected, and which he levied after a fixed rate from the Canadians in the neighborhood, and distributing them again to his forces; rigidly protecting the farms from depredation, and even making his followers avoid trampling on growing crops.

Not less remarkable were the bravery and versatile skill employed in the operations for attack. All the slender means of Indian warfare were exhausted in assaulting the palisades of the fort. Repeated attempts were made to burn the two vessels, by fire-rafts sent down the river. A detachment of nearly a hundred men, sent to relieve the fort, was surprised by a party of Wyandots when within thirty miles of their destination, sixty of them taken or slain, and the rest driven back to the eastward in but two of their eighteen boats; and the ample stock of provisions and ammunition intended for the besieged, all fell into the hands of the Indians. The schooner Gladwyn, one of the two vessels attached to the fort, was fiercely attacked by the Indians while in the river below, on her way up with a small reinforcement, and was driven back to the lake, though a second attempt carried her up to the fortress in safety, with her men and supplies. Captain Dalzell, a companion in arms of General Putnam, arrived at the fort toward the end of July, with a second reinforcement of nearly three hundred men, and obtained with difficulty from the cautious Gladwyn, permission to lead a party to endeavor to surprise Pontiac's camp. But the wary chief, informed by some Canadians of the intended attack, ambuscaded them on their way, and they were only able to return to the fort by the exercise of great skill and coolness in manœuvring, and with the loss of fifty-nine killed and wounded. One of the English schooners was attacked again, while returning from Niagara, and in spite of cannon and small-arms, and a most heroic defence by her little crew of twelve men, would have been taken, had not the Indians been scared at the sudden order of the mate to blow up the schooner, and all jumped overboard to escape.

But the obstinate resolution of Major Gladwyn; the reinforcements from the east; the weariness of this long siege, now severely felt by the Indian host; the failure of their ammunition; the receipt of a letter which the French commander at Fort Chartres had reluctantly dispatched at the demand of Sir Jeffrey Amherst, and which informed Pontiac that the French were at peace with the English, and that he could expect no aid from them; and the approach of winter, when the Indians must of necessity scatter themselves abroad in the forests to keep themselves alive by hunting—all these causes conspired to disappoint this central portion of the great design of Pontiac. The Wyandots and Pottawatomies had made a peace during July, which, however, they afterward broke; but in October they sought, together with the Ojibwas, to make a regular treaty. Gladwyn consented to a truce, and instantly taking advantage of the opportunity, soon had his garrison provisioned for the whole winter. And Pontiac, cruelly enraged and disappointed, with no forces left but his own Ottawas, and now at last giving up his hopes of French aid, left Detroit, and departing to what is now the northwest part of Ohio, set about stirring up the Indians of that region; intending to resume the siege of Detroit in the spring.

The brief sequel of his war and end of his life are soon told. In the spring of 1764, the English government resolved upon a judicious scheme for the organization of trade and intercourse with the Indians.

As a necessary preliminary, however, they sent two armies, one under Col. Bradstreet, along the lakes, and another under Col. Bouquet, through Pennsylvania into the heart of the Indian country, to bring the tribes to submission. Of this latter commander and this expedition, it is fit that some account should here be given.

Col. Henry Bouquet was a native of the Swiss canton of Berne, was a soldier from his boyhood, and had served under Sardinia and Holland, before he became lieutenant-colonel of the Royal Americans, a corps raised in America, chiefly of Germans, and officered by foreigners. It is now the 60th Rifles. In this command, Bouquet had already gained a high reputation in Pennsylvania, as a noble and accomplished man and soldier. During the previous year, while in charge of a small force and a convoy for the relief of forts Bedford, Ligonier and Pitt, he had commanded at the desperate battle of Bushy Run, one of the hardest fought fields ever contested between whites and Indians. This was on August 5th, 1763, when Bouquet's little army, of only about five hundred men, many of them invalids from the unhealthy service in the West Indies, was suddenly attacked while on the march, about twenty-five miles from Fort Pitt, by a force of Indians about as numerous as the English, but having the great advantages of complete knowledge of the forest and its warfare. Bouquet, with ready skill, formed his men into a circle round his horses and baggage, and from one o'clock until eight sustained a furious and incessant attack. The yelling savages, with a boldness very rare in their system of fighting, rushed against the slender line of English, with a close and heavy fire; and then, when the Highlanders, after one sharp volley, charged with the bayonet, they leaped back out of reach, and a moment afterward dashed at another portion of the ring. At nightfall they drew off, having lost very few, while 60 of the soldiers, besides officers, were killed or disabled. Bouquet made his men encamp in their order of battle, upon their arms, making every preparation against a night attack; and thus, in momentary expectation of the foe, weary and thirsty —for the hill on which they were afforded no water, and none dared seek it—and without fire, lest the light should guide the forest marksmen, the beleagured little army awaited daylight, the wounded being deposited within a sort of little breastwork of flour-bags. At early dawn next morning the Indians resumed the battle in the same manner, attacking furiously, firing, and vanishing into the forest whenever the English charged forward from their narrow ring. Thus they fought until about ten o'clock, suffering actual agonies of thirst, their little force gradually thinning under the fire of the Indian rifles; and now the weary ranks began to lose strength and courage. Perseverance in their cunning tactics must infallibly have given the savages the victory; but at the moment when this became evident, the cool and shrewd Bouquet snatched it from them by a well-planned stratagem. He caused two companies to withdraw from the line of defence, as if retreating, toward the centre of the circle. The Indians, perceiving this, charged with redoubled fury upon the weakened line, and were on the point of breaking through, when the two companies, who had taken advantage of some low and wooded ground for their manœuvre, and had passed out of the circle and made a short circuit in the forest, burst upon the flank of the Indians, and delivered a heavy and deadly volley. The savages, though taken entirely by surprise, faced about and intrepidly returned the fire; but fled, when these new opponents charged violently with fixed bayonets. Two other companies, placed in ambush for the purpose, as the routed savages fled across their front, rose and gave them another destructive volley, and then all the four charging again together, the savage foe fled, routed and entirely broken and discouraged, leaving about sixty of their number dead on the ground—an enormous loss for them. The command, setting out again next day, reached Fort Pitt in safety; and Col. Bouquet received for his courage and conduct in this important battle, the thanks of the Pennsylvania Assembly, and of the king.

Col. Bouquet was thus naturally selected to head the southern of the two expeditions of 1764 against the Indians, as he had proved his judgment and skill upon the very ground now to be traversed again; and accordingly, a force of about eighteen hundred men, regulars, Pennsylvania provincials, and Virginia riflemen, having been mustered at Carlisle on the 5th of

August, Bouquet assumed the command, after the troops had been addressed by Governor Penn, and in a few days the army marched for Fort Loudon. Their commander, well aware of the danger of the enterprise, used every precaution that experience and foresight could suggest. He established the strictest discipline, shooting a couple of deserters at Fort Loudon before he could enforce it to his mind; allowed not one woman to accompany the army except one to each corps, and two nurses; and arranged a careful and well-protected order of marching, in open order, in a parallelogram, the baggage and cattle in the centre, and with many outlying parties and scouts in the woods in advance. When he reached Fort Loudon, three hundred of the Pennsylvanians had deserted, and he remained here some weeks to recruit. Bradstreet, commanding the northern expedition, had now reached Presqu' Isle on Lake Erie, where a pretended Indian embassy met him and fooled him into negotiations, intending on their part merely to prevent his advance, while all the time their warriors were murdering and burning on the frontier. But Bouquet disregarded the peace thus made, and Gage annulled it.

Setting forward again from Fort Loudon, Bouquet reached Fort Pitt in September, and there delayed again until October 3d, when, leaving the fort, he plunged into the untraversed forest, marching to ward the Indian towns on the pleasant banks of the Muskingum. In the same careful order, ready at any moment to form in a defensive ring around the baggage if attacked, and filling the woods far in advance and on the flanks with the Virginia scouts, he proceeded, unable to advance more than from five to twelve miles a day; until after ten days' difficult progress, he fixed himself in the heart of the Indian country, and within striking distance of all their villages except the Shawanee towns on the Scioto.

Here the fierce tribes, dismayed at the presence of what was to them a mighty host, and conscious that they could offer no adequate resistance to Bouquet and Bradstreet, met the former; and after some negotiations, in the course of which their mortification and sullen pride, mingled with an evident fear almost abject, rendered their speeches, usually so figurative and vivid, even dull, spiritless, and common-place, the Indians complied with Bouquet's demands, delivered up more than two hundred prisoners, and faithfully promised to send in the rest in the spring. After deposing a contumacious Delaware chief, and causing a successor to be appointed, exacting hostages for good behavior, and prescribing the immediate sending of a deputation to Sir William Johnson to agree upon terms of peace, Bouquet, who had hitherto treated the terrified savages with chilling and overawing sternness, relaxed his demeanor, and held another council, in which he treated them in a friendly manner.

Many accounts have been given of the extraordinary scenes at the delivery of the Indian prisoners. Numbers of the frontiersmen who had accompanied the expedition, had done so in the hope of regaining wives, children, or relatives, in captivity in the wilderness. The whole annals of human history could scarcely furnish a record of another scene so moving and so wonderful as this for the exhibition of varied and violent human passions. Day by day the lost white people came back in troops, many of them, powerfully held by the strange love of the wilderness, coming with reluctance, and even bound as prisoners to prevent them from fleeing back into the forest. Women, even, would fain have remained in the cabins of the dusky husbands of their captivity, to train their young half-breeds in forest nurture. In truth, the strangest feature of the scene was the comparative indifference of the rescued captives, contrasting so strongly with the overwhelming agitation of the friends who sought them. Husbands sought wives, and parents children, trembling and weeping, doubtful of them when found, changed as they were by the growth of years and the exposures of forest life; and the strange magnetism of human passion, seizing upon all around, even infected the rudest of the soldiers, who sympathized in the sorrows or the joys of the occasion; many of them not even able to refrain from tears.

One of the most affecting occurrences of the occasion was the recognition by an aged mother of her daughter, who, carried away nine years before, was among the captives. The eyes of the parent, sharpened by natural affection, discerned the features of her lost child in those of a swarthy and sunburnt young female; but her long captivity had deprived the girl of almost every word of the English which she had acquired at the early age when she was stolen, and she quite failed to recognize her old mother, who lamented with rude, affecting sorrow, that the daughter whom she had so often sung to sleep, had so utterly forgotten her. Bouquet, a man of kind feelings as well as ready intellect, seized the hint which the sorrowing mother did not perceive, and told her to try the experiment of singing the song with which she had put her child to sleep. She did so; and the long-forgotten, simple strain unsealed the daughter's memory and awoke her affections at once; and weeping and rejoicing, she fell upon her mother's neck.

But the wondrous magic of the wilderness, the innate savagery that is somewhere hidden in almost every heart, were singularly proved by the actions of some of the captives this day redeemed. Of all the white women who had taken Indian husbands, not one, even though her children came with her, returned willingly to civilized life; and several of them afterward actually escaped back to their red lords, their wigwams, and the forest.

The business of the expedition thus prosperously accomplished, Bouquet and his little army returned upon their footsteps, and safely regained the settlements. The successful leader received a vote of thanks, most flatteringly worded, from the Pennsylvania Assembly, and another from that of Virginia; and also a more substantial token of the appreciation of his services, in his appointment by the king to the rank of brigadier-general, with the command of the southern department in North America. Col. Bouquet did not, however, long survive to fulfill the hopes inspired by his remarkable excellences and success; for he was carried off by a fever at Pensacola, only three years afterward.

Colonel Bradstreet, permitting himself to be deluded by the Indians as I have stated, accomplished but a small part of his intended purposes; but he effectually relieved Detroit, which had now been besieged more or less closely for fifteen months—for Pontiac had recommenced the siege in the spring.

Shut out from hopes of success elsewhere, Pontiac now passed into the Illinois country, whither the English forces had not yet penetrated, and with untiring activity began to organize a new league of those tribes that inhabited Illinois and dwelt along the banks of the Mississippi River. His design was to keep closed to the English the rich country of the Illinois, by guarding the two approaches to it, by the Mississippi and by the Ohio. But although two attempts to ascend the Mississippi with detachments of British troops were unsuccessful, this last plan of the great Indian leader was frustrated by the negotiation of an English envoy, the fur-trader George Croghan, who moved westward to prepare a path for the troops which Gage, Amherst's successor, proposed to send to take possession of the ancient French stronghold of Fort Chartres. Finding himself deserted by one discouraged tribe after another, and failing to obtain any aid from the French, either in Illinois or at New Orleans, he at last resolved to seek peace with the English; and meeting Croghan at Fort Ouatanon on the Wabash, he concluded an alliance with him, which he confirmed at a great council of the northern tribes held a short time afterward at Detroit; ending his speech as any other Indian would, by begging for rum.

Next spring the great chief proceeded eastward to Oswego, where he again confirmed his alliance with the English, and gave up the vast plans which he had conceived for the preservation of the Indian race. Carrying many valuable gifts, he returned westward to the Maumee. Here we lose sight of him for four years, which he doubtless spent in hunting or in feud, like his warrior brethren.

In April, 1769, he suddenly and for the last time reappears, coming out of his woods into the Illinois country, to the great uneasiness of the English traders in those parts. He crosses the great river and visits his old friend St. Ange de Bellerive, now commanding at St. Louis for the Spaniards. After a time he hears of some meeting of Indians across the river at Cahokia, assembled there for pleasure; and in spite of the persuasions of St. Ange, who knew the enmity of the brutal British fur-traders, he persists in going; expressing his contempt for the English. At Cahokia, he receives invitation after invitation from one friend and another, and accepts all. Drinking himself drunk, he goes out of the village into the woods, singing magic songs. An English fur-trader, seeing him, promptly gives a miserable Kaskaskia Indian a barrel of liquor to kill him, and promises him something more. The wretch followed Pontiac, crept up behind him, and clove his head with his hatchet.

The few followers of the murdered chieftain who would have avenged his death, were driven out of the village. But the news of the death of the great war-chief spread quickly and far; and his Ottawas and their confederate tribes, gathering together, came down upon the treacherous and cowardly

Illinois, exterminated all but thirty families of them, and a few years afterward cut off all this wretched remnant, utterly extinguishing the tribe by the adoption of the few children who alone were saved alive.

St. Ange caused the body of the slain warrior to be brought across the Mississippi and buried. No man knows the place of his grave; but it is somewhere beneath the multitudinous tread of the busy crowds that throng the city of St. Louis. There he sleeps; and far away to the northward still are vanishing into further wildernesses, into the spirit land, the decreasing bands of the Algonquins, who yet retain the memory of their greatest chieftain. Over them is rushing, as it already rushes over his forgotten bones, the vast irresistible ocean of the power of the white race. And as most of them are already laid, so their scattered remainder soon shall lie, trodden under foot, unknown, unremembered; existing, even in history, only as a legend and a tradition. Pontiac, sleeping beneath the lofty, crowded houses of St. Louis, lies there, the symbol and the prophecy of his race, and of its doom.

Besides Pontiac himself, there are perhaps none of the actors in this story whom we need follow further, unless it be the beautiful Ojibwa girl, Catharine, whose warning saved Detroit. She was, it is said, severely whipped by Pontiac himself. And there is a further tradition that she grew old, haggish, and drunken, as the Indian women do; and that in a drunken fit, she fell into a great kettle of boiling maple sap, and died miserably.

Lecture V.

THE

CABIN HOMES

OF THE WILDERNESS,

AT THE BEGINNING OF THE REVOLUTION.

CABIN HOMES OF THE WILDERNESS

AT THE OPENING OF THE REVOLUTION.

In the year 1768, there was assembled at Fort Stanwix, in central New York, on the site of the present city of Rome, a council of the confederated Six Nations, or Iroquois, under the supervision and influence of Sir William Johnson, the British agent for Indian affairs. It was much desired by sundry parties interested, that a title to an immense region of country lying west of the mountains should, in some way or other, be secured from the Indians; and as these bold adventurers, the Iroquois, the wild rovers, who laid under contribution their red brethren from the seaboard coasts of Maine upon the east, to the fast-rushing flood of the Father of Waters upon the west, exacting taxes paid equally by the Shawnees and Illinois, and by the Delawares and the Hurons— as these wild rovers claimed large districts of country besides those which they themselves occupied, the agents of the British government thought it well to secure this title from them. They claimed, in virtue of their conquests, the whole region of country lying upon the south of the Ohio, running from that river on the north through the whole extent of the country traversed by the Cumberland and Tennessee rivers. At this council, assembled about the 1st of November, 1768, Sir William Johnson, who had arranged the details and particulars beforehand, with an unscrupulous skill worthy of a modern politician, and by means of a series of gifts and presents to these hardy warriors, made the purchase, securing, in the first place, that whole region lying between the mouth of the Cherokee or Tennessee River upon the westward, and the Kanawha at the east, for the crown of Great Britain; and the lands from the Kanawha on the west to the Monongahela on the east, for such traders as had been defrauded or injured during the war of Pontiac. Let it be remembered that these Indians had, in truth, no more right and title to that land than you; and yet, by the action of its agents and officers, the British government executed this agreement, and by virtue of it, henceforth claimed all that district of country lying west of the Monongahela and south of the Ohio river.

Under this treaty it was determined to make a grant of 200,000 acres to such officers and soldiers as had been engaged in the old French war, and to locate it just west of the Kanawha River, within the limits of the present State of Kentucky.

And now—casting a rapid glance to another portion of our present vast territory—about the year 1770 we shall find coasting along the borders of Lake Superior upon the northward, ascertaining particulars and gaining information regarding the copper mines of that district, passing thence westward across the Mississippi River, and making a long and perilous journey into the country of the Dacotah or Sioux Indians, a bold and hardy captain from Connecticut, one Jonathan Carver. He called the attention of the British government and of the eastern colonists to the boundless mineral and agricultural wealth within the district he had traversed, and bore the first intelligence of a credible and authentic character in regard to the Oregon or Columbia River, and the country lying west of the Rocky Mountains.

We shall find at the same time floating down the Beautiful River of the French—the Ohio—a person to whom we have had occasion before to allude, the young athletic Virginian, George Washington; having, in common with his brethren, that American peculiarity, a powerful instinct for good land, a strong desire after real estate. Pursuing his meandering course, in flat-boat or canoe, down the peaceful current of this river, comes this young Virginian, to locate his own right as an officer in the French war, and also the claims of his brother soldiers and officers. His eye having been early disciplined in his pursuits as a surveyor, and long accustomed to wander as forester and woodman, he became familiar with all forms and phases of nature, a lover of beautiful scenery, and at the same time skilled in estimating and selecting good lands. He revels in the panorama of magnificence outspread before him. Here a stately deer is browsing upon the river bluff, and yonder another of his brethren steps proudly down to slake his thirst in the peaceful stream. Here herds of buffalo are quietly wandering and grazing at their will. The woods are crowded with flocks of wild turkeys; and everywhere around him, in the beautiful summer season of the year, everything on earth wears the brightest smile of benignity and beauty; and heart and eye of our Virginian gladden and are ravished with delight. He forms the purpose of becoming a settler of the West, and but for the near outbreak of the American Revolution, no doubt George Washington would have been a great pioneer of western civilization, leaving his impress upon its grateful and virgin soil, as durably and lastingly as he has now left it upon our whole continent.

Just before this period, a long series of outrageous and oppressive proceedings by the government officers of North Carolina, supported and encouraged by the royal governor himself, the rigid, overbearing and haughty Tryon, had thoroughly alienated the affections of that colony from the English government. The sheriffs, as collectors, had levied enormous illegal taxes, for their own private gain; and the courts were courts of anything but justice. In their well-founded indignation, all the inland inhabitants formed themselves into bodies of so-called "Regulators," and while they administered a rude but honest justice among themselves, broke up and prohibited the sitting of the oppressive regular courts. These hardy men violently and successfully opposed the stamp act; and Governor Tryon, irritated by their continued resistance to the tyranny of himself and his creatures, issuing from the executive palace, headed a levy of the militia, and on the river Alamance, gave battle to the forces of the Regulators, in the year 1771. The brave countrymen, like their fellows at Bunker Hill, fought until their powder was all expended, and then sullenly fled, having lost nine of their own number, and killed just thrice as many of their foes.

Expecting no justice while under the sway of the British lion, and exasperated beyond all patience at the oppressions, the official injustice and social indignities they had vainly opposed, these bold and determined men resolved to flee to the wilderness; from ancient times the refuge of the oppressed and the poor. Deserting their homesteads and the hearthstones by which their children had been nursed, and where their fondest memories were garnered, with their teams, their flocks, their wives and little ones, they toil up the steep ascents of the Alleghany Mountains, and pass westward till they find the broad alluvial lands of the river Watauga. Here, entering into a league with the chief men of the Cherokee nation, which held possession of this country, they make just and legitimate purchase of a sufficient extent of territory to answer their purpose of agricultural pursuits. And here, under leadership of Col. James Robertson, one of the noblest pioneers our history speaks of, they establish the first Republic ever founded upon the soil of the American continent—despising and eschewing the authority of England, from which they had only received wrong, outrage, betrayal, and their compatriots' deaths. Surrounded by the grandeur of the great primitive forms of nature, the towering mountain lifting its great peak to the clouds, the plains all beautiful with the white of the abounding strawberry blossom, or the rich red of its fruit; the rhododendron, with its bright and genial hues, and the azalea, making all the forests crimson with a touch of fire—here these hardy men plant themselves, and begin to carry their explorations and surveys far to the westward. This is the germ and the birth-place of the present State of Tennessee.

Still further to the southwest, we find strange events transpiring upon the banks of the Mississippi River, in the neighborhood of the present city of Natchez, where stood the old French Fort Rosalie, named after the fair dame of the great French nobleman, Count Pontchartrain. During the old French war, in 1755–6, General Phineas Lyman, of Durham, in Connecticut, had buckled on the harness of war, and had approved himself a valiant and noble leader, doing faithful service in behalf of the colonies until the conclusion of the war. His valor and constancy, his rare power of combination, masterful accuracy in details, and able generalship, had gained him a place so high in the confidence of his countrymen, that the reputation which he won so well in his office of major-general and commander-in-chief of the Connecticut forces, and as commander of the expedition to Havana, in 1762, was second to that of no man in America. Men high in place in England had also repeatedly invited the able, eminent and accomplished provincial soldier to visit the mother country. Organizing an association under the name of the "Military Adventurers," of the soldiers and officers of the war just ended, he accordingly proceeded to England as its agent, to solicit for it a grant of the desert lands lying on the Yazoo and Mississippi rivers. For these associates had heard marvellous stories of the richness of the land in the Southwest, and desired to settle upon so fair a domain; judging that they had a right to claim the grant in return for their services to the British government. Gen. Lyman arrived in England; but instead of meeting a kind reception and a cordial acknowledgment of his services, was treated with coldness and contempt, and with mean and cruel ingratitude. He was deluded with promise after promise, and delay after delay, even for years; until the discovery of this long series of cheatings came upon him with such crushing violence that he fell into absolute listless despondency. The noble soldier whose spirit had passed undismayed through perils of sea and land, Indian ambuscade and pitched battle, unable to bear the thought of returning, deluded, to his deluded friends, sadly determined to bear his fancied ignominy as best he might, in distant England, and to lay his dishonored bones there.

Thus the unhappy General Lyman wasted eleven years of the prime of life, absent from that home which he had left in the flush of present success, and with still more radiant hopes beaming from the future—a home made sacred and beautiful, and happy, by a lovely wife, by beloved, intelligent, refined and highly educated children. And when the faithful and patient wife could endure the long heart-break no more, she sent her eldest-born to England to bring back his father.

The unhappy father, his paternal affection awakened at the sight of his boy, consents to return ; and the more readily, as the British government has, with a liberality too late exercised, at last made the desired grant, at the intended spot, within the limits of the present State of Mississippi, and in what was then called western Florida. To General Lyman himself was given a special grant of lands broad enough for future wealth; and a promise—never fulfilled—of a pension of £200 a year. But many of the grantees were now hoary old men, and all were aged beyond the period of life when men remove into wildernesses to undertake the rude, exhausting labors of founding new communities. But Gen. Lyman came home, with his grant. His oldest son, a youth of brilliant promise, had completed his studies, received and held a commission in the army, and given it up for the practice of law; had felt to the full the effects of all these high hopes so long deferred, which prevented him from earnest devotion to the law. The long weary suspense and doubt hanging over his own prospects, had destroyed health of body and mind together, and when the wretched father met him, he had sunk from brokenheartedness into lunacy. But he carried the hapless youth away, hoping that new atmospheres and new scenes might give him back his health; and with a few friends proceeded to West Florida, and located his grant. Scarcely had he done so, when his son died. In the next year, 1775, the desolate father followed him to the grave. In 1776, Mrs. Lyman came to this fatal country, with her only brother and all her child ren except one son. She died in a few months; and next summer her brother died.

This expedition, which sailed from Middletown, May 1st, 1776, passed through a battle with misfortune so long, so varied, and so terrible, that it deserves something more than a mere reference. Let us briefly trace the affecting story. Reaching New Orleans, August 1st, 1776, they begin to ascend the Mississippi in open boats. Day after day passes; and they are yet dragging their heavily-laden craft against the furious current, through sickly airs, and under the exhausting southern sun. The malaria of the swamps begins its fearful work, and one and another of the hardy emigrants sicken and die; while the fated survivors, with diminished strength, more slowly drag the heavy boats up stream. Boat after boat is left—the crew too feeble to draw it—fastened to the willows or anchored in the current; among them that of Captain Matthew Phelps. Reaching Natchez, the minister of the party, Mr. Smith, who, in genuine Puritan style, had accompanied them from Connecticut, falls a victim to the fever. The remainder of the party at last reaches the site of the intended settlement, where General Lyman had, before his death, made some small improvements; and here it is that Madam Lyman follows her hapless husband to another world.

Captain Phelps, who was left below on the river still remained there, his family so reduced by fever and-ague that they could only, at intervals, wait on each other at all. His daughter Abigail soon died, and the mourning father buried her on the bank, digging her grave with his own hands. This was in the early part of Sept., 1776. On the 16th, an infant son, born at sea on the voyage out, died, and the father again dug a grave and buried his boy by the side of his daughter. A companion in misery, named Flowers, who had lost all his family, now overtook Phelps, and joining forces, they put the property of both in a larger boat, and worn down almost to skeletons, began again the ascent of the river. They were still toiling upward on the 12th of October, when, a little above Natchez, Mrs. Phelps died, at the house of a hospitable planter named Alston, who gave her a decent burial. Moving onward again, Capt. Phelps reached the mouth of the Big Black, on which river his lands lay, on the 24th of Nov.; having been almost a hundred days in making the trip from New Orleans, which now occupies a few hours. Weakened by disease beyond the power of labor, Phelps here hired a man and boy to help him up the river, and himself, with the boy, labored at the tow-line, leaving the man on board to steer. The boat glides into an eddy, or 'suck," and her stern catching under a willow, the steersman is thrown out, but being a sturdy swimmer, escapes to the shore. Phelps's two remaining children, a boy of five and a girl of ten years of age, worn down by their long and clinging sickness, are sitting listlessly upon the bed where they have suffered so much. The father, from whose arms one after another of his beloved has been wrested so terribly, in a transport of agony, seeing the boat circling in the whirlpool, hastily ties the line to a tree, and not being able to swim, creeps out on the willow that holds down the boat, hoping to rescue the children and carry them ashore. He reaches the boat, and his added weight bears down the treacherous willow, and the stern under it. But begging the sister to sit still while he saves her brother, the frightened man calls his boy; the little fellow is wading through the water in the boat toward his father, when a high wave strikes the bow, it is carried instantly under, and the two children are swept almost out of his very arms into the devouring whirl of the river. Standing helplessly upon the dangerous tree, the miserable man sees them rise once, clasped in each other's arms, and then they disappear forever beneath the boiling muddy water; and bereft before of wife, daughter, infant, and now of all his little ones—every tie to earth thus rudely severed, and, though it is scarcely worth the naming in addition, his little property swept into the gulf, too—the lonely, desolate man sadly escapes to the shore and ascends slowly to the place of his proposed settlement. A brutal squatter has usurped his claim, and under the protection of the custom of the land, defies him. Thus left absolutely alone and penniless, he turns his face again to his distant native State; and there, it is pleasant to know, after so many bitter sorrows, he passed the remainder of his days in peace and comfort; and saw another wife, and other little children, within a happy home. He often told the story of his sufferings to friend or neighbor, narrating one disaster after another with the steady resignation of a Christian—all but one terrible sight. He could not speak of the moment when the flood swallowed down his two youngest close before his eyes.

The survivors of this sturdy band of Connecticut farmers, after struggling through so many obstacles, became thrifty and successful planters in the country round Natchez, with handsome dwellings, large estates, and scores of slaves.

But time passed on, and the American Revolution broke out. All these Connecticut people were ardent loyalists. The contagion of independence had not been carried so far as their distant dwellings. An agent of the American Congress, Oliver Pollock, had descended from Pittsburg to New Orleans, then in the possession of the Spaniards, and made arrangements with the Spanish authorities to supply the settlements upon the Kentucky, the Cumberland, Tennessee, and other whig American settlements, with ammunition to carry on the war. And a little after, in 1779, there descends the river one John Willing, a citizen of Philadelphia, with an American commission as colonel. He is plausible of speech and of winning address; he visits these loyal settlers in the neighborhood of Natchez and in other parts of Mississippi, gathers them together, makes them many orations, wins their confidence, and binds them by oath to strict neutrality. They are unwilling wholly to renounce allegiance to the British crown, but promise not to interfere in the struggle then going on. Willing then, ascending the river with a small force, seizes, by stratagem, a British war vessel lying there, carries her to New Orleans, sells her to the Spanish authorities, and with the proceeds spends his time, with his companions, in riotous living and debauchery, instead of applying the money to the purpose for which it was intended—the purchase of arms. Having wasted the whole, he reascends the river, ravages and pillages the estates in the neighborhood of Baton Rouge, then in the possession of the English, and commences the reascent of the Mississippi to do the same at the settlements of Natchez. Our Connecticut settlers in that region, and their neighbors, valorous men, hearing of the conduct of the desperado, and all faith in him—and, unfortunately, in the American cause—thus destroyed, collect themselves together, armed and equipped, to punish him, or at least to prevent his piratical designs. He reaches the neighborhood of the spot where they are fortified, crosses to the other side of the river, and then, by means of his artillery, treacherously opens fire on them under cover of a flag of truce. This they return with such hearty good will that some of his men are killed and some taken prisoners. He and the remainder of them return to New Orleans, and from there he escapes into the country on the banks of the Alabama River. The conduct of this desperado shook all confidence and faith, on the part of the settlers, in the integrity and character of the American struggle for independence; and very justly considering themselves absolved from their oath of neutrality, they resolved to remain loyal to the crown of England.

About this period France gave evidence of its leaning to the American cause of independence; whereupon the English government, in anger, declared war against France. Spain, also, which had been the firm ally of France, gave favorable consideration to the designs of the revolutionists; and England, including her within the ban, declared war against Spain. The Spanish government decided to attack the British in Louisiana; and Don Galvez, governor of New Orleans, ascended the river, took all the British posts as far as Natchez, and then returned to capture Mobile and Pensacola. The loyalists, including Col. Philip Austin, John Austin, Col. Hutchins, Mr. Lyman, Dr. Dwight, and various other of the Connecticut emigrants before named, now large holders of real estate, were unwilling to submit to the authority of Spain. Arming themselves, they attacked the weak garrison left in Fort Panmure, formerly Fort Rosalie, at Natchez, and succeeded, by stratagem and other means, in dispossessing the Spanish. They heard, furthermore, that a large British fleet was coming to chastise the Spanish upon the Gulf; but, sorrowful to tell, just after their success in ejecting the Spanish from the fort, they learned that these accounts of coming fleets were all deceptive and untrue. And now Don Galvez, having taken Mobile and Pensacola, invested with great honors and powers, is about to come and punish these disobedient British subjects of Spain. But they, well knowing the treacherous and cruel nature of the Spaniards, resolve, rather than to await their coming and to abide their revenge, to abandon their homes and undertake the long and adventurous journey to the settlements in Georgia. Before them is a trackless wilderness, then lying between the Mississippi River on the west and the Ogeechee upon the east—a tract of country inhabited only by wild beasts and wilder savages. With the bloodhounds of Spain upon their track, more than one hundred of these people set out, mounted upon horses with their wives and little ones, some of the children in arms, with their servants and moveables upon pack-horses, and proceed norteastwardly, in hopes to reach the prairie region of Mississippi. This is the month of May, 1781. It is an unusually dry spring. They gain the prairie country, and no water is to be found. Far in the distance before them, as the mariner at sea beholds what he supposes islands near the blue horizon, so rise upon the level prairie clumps of trees, and here they hope for water. Toward that they press, only to be disappointed. Thirty-six hours have passed, yet no drop of cooling liquid has touched their lips or tongues. At length a camp is formed. The women and children are deposited here, and the men start out in parties to search for the precious liquid. The whole day is passed; they return, faint, weary, and despairing, their tongues hanging out of their mouths, and fall upon the ground utterly dejected and brokenhearted. In this emergency, when man's hardihood and courage has failed, female instinct and energy step forward. Mrs. Dwight, wife of Dr. Dwight, sallies from the camp, attended by several women and one or two men. They reach a tract of ground at the foot of a couple of hills, where, in a spongy spot, she bids the men to dig. The spades are stoutly handled; they come to moist earth, to trickling drops, and after a little they stay their hands; for a pure and beautiful fountain of water gushes up. Thank God! is the universal exclamation. The news is borne backward to the camp, and now all the party, men, women, and children, and their patient, suffering beasts, rush wildly to the fountain—a fountain of life in a parched and thirsty land. Dr. Dwight stations guards about the spring, to prevent an intemperate use of the pure element; and all through the livelong night, men and women, and jaded horses, allowed to slake their thirst quietly and by slow degrees, drink and drink, with a thirst almost unquenchable. And now they turn to the northwestward to avoid the Indians, the Chickasaws on the one side and the Choctaws on the other, who, it is feared, are in league with the Spanish.

Their compass is lost, and they have no guide except the sun in heaven, which is often concealed by clouds, for now the weather becomes rainy and inclement. Ever and anon a prowling party of Indians, under the shadow of the night, creep into camp and run off horses or plunder baggage. And worse than all, a loathsome disease infects the worn-out company. Having wandered northward, nearly to the Tennessee River, they turn about and march nearly straight south again to near the present city of Aberdeen, Mississippi, where they cross the Tombigbee on rafts of logs. Thence they struggle through the wilderness to the Black Warrior River, which they cross at Tuscaloosa Falls; and thence, afraid to follow any trail for fear of enemies, they go wandering up and down in their helpless misery, until they find themselves in the mountainous regions of the upper part of Alabama. Then they direct their steps toward the Georgian settlements, hoping to reach them by way of the Cherokee nation. One day, to their terror—for a human form inspires them with nameless fears of Indian ambuscades and savage tortures—they see three men advancing on the rude path which they are pursuing, to meet them. The strangers advance, and are found to be an old trader among the Indians, and two Chickasaws with him. The rugged frontiersman, shocked at the wretched appearance of the forlorn and famine-stricken troop, served out to them all his provisions, and his last gallon of tafia or trading-rum. He added to his kind gifts, kind advice, admonishing them to avoid the Tennessee mountains, and the Cherokees, who were mostly whiggish in alliance and feeling, and rather to turn southward and venture themselves among the Creeks, trusting to their loyalist attitude, and to the influence and well-known humanity of their chief, the celebrated Colonel Alexander McGillivray.

This advice they implicitly followed; turned southward once more; once more crossed the intervening ranges of mountains, for two hundred miles, often walking with feet bare, torn and bleeding; obliged to lead their laden horses along the perilous and pathless rocks. And now they reach the Coosa

River, in Antauga County, in central Alabama. Exhausted and feeble, the deep, strong and rapid current and the dangerous obstructing rocks of the noble river are obstacles which they have not strength remaining to overcome, and they lie down upon the banks in listless despair, unable even to build a raft. They might all have perished in their stupid discouragement, had it not been for the courage and resolution of the same Mrs. Dwight who discovered the fountain that saved their lives before. She declared that if there was even one man bold enough to go with her, she would at least try to cross the river, and find a canoe or some better ford. Her husband and one other man, inspired by her brave spirit, swore she should not risk her life alone, and all three swam their horses across the stream; carried down by the current, and at least once plunged completely under water, by leaping from a ledge. On the other side they found, a mile above, a large canoe, stove on the rocks. They repaired it as well as they could, and leaving Mrs. Dwight with the horses, the two men took it down to their friends; and by the end of the next day they were all safely across.

Resuming their march, after proceeding about twenty miles they approach a Creek town, known as the Hickory Ground, at the present town of Wetumpka. Colonel McGillivray, the celebrated Creek ruler, has a residence there, but is absent. Afraid to enter the village, the trembling loyalists send in three deputies to explain their condition and ask relief. The ambassadors ride into the Indian town, along the path, amongst squaws hoeing corn, and between pleasant cabins, and lazy warriors, basking in the sun. But at the sight of strangers the fierce savages quickly gather about them in a dissatisfied and increasingly angry crowd, for they see that the saddles are not Spanish, like those of their allies, but English, like those of their unscrupulous and bitter foes, the Georgians. The wretched deputies in vain set forth the truth, that they are royalists, friends of King George and of the Creek nation; in vain explain whence and why they have come, and urge their helpless state, the misery of their company, and their frank and confiding application. The savages converse and argue together; their tones grow ferocious, their eyes begin to gleam with fury, and they handle their weapons. The unhappy men see death close before them; they and their hapless friends will end their long desperate journey under the tomahawks and knives of these fierce Indians.

A negro rides up, and with some seeming authority demands the cause of the excitement. It is Paro, body-servant to Col. McGillivray, this moment returned from a journey. The Indians answer that these are some Georgians whom they propose to kill. But the deputies quickly tell him their sad and truthful story, and he believes it, and tries to convince the warriors. But though he adds violent reproaches to persuasions and arguments, they simply answer that all the company must die. An ignorant but fair-minded warrior, now bethinking himself of the strange custom—which he takes it for granted is universal among all the whites—of putting talk on paper, all at once calls out—for he would be just, and appeals to the records—"If you tell the truth, make the paper talk!" The quick-witted negro takes a hint from their demand and asks them for a journal of their trip. They kept none. Then have they any paper with writing on it? They search in terror. At last, one of them finds an old letter in his pocket. Paro tells him what to do, and how; and accordingly he reads as if from the letter, in a slow and solemn manner—it may be believed he would not lack earnestness—a full and detailed account of their journey, and of its causes, Paro interpreting with much spirit and many gestures. As the reader proceeds, the wild faces of his audience soften and light up, and putting aside their weapons, they all come up to the deputies, at the end of the account, shake hands all round, welcome them to the town, and presently bringing in the whole company, furnish them good lodging and bounteous entertainment.

After abundant rest and refreshment, the party

proceeded eastward, separating into two divisions. One reached Savannah, and the other was taken by the whigs, though soon released. During the whole of this terrible journey of one hundred and forty-nine days from Natchez, not one of the party lost his life.

The fatigues and dangers of the way, however, had undermined the health of some of the travellers; and two daughters of Gen. Lyman died after reaching Savannah. Three of their brothers were also members of the expedition; of whom, when the British left Georgia, one went to Nova Scotia, one to New York, and one to New Providence in the island of Nassau. It is said that all these sons died of broken hearts; and as Dr. Dwight observes, in his account of General Lyman's misfortunes, this may well be termed "the Unhappy Family;" so long and uninterrupted was the series of crushing misfortunes which bore them, one after another, down into obscure graves.

In western Pennsylvania had settled, in the early part of the century, a stout Englishman and his wife, whose lands had increased, and his children had multiplied around his board. To him was born, in 1735, his son Daniel Boone. The boy, a hunter by birth and nature, early became a daring and skillful woodsman, strong, fleet and active, and unrivalled in the use of the rifle. He was but eighteen when his father removed to the upper country on the Yadkin, among the mountains in the west of North Carolina; rejoicing in the wild and noble scenery, the primeval forest, the richness of the virgin soil and the abounding game. Here Boone married, while yet young, and lived for some time, hunting and farming; loving and beloved by wife and children; but yet essentially a wild and solitary man, spending his happiest hours alone in the woods, hunting sometimes, and often enjoying with a strange delight, for a man so rude and unlettered, the numberless beauties of the mountain and river landscapes.

In the spring of 1769 he had already become uneasy at the approach of other men; for other settlers were planting themselves along the streams, other hunters were wandering in the woods; so he meditates an expedition into the unknown forest world beyond the mountains. The handles of the plough are dropped in the furrow, he hastens to his house, gathers his rifle and accoutrements, and starts in company with an old Indian trader and hunter named Finlay, and four other men. They commence their journey on the 1st of May, 1769. A long, toilsome way they follow for six weeks. Crossing the Alleghany, the iron mountain, to the Cumberland Pass, they come out upon the headwaters of the Kanawha, and now have reached the goodly land. And truly, is it not an Eden? During a sojourn of six and a half months, feasting his eyes with the glories which he can enjoy there without end—herds of buffalo which no man can number, beautiful springs gushing from every hill-side, wide, wealthy savannas, broad tree-fringed rivers, noble forests, and all the unimaginable, solitary splendors of a rich land, without human inhabitant. At the expiration of this time, Boone and William Stewart are taken captive by the Indians. The remainder of the company are frightened, and hurry homeward. Boone and his companion remain in the hands of their captors, pretending quiet satisfaction, for a week; then easily escape. Not a great while thereafter, William Stewart is shot by the Indians; and now Daniel Boone remains alone. The spring of the year comes to this lonely hunter, wandering here through all these wide and pleasant lands of forest and prairie and canebrake, which the Indians call "The Dark and Bloody Ground." Now he is joined by his brother, Squire Boone, a man who shares many peculiarities with himself. For a year and a half longer do these intrepid men remain in Kentucky, when Squire Boone returns to the settlements for a fresh supply of powder and lead, while Daniel remains alone in the wilderness, surrounded by savage foes seeking his trail; yet unfearing and defiant. They go in groups; he without an associate, without even a dog to bear him company. This strange safety was assured by a weed—a thistle—which grew in abundance throughout Kentucky, as if Providence had spread a carpet of safety over the land for this solitary wanderer. On this humble herb the foot of the traveller leaves a peculiar impress, which remains long and distinctly; and the Indians, the lords of the soil, numerous and bold, tread carelessly as they rove across their hereditary forests and prairies, and leave patent to the trained unerring eye of the solitary white man the record of their number and their journey; while he, avoiding the tell-tale herb, moves unknown and safe from one hunting-ground to another. Thus, to his eyes, the ground is covered as if with a sheet of snow, bearing the impression of his enemies' trails; while, for their eyes, no snow is on the ground, and his step has left no trace. Thus wanders this one solitary Anglo-Saxon, glad at heart in the revelation of a new apocalypse of earthly beauty; a man untaught in books and erudition, but whose eyes often overflow with happy, grateful tears as he looks abroad upon the loveliness of nature, tasting the sweetest and profoundest things of God; reading, with clear, keen eye, the open secret which nature reveals to all her children, and pursuing his way of peril to find it a way of delight and joy. Having fully explored the country in company with his brother, he returns to the settlements. The tidings he brings are hailed with rapture by the people; but two years are allowed to pass before active measures are taken to assume the occupancy of the new soil. At length Boone departs with his family, having first shaken hands with all his neighbors twice round; for, notwithstanding his silent ways, he is much beloved, because he never omitted an opportunity to do a kindly office to his brother man, at whatever inconvenience to himself.

With five more families he sets out, with wife and children; is joined, in Powell's Valley, by forty well-armed men; and advances prosperously, until just as the last mountain pass is before them. Even as they are ascending the rugged way, the rear of the party is attacked by the Indians, and at the first fire, Boone's oldest son, a promising youth of about twenty, falls—the second victim. William Stewart was the first; and they two are the precious first-fruits of that fearful hecatomb offered so cheerfully by those dauntless and uncompromising men, the heroic forefathers of the Mississippi Valley.

After the Indians are vanquished and driven from their coverts, a halt is called; and though the parley which ensues is attended only by the men, the women and children are represented. The company determine to fall back upon Powell's Valley. Here they take up a position, put themselves in a defensive attitude, and month after month is passed away in hunting or dreaming. Boone sits one day in the porch of his humble cabin, when down the valley comes, all foaming with his haste, an express messenger from

Lord Dunmore, the Governor of Virginia, looking for Daniel Boone. This is in 1774. He is wanted by Lord Dunmore to go westward four hundred miles, to the falls on the Ohio River, at what is now Louisville, to bear tidings to a party of surveyors and land jobbers there, that the Indians are about to break into hostility; and then safely to convoy these men home again. One furtive glance at Mrs. Boone, who nods assent, and his rifle is grasped, and Daniel, with a quiet and easy heart, starts alone upon his wild and terrible journey. He reaches the Falls, surprises the surveyors and speculators, and brings them back in safety, performing the journey of 800 miles in six weeks; and receives not only the thanks of the men thus rescued from the clutches of the savages, but also of the lordly Governor of Virginia.

And now it is not needful for me to stop to detail the peculiar transactions of Logan's War, or that other war of Lord Dunmore, whose scene was the western border in 1774. The Indians, wronged and outraged by the conduct of the squatter settlers, who had grasped their land without remunerating them, had again risen; but after a brief campaign, were overcome, and forced to yield their lands to the whites; and Lord Dunmore hastened back to uphold and maintain the tottering authority of the British Crown within the territories of Virginia.

And now, in 1774, there has penetrated the interior

of Kentucky another lone hunter, James Harrod. James Logan also has come. Daniel Boone is engaged as superintendent by one Col. Henderson, who purposes to be a great land-jobber in the west; a man who taught himself to read and write after attaining adult years, and who began life in the province of Carolina. He was a man of strong sense, and of much practical skill and enterprise. He ran for and obtained the lofty office of constable, next became a magistrate, and afterward lived to reach the bench of the Supreme Court of North Carolina. He was not a cross-grained ascetic, not a studious scholar, but a free, bold, dashing, spirited fellow, who had made his money easily, and spent it yet more easily—generous and jovial to all, and expending in good living and speculation all that he earned. At this time he was bankrupt; and casting his eye about the world to see from what quarter he could gather new supplies, he thought of western lands. He would found an empire in the West. He makes a treaty with the Cherokees for some land which did not belong to them; but that is a small matter; his title is as good as that of the British government to American lands. He buys the vast region of country lying between the Kanawha and Cherokee rivers. Here he proposes to establish the Republic of Transylvania; and Boone is sent out as a pioneer, to found the first settlement. And now, in conjunction with the settlements of

Harrod and Logan, Boonesborough is established, and into this new home comes Mrs. Boone, with three other women. These were the pioneer women of the West; the women who, with their children, braved the perils of the way, the dangers of the forest, and the more fearful wiles of the bloodthirsty, insidious foes who lurk in every thicket, and ambuscade every ravine.

As the war of the Revolution broke out in the eastern colonies, the aristocratic ministry of England contrived a grand *coup d'état*, to arm the Indian savages against the western settlements; that, having destroyed these, they might sweep eastward over the mountains. The colonists, thus attacked at once in front and rear, it was imagined must quickly succumb; and in truth, had it not been for these infant settlements in the land of the canebrake—these three little forts of Boonesborough, Harrodsburg and Logansport—manned altogether by not more than one hundred fighting-men, which stood, a slender but impregnable breakwater, against the wild, tempestuous rush of the forest tribes of the Northwest—there is reason for believing that the onset of those fierce warriors might have turned the wavering balance of the war, and given the victory, in the bitter struggle of the Revolution, to the British.

But there is another life, less known than Daniel Boone's, but, if possible, still more hardily adventurous, and certainly more closely characteristic of the men and times of which I am speaking. Let us follow it, and see what were the deeds and the dangers of one whom we may well call the ideal man—the representative man of ante-Revolutionary Kentucky. I mean the life of General Simon Kenton, the refugee, hunter, spy, horse-stealer, Indian-fighter, soldier and officer; and withal the perfect hero, true friend and brave protector of the scattered, imperilled outposts of civilization that scantily dotted the blood-stained forests of Kentucky.

Simon Kenton was born in Fauquier County, Virginia, in 1755. He was of the wild and insubordinate, but cool, adventurous and daring Scotch-Irish blood—his mother Scotch and his father Irish. The parents were so poor that the boy's education, to his lasting disadvantage in life, was quite neglected. In those wild days, and in the hardy, healthy life of the mountains, marriages were early made. Kenton was only about sixteen when he was in love; and lost his sweetheart, too, by the success of a preferred rival, his own most intimate friend, one Veach, who was, for all that appears, as young as he. Desperate with disappointment, he recklessly, as the old song says, "came to the wedding without any bidding," and finding the happy couple among their friends, seated on a bed, he seems to have quite lost his wits, and crazily and rudely thrust himself between them. Upon this,

Veach and his brothers pounced upon him, gave him a sound thrashing and turned him out of the house. But meeting Veach alone in the woods, soon afterward, Kenton intimating that he was still dissatisfied, they had a long and severe pitched battle, which ended in Kenton's thoroughly squaring accounts by beating his adversary to helplessness, and leaving him on the ground for dead. Frightened at his work, fearing the revenge of friends and the rude penalties of border law, his friend and his love both lost, a sudden mighty sense of loneliness and hate for civilized life came upon him, and he fled to the mountains and the woods. Journeying by night, and hiding by day, he pushes westward, and in April, 1771, reaches Cheat River; works for hire until he earns a good rifle; goes on to Fort Pitt; engages himself to hunt for the garrison; and forms a strong friendship with that Simon Girty who stands amidst the blood and fire of the fearful Indian wars of those times, a figure infernal with murder and treason, a renegade among the savages, and yet—as if to prove that the worst men are not all bad—more than once proving himself an eminently faithful and unflinching protector of the very few to whom he felt gratitude or affection.

In the autumn of 1771, with two hunters named Yeager and Strader, the first of whom had excited his fancy with wonderful stories of the cane-lands of Kentucky, he went down the Ohio to find them. Not succeeding, they returned to the woods of the great Kanawha, and hunted for a year and a half. In the spring of 1773 the Indians, then becoming excited against the settlements, suddenly fired upon the three hunters while asleep in their camp, and killed Yeager; Strader and Kenton fled into the woods naked, as they lay in their shirts only, without arms or food, and after wandering six days, torn, bleeding, and famished, so footsore that their last day's journey was but six miles, and so exhausted that on that same day they repeatedly lay down to die, they met some hunters, obtained food and clothes, and returned to a settlement. Kenton now went to work again, until he had obtained another rifle and hunter's outfit; accompanied a party searching for Capt. Bullitt, who had gone down the Ohio on a surveying expedition; guided it, when unsuccessful, back to Virginia; volunteered into Dunmore's army in 1774, doing good service as a spy; and being discharged in the fall, hunted on the Big Sandy that winter; and the next summer made a second trip with a hunter named Williams, in search of the cane-lands of Kentucky, the glowing descriptions of his dead friend Yeager still dwelling in his mind. He discovered the long-wished-for cane by accident, not far from Maysville, in Mason County; cleared some land and planted an acre of corn upon one of the richest and loveliest spots in Kentucky, and that season ate the first corn raised by a white man in the "Dark and Bloody Ground."

Kenton now passed two or three years in a series of hunting and fighting adventures, almost monotonous for daring, and the extremest and most incessant peril from the savages, who haunted every covert of the beloved land into which the whites were crowding with increased rapidity. In the spring of 1777, while he was residing at Harrodsburg, he was sent out with a small party, and driven back by the Indians. Sending his men into the station, he went off alone to warn the garrison of Boonesborough; delayed entering until dark, to avoid the ambushes which the Indians frequently laid to shoot any persons coming or going; and on his entrance found the garrison bringing home the corpses of two men who had ignorantly or carelessly violated this prudent rule, and would have entered in daylight on the path he had followed.

The Indians were now becoming more and more enraged at the occupation of the beautiful land of Kentucky, and made incessant and furious incursions ito the settlements, closely besieging every station. Boonesborough was thus assaulted three times.

Gen. George Rogers Clark, then a major, was in chief command of the settlements; and with his concurrence six spies were appointed as a scouting force to watch the Indian frontier, two for each of the three chief stations, Boonesborough, Harrodsburg, and Logansport. Of these Kenton was chosen from Boonesborough, by Boone himself. These fearless and wily woodsmen for a whole year gave timely notice of every attack, going out by twos, each party in its week; except once. Kenton and two more were about going out of Boonesborough to hunt, when two men at work outside the fort were fired at by Indians, and fled unhurt toward the fort. One escaped, but a bold warrior tomahawked the other within seventy yards of the fort, and was scalping him when Kenton shot him, and with his two companions sallied out upon the others of the savage party. Boone himself also quickly came out with ten men to support the attack. Kenton, turning round, saw an Indian aiming at Boone's men, and taking a quick aim, shot him. Boone now discovered that his company was cut off from the fort by a large force of Indians who had thrown themselves between. There was but one resource, a prompt attack. "Right about!" he cried, "fire! charge!" and the little band sprang desperately at their red foes, whose first volley wounded seven of the fourteen, and breaking Boone's leg, brought him down. An Indian leaped on him, hatchet in hand, but the keen-eyed Kenton, cool as ice but quick as lightning, shot him through the heart, lifted the old leader in his arms, and carried him into the fort.

The rest all got in too, and after the gate was shut, Boone, a silent man, and much more chary of words and praises than a conqueror of crowns, sent for Kenton to give him his meed of praise for having saved his own life and killed three Indians without getting hurt himself; though the urgency of the case had prevented him from taking the scalp of any of them. This was the eulogy of the veteran Indian-fighter:

"Well, Sam, you have behaved yourself like a man, to-day; indeed you are a fine fellow!"

Kenton continued in this little force of spies until June of the next year, when he accompanied Gen. Clarke's remarkable expedition against Kaskaskia and Vincennes; and at his return, joined Boone, who was about marching against an Indian town on Point Creek, with nineteen men. He was in advance of the party when he heard loud laughter in the woods, and had barely time to "tree," when a pony approached, carrying two Indians, one facing the tail and the other the head, and in high spirits. Instantly firing, Kenton's bullet killed one and dangerously wound the other. Springing forth to scalp them, about forty savages attacked him, and he commenced dodging about among the trees, feeling exceedingly hurried and very unsafe until Boone's force came up, charged furiously, and drove the enemy. But having learned that a large war-party had gone out against his own station, Boone now turned short round, and hastened homeward. Kenton, and a fellow-woodsman named Montgomery, however, remained, lay within rifle shot of the Indian town two days, stole each a good horse, and rode into Boonesborough the day after the Indians, who had been besieging it, had disappeared.

A few weeks afterward they set off to steal more horses, taking one Clarke with them. They secured seven near Chillicothe, and got away; the Indians, however, being close behind. Reaching the Ohio, the three men tried in vain to drive their prizes across the river, roughened under a high wind. After delaying, with the most astounding recklessness, for almost a day, waiting for a calm, they decided once to leave four of their beasts and ride home on the other three. While trying to catch them again (having changed their minds), the Indians came up, shot Montgomery and took Kenton prisoner—even then only in consequence of the very extremest folly on his part, in turning back to get a shot at them. Clarke alone, who fled as fast as possible, escaped.

The Indians, themselves most thoroughgoing offenders in the same line, professed the most violent indignation at Kenton's offence, and reproached him for a "hoss steal," beat him until they could not beat him longer, and then secured him for the night, flat on the ground, his legs stretched out and tied tight to two saplings, his arms lashed at length to a strong pole tied across his breast, and a stout thong, so tight as barely to permit him to breathe, strained back to a stake. He remained a captive eight months, ran the gauntlet eight times, was once nearly killed by a blow from an axe, and was three times tied to a stake to be burnt, being twice saved by the renegade Simon Girty, his early friend—who, in this, showed himself capable of the strongest attachment and the most energetic and disinterested efforts for another—and once by Logan, the Mingo chief, who induced a Canadian trader to buy him. His owner finally took him to Detroit, where he remained, laboring for small wages, until the summer of 1779.

Being in the flower of his youth—he was now twenty-four—an exceedingly handsome man, tall, straight and graceful, dignified and manly in deportment and speech, already famous for his bravery and skill in Indian warfare, with a soft and pleasant voice, and always a favorite with females, he was so fortunate as to excite a deep interest in the bosom of a Mrs. Harvey, wife of an English trader. Conceiving hopes of escape by her means, he intrusted her, after long doubt, and with great circumspection, with his scheme. After a little hesitation she consented to aid him, and procured and concealed for him and the two fellow-prisoners with whom he proposed to escape, provisions and ammunition. During a grand drunken frolic of the Indians, she also stole for them three good rifles, and on the 3d June, 1779, they set out, and reached Louisville after thirty-three days of great hardship.

After resting a little while, he went alone through the forest to visit Gen. Clark, at Vincennes; then returned to Harrodsburg; and the next spring accompanied Clark on his expedition against the Indian towns, commanding a company; and, being now the best woodsman and forest spy in the western country, he was the principal guide to the expedition. During two years after the return of these troops, Kenton was occupied, as usual, in spying, hunting, or surveying; and in the autumn of 1782, after eleven years of exile and remorse for supposed murder, he learned at the same time that his father was yet alive, and that Veach was not dead, but living and well. Hitherto, since his flight, he had always been known as Simon Butler; but now he gladly resumed his own name, and with the weight of shame, banishment and guilt removed from his mind, "felt like a new man."

In this same autumn, Kenton again commanded a company and acted as guide for the army on Clark's second expedition against the Indian towns. After his return, he made a clearing on one of the many tracts of valuable land of which he had become the owner, and a year afterward, having raised a good crop of corn, returned home, visiting his friends, who had supposed him dead, and Mr. and Mrs. Veach, who received him without any remains of rancor for his ancient misdoings. He took his father with him on his return, but the old man died and was buried on the way.

During the subsequent years, Kenton, now at the head of a thriving frontier settlement and a large land-owner, led a company in two more expeditions into the Indian country, and in 1793, with a party, ambuscaded a troop of savages at their crossing-place on the Ohio, and, as they came up on their return, killed six and drove the rest away. This was the last incursion they ever made into Kentucky. The whites were now too strong for them, and, discouraged and beaten, they confined themselves within the territories north of the Ohio. All this time—that is, from about 1784 until the end of the century—Kenton was the foremost man on the Kentucky frontier. His landed property was large—he even gave away at one time one thousand acres of land, upon which was founded the town of Washington—and his noble and kindly character, as well as his preëminent skill and valor as a woodsman and forest soldier, rendered him beloved and esteemed by all.

After the expedition of Wayne had given a final blow to the power of the Indians, and the infant commonwealth of Kentucky was beginning to stride forward toward wealth and power with the long, rapid steps of the young giant States of the West, a sad series of reverses, disgraceful to the State for which he had fought so bravely, overtook Kenton. True as steel, and confiding and unsuspicious to a degree almost incredible and quite unknown except as the companion quality of such crystal honesty and child-like sincerity as his, and a rude and unlettered man withal, what should the heroic wanderer of the woods know of the details of legal formularies? How could he, spending thirty years in incessant, exhausting perils and combats, exposed to a thousand deaths and to tortures unutterable, worse than death, in the long defence of the infant settlements of Kentucky—how could he dream that any one would rob him of the land he had bought with his blood—that the commonwealth he had done so much to establish would suffer him to be beggared within her own limits by speculating knaves, engineering him out of his rightful property by the shrewd villainies of laws misapplied, and principles of justice perverted into instruments of oppression? But those who rushed so rapidly into Kentucky, after her borders were freed from the Indians, gave small heed to the men who had secured them peace. Kenton, like Boone and so many more of the pioneers of the forest, had ignorantly omitted one and another form, or entry, or item of description, in the proceedings taken to secure the lands selected in so much peril, and deserved by such inexpressible hardships and toils. One knave after another brought suit, founded on subsequent and more formal proceedings, for clearing woodland or prairie. Kenton's estate was wrenched piece-meal from him; his body was taken for debt, on covenants in the deeds to those very lands which he had substantially given away; and he was imprisoned for a year on the very spot where he had planted the first corn raised by a white man in the north of Kentucky, and had afterward built his frontier station.

Reduced almost to beggary, he moved out of his ungrateful adopted State in 1802, and settled at Urbana, now no longer young, and with the cheerless prospect of an old age of penury among strangers. In 1805, he was chosen brigadier-general in the Ohio militia. Five years afterward, being at a camp-meeting, under the influence of the rude but effective preaching of a strong, simple-hearted man of God, he became convicted of sin, and would fain range himself within the church of God. With a natural reluctance to expose his spiritual moods and exercises to the observation of others, he requested a minister present to accompany him into the woods and pray with him, saying at the same time, "But don't make a noise about it!" The plain and sincere clergyman knelt down with the old frontiersman and wrestled with God in prayer for him; restraining his fervor however, as required. And now the powerful appeals and sympathies of the wise, though homely, preacher, and the influences of Him that answereth prayer, worked mightily within the honest, simple soul of the old man; and in a great whirlwind of fears and terrors, and mingled joy and pain, in the new feelings and perceptions that break in upon his soul, he rises almost distracted and hastens back toward the crowded meeting, crying aloud in his trouble, and borne far beyond any regard to human criticism or human presence; while the quaint old preacher, with that wonderful mingling of profound admonition and comicality, so strangely characteristic of his class, and so eminently effective upon their peculiar people, halloed after him, retorting his late request,—" Look here; don't make a noise about it!" But Kenton found peace in believing, and became a sincere member of the Methodist church.

In 1813, when Shelby and the Kentucky volunteers so bravely marched to the aid of Harrison, against the banded tribes of the Northwest, Kenton accompanied the army, and was present as a privileged member of Gov. Shelby's family, at the battle of the Thames, his last fight. Returning home, he lived on in obscure poverty, in his hut in the woods, until 1820, when he removed to near the head of Mad River, in Logan County; within sight of Wapatomika, where, forty-two years before, the Indians had tied him to the stake to burn him to death.

In this distant spot he was still plagued with lawsuits and executions in Kentucky; and in 1824, being seventy years old, in rags, and on a wretched horse, he journeyed to Frankfort, to petition the State of Kentucky to release from forfeiture for taxes some poor tracts of mountain land still left to him. Rambling up and down the city, which had grown up where he had wandered in primeval woods, a spectacle to boys and a stranger to men, he was recognized by an old friend or acquaintance, well clothed and hospitably entertained. And soon, when the news went out that General Simon Kenton was in the town, the fame that such noble and ancient men get in their old age, as if they were dead, gathered many to see the renowned hunter and warrior of two generations back. They carried the old man to the capitol, placed him in the speaker's chair, and introduced him to a great multitude of men, after our wonderful American fashion which thus gratifies the curiosity of a multitude under the shallow pretence of doing homage to one. And the simple-hearted old man, believing in every word and every smile—and indeed, doubtless no small share of that inexpensive admiration was sincere enough as far as it went—was wondrously lifted up, and was afterward wont to say, that that was the proudest day of his life. His petition was granted, however, at once. Judge Burnet and Governor Vance, of Ohio, then in Congress, a little afterward also obtained for him a pension of twenty dollars a month, which preserved him for the rest of his life from extreme want. Living twelve years longer, loved and respected by all who knew him, quiet and obscure, Simon Kenton died in April, 1836—in fullness of years, for he was eighty-one.

I have ventured upon all this detail, and have followed the life of this famous old pioneer so far beyond the period described by the title of this lecture, because that life is such a full and vivid picture—such a complete epitome and type—of a life which was led by so many of those who dwelt in the cabin homes of the wilderness in that wild and perilous period. Nor do my contracted limits suffice for more than a swift and shadowy outline of the story. The multiplied details of Kenton's life of hardships, enterprise, battle, peril and escape, would fill volumes. And the full history of all the startling dangers, the bold and wild exploits, the desperate escapes, the fearful miseries of those times, would make a library of strangest adventure.

Lecture VI.

THE CABIN HOMES OF THE WILDERNESS DURING THE AMERICAN REVOLUTION.

CABIN HOMES OF THE WILDERNESS,

DURING THE AMERICAN REVOLUTION.

THE wilderness hath a schooling all its own, and its tuition is not one destitute of profit or compensation. I would not undervalue the worth of literature, the acquisition of science, or the training imparted in colleges. Perhaps few men have paid a higher price for these. And yet there is a majesty, a splendor, in a lonely forest, a boundless prairie, in the great primeval forms of nature while they are yet untainted and undesecrated by the play of human passions and human appetites, fresh as a virgin world from the hand of the Creator, which imparts to the human soul a grandeur and nobility of character rarely acquired in the pursuits of trade or commerce, or in the common, fixed and plodding occupations of every-day life. A peculiar muscularity is given to the form, a vigor to the step, a freshness to the thought; the will is untrammelled, scarcely even limited by the thought of any impossibility; self-reliance is developed to the very highest point; an independence of action and of being that leans only on the Everlasting arms that are around and underneath us all. Here, in the spring or early summer, when the grove perfumes the atmosphere, and loads it as with fragrance from on high—when the prairie stretches its illimitable ocean-like surface before the eye—when the tall and rustling grass is interspersed and interwoven with flowers of a thousand hues and a thousand aromas—here, where the buffalo roams at his own wild will, and the deer stalks proudly on, clad in his red summer garment—where the stately elk, with his spreading antlers, seems the monarch of the forest, and where the low growl of the bear is heard ever and anon, and at nightfall comes upon the breeze the howl of a pack of wolves from the far distance—here, where man is surrounded by nature in her simplest, and sternest, and most inviting forms, does he cultivate to the very utmost all the vast self-supporting powers of humanity; his gun, his own sagacity, an unerring and unblenching eye, an unquivering muscle, his only supports this side of Providence. If he is wanting to himself in the wilderness, he is lost indeed.

Such a wilderness as this was the boundless West at the commencement of our Revolution. Here was the great normal school for western character, and admirably were the pupils that came to receive the instruction of this university qualified to enter it. Men for the most part destitute of the culture of the schools, unblessed with the tuition of art, or science, or literature, accustomed to battle with the storm in the wild mountains and wilder woods of the western skirts of the colonies, trained in the fierce sports of the border, now rush like a tide down the western slopes of the Alleghany Mountains, to take possession of these illimitable and magnificent regions; to transfer them from the sway of barbarism and solitude, and transform them into busy and peopled haunts of living and working men. These new-comers were men strong of frame, compact and muscular, Herculean of stature, of dauntless courage, of determination incapable of discouragement or fear, carrying their lives in their hands, ready, if necessary, to crimson the soil of that new world with their heart's blood. There is hardly a more striking commentary upon, or interpretation of, the pristine radical elements of Anglo-Saxon character in the whole range of the records of our race, than is to be found in the history of its occupancy of Kentucky and the Northwestern Territory.

These men thus came to take possession just at the period when the Revolutionary struggle was beginning; when the whole firmament of the political sky of America was overcast and darkened by lowering and thunderous clouds; when the might of the mother country was lifting itself in all its majesty to chastise the rebellious colonies; when white men in red coats, with epaulettes upon their shoulders and commissions from the third George in their pockets —men who claimed and acknowledged the ties of human kindred with the colonists upon this side the water—were absolutely suborning the red savages of the West to deeds of unparalleled cruelty and blood-thirstiness; when these servants of the third George actually set a price upon the scalps of their brethren, and not only this, but upon the scalps of women and children of Anglo-Saxon blood. Col. Hamilton, commandant at Detroit, acting, as he affirmed, under the authority, the advice and consent, of the government of England, absolutely offered a price for the scalps of women and children, torn from their bleeding skulls by the ruthless savages of the border. Thenceforth and forever, as long as that man's name finds a place in history, let him be called by the homely but terrible name given him by the heroic General Clark, who took him prisoner at Vincennes, "Hamilton the hair-buyer."

And now, when to the dangers of the wild, dark woods, the perils of those lurking savages, to whom the perpetration of the most treacherous murders, and of the most horrible cruelties, is as the breath of their nostrils, are added the intensifications and reinforcements of that gloomy time; when the wild invading fury of the red men, already savage and devastating enough, was stimulated by these inhuman promises of gain, and by the prospect of immediate and powerful foreign aid; when the forces of England were mustering all along the borders of the lakes; when the British commanders and agents were subsidizing, and enrolling and equipping, the half-savage Canadians of Montreal and Detroit, and the savages of so many boundless forests from Niagara to distant Chicago, from the headwaters of the Susquehanna and the great Council House of Onondaga to the distant shores of Huron and Superior; when this furious and redoubled tide of desolation and slaughter was gathering, to be poured out upon these infant and seemingly helpless settlements of the West, were not these pioneers, who, daring to take their lives in their hands—yea, and the lives of their wives and young children—and trusting in nothing besides their God, except their woodcraft and their rifles, plunged far beyond the mountain boundaries of civilization into that blood-stained borderland; and who maintained and protected the infant settlements so long, so well, against such overwhelming and desperate odds—were not these of heroic mold, of even gigantic resolution and valor, and most justly entitled to our admiration and our love?

Such were Boone, Kenton, Logan, Harrod, Calloway, McGary, Todd, and many more than I can even name here; all the leading settlers of Kentucky. In the preceding lecture were presented sketches of one or two lives among them, in the account of which I somewhat transgressed the limits of the period strictly under consideration, but no further than was necessary to complete the picture of the *men*, which is that of the times. The present lecture is in its nature necessarily a continuation of that; and in it I shall aim to afford such glimpses of some of the more important of the varied movements and adventures which took place in the great valley during the Revolution, as may enable the student to gain a broad and connected view of the complexion and progress of this stirring chapter in our history.

Perhaps almost enough has already been said for my purpose, so far as regards the territory of Kentucky. But it will not be inappropriate to afford the means of a still fuller apprehension of the perils and the bravery of the times, by a brief account of some of its innumerable adventures.

In the year 1776 there were but about one hun dred fighting men in Kentucky. Of these from thirty to fifty were usually in garrison at Boonesborough, or absent on expeditions thence.

Let me delay a moment to describe this famous old fort, whose site is now occupied by an obscure and decaying village of the same name. Boonesborough was the first fort built in Kentucky, and was established by Daniel Boone in 1775. It stood in a small cleared space on the bank of the Kentucky River; and occupied a parallelogram about two hundred and sixty by one hundred and fifty feet, one angle resting on the river bank. Its rude but sufficient fortifications consisted of two cabins on a side, with a gate between, one at each end, and at the corners block-houses, which were merely houses built with larger logs than a common cabin, and more carefully and closely constructed for defence. These cabins and block-houses were connected by high strong fences of large pickets or timbers driven close together into the ground. All the outer walls were loopholed for musketry; and this wooden fort, that could not have resisted a six-pound field battery, was to the children of the forest an impregnable stronghold, proved by many a desperate assault urged on by the bitter sorrow and anger they felt at each successive extension of the white man's hold on their favorite forests and savannas.

One of the men employed on the work was killed a few days after the foundations were laid. The fort was incessantly beleaguered for years, and sustained three furious sieges by large bodies of Indians; the last time in September, 1778, under the command of British officers. The settlement had grown so dense and spread so far by this time, that the savages could no longer penetrate to the walls of the fort without leaving too many enemies in their rear.

The following incident well illustrates the dangers

to which the inhabitants of these little fortresses were daily exposed.

One fine summer afternoon, while the garrison was not dreaming of danger, some of the men lounging idly around the gate, or under the shadow of the stockade, were looking upon three girls, two of them daughters of Col. Richard Calloway, the other of Daniel Boone; the oldest fourteen years of age, the youngest nine or ten. The three girls were playing in a light canoe upon the placid bosom of the stream, dancing, and seemingly in danger of upsetting the light bark, but yet with practised skill preserving its balance; their sweet and merry peals of laughter ringing far, far away, through the silent air. By the movements of the girls the canoe is driven further and further from the southern bank, until they are two-thirds of the way across the stream; when suddenly, by an unseen yet irresistible impulse, it begins to move directly toward the northern shore, while the girls, surprised and wondering, look all around to see what may be the cause of the motion. Just as they are gaining the edge of the northern shore, the hand of a savage, and then his eye, fierce and glaring as that of a panther about to leap upon its prey, is seen within the shade of the bushes that fringe the stream, and as the boat is pulled within the same dark covert, they see other fierce eyeballs gleaming there, and strong arms inclose them. One shriek from the poor affrighted girls, and their mouths are closed, and they are hurried off in the grasp of their Indian captors. That scream had been heard at the fort—the men had seen the motion of the boat, and quickly understood what had happened. No other canoes were in the neighborhood, and there was every reason to apprehend that other savages were still lurking in the bushes to pick off any men who might seek to pursue. How they finally succeeded in getting across, whether by swimming or the rescue of their canoe, is not known. Those in the fort waited the return of Boone, who was away on business. After several hours he returned; but as it was near nightfall, he waited until morning, and by daylight set out in pursuit, with seven men. They had made a march of but a few miles when they reached a cane-brake where the savages had entered, and had taken such special pains to obliterate their traces that to follow the trail through the brake would consume time most critically precious, and might probably allow the Indians to escape.

In this emergency, Boone strikes on a happy device, to "circumvent" the savages, to use a favorite word in western parlance—by making a detour around the entire brake, so as to strike the trail of the savages on the other side, wherever it might be. The plan is fortunately successful, and after travelling thirty miles with incredible speed, they find a buffalo path where the trail is quite fresh. Hastening ten miles further, they come suddenly upon the savages lying down or preparing a meal, and little thinking of danger, supposing that they had distanced pursuit; but having the girls in close and careful custody.

The two parties saw each other at the same time; but the whites, firing a volley, charged so furiously upon the Indians, that they fled, leaving packs, ammunition, and weapons, except one empty shot-gun. The girls were uninjured, except by excessive fright and fatigue; and their rescuers were so rejoiced at their recovery that, without pursuing the Indians further, they returned at once to the fort.

In this same summer, one or two other feats were performed which merit our notice. Harrod's, Logan's and Boone's stations were this year attacked by Indians at the same time; large numbers of them besieging each fort, and innumerable parties prowling through the wilderness for the purpose of cutting off isolated settlers. Harrod's fort was attacked by a large body of Indians, who were determined to starve the garrison out. Their cornfields were destroyed. The body of savages attacking them was some five or six hundred in number, while there were only about forty men inside the stockade. The woods for many miles were infested by the Indians, so that the crack of a white man's gun, if heard within them, would have secured his instant death. Nevertheless, a lad sixteen or seventeen years of age, named James Ray—several older hunters having tried in vain to supply the fort with provisions—volunteered his services. He was a married man, for they married early then; a son-in-law of Col. McGary. Taking the only horse of his father-in-law, all the others, of forty, having been stolen or destroyed by the Indians—an old, worn-down beast—and leaving the stockade between midnight and daylight, taking his pathway in running brooks of water so as to leave no trace—thus the shrewd bold boy pursued his way for many miles, till far beyond the savages; hunted the remainder of the day, slept a portion of the evening, and then came back as he had gone, his horse loaded with provisions. Thus for months, did this gallant young Virginian maintain the fort by his single rifle.

One other instance. All the stations, as I have said, were attacked; and Logan's, containing fifteen men, shared the fate of the others. Early in the morning, a small guard of men are outside the gates, guarding a party of women milking the cows. This party is saluted by a sudden hail of bullets. Three of the men are killed; the women all succeed in making their escape. The entire party rush into the gate of the fort, and enter in safety; but the bodies of the three slain men and one poor wounded fellow are still outside the gate. The wounded man, Harrison by name, runs a few steps and falls, in sight of both attackers and defenders. Here he lies, and unless rescued must quickly be scalped. The Indians refrain from firing upon him further, hoping to lure other of his friends to his help. The cries of the wounded man for aid, the frantic grief of his wife, seem to fall upon deaf ears. The men say: "There are only twelve of us, and not one can be spared for less than a hundred red-skins, at least. No man's life can be given, and it will cost any man's life to attempt the rescue. But his wife, with terrible urgency, with cries and implorations of heartbreaking intensity, solicits all in turn. Col. Logan, the commandant of the station, cannot withstand such entreaty and helplessness. He says, "Boys, are there none of you will go with me?" John Martin rallies his courage, and says, "I am as ready to die now as I ever shall be; I will go with you." The gates are opened, and out they rush. A storm of leaden hail greets them. Martin finds he is not as ready to die as he thought, and runs back again. But out among the rifle balls rushes Logan; bends over the wounded man; raises him in his arms as if he were an infant; and while the bullets are flying all around him, and more than one lock of his hair is cut off as by scissors, succeeds in entering the gates again, and delivers the wounded Harrison into the arms of his rejoicing wife.

Still the Indians maintain the siege. There are only twelve men left; their powder and ball are running low; a fresh supply must be had, or all the horrors of Indian captivity must be the consequence. None can be had nearer than at the settlements on the Holston River, two hundred miles distant. There was scarcely a chance that any messenger could pass the Indians, or that if he could, the fort could hold out until his return. Rash and desperate as the bold woodsmen were, they all hesitated to make this fearful experiment. Col. Logan himself, with that reflective, resolute, deliberate bravery which carries the nobler sort of men, in time of need, so much further than the animal impulses of common hardihood, then volunteers, and selecting two companions, creeps out at night, and the three bold men noiselessly pass the Indian lines. Avoiding the usual road, he strikes off into the forest, pushes at almost superhuman speed over trackless mountain and valley, reaches Holston, secures the ammunition, puts it into the hands of his two companions, and himself preceding them, that his little garrison may the sooner receive the good news and strengthen their hearts, returns again, arriving in ten days after his departure; thus making this trip of four hundred miles through a rugged wilderness at the rate of forty miles a day, on foot, and with scarce aught to live upon. The powder and ball is successfully brought in, and the Indians are driven away.

About this same time, or just before it, there comes to Kentucky a young man. Born in 1752, when he enters Kentucky in 1775 he is twenty-three years of age—a fine soldier-like fellow, who has been in Lord Dunmore's war, who commenced life as did most of the young men in Virginia and thereabouts, as a surveyor, this being the surest highway to fortune and distinction. He had been in Logan's war as a volunteer in the personal staff of Lord Dunmore, and now comes to Kentucky to see what manner of persons are there, and if the country be fit to settle in. Of stalwart bearing, noble in person, winning in manners, yet commanding, this man's courage and conduct through all the subsequent struggles of the pioneers of the West well entitle him to the lofty appellation of the Washington of the West. His name is George Rogers Clark, a man, singularly enough, as yet without a biography; and yet, excepting Washington, Franklin, and a few others, there is not a man in all the annals of our country who so well deserves the tribute of the biographer, the panegyric of the historian, and the applause of his countrymen. He came to Kentucky, examined the condition of the province, returned to Virginia in the fall, and came back to Kentucky in early spring for the purpose of making it his home, and taking part with his brothers of the frontier in their arduous defence of their lands and lives. He spent much of his time, alone, hunting or wandering through the woods; visiting all the stations; and easily making himself acquainted with the pioneers, from the smallest children upward. And now, having acquainted himself with all the features of their life and needs, he recommends their calling a convention for the purpose of acquiring for themselves some political rights and position. He is appointed by this convention, with one Gabriel Jones, a representative or delegate to the legislature of Virginia; and proceeding to Williamsburg, then the capital of Virginia, finds the legislature adjourned. He submits his credentials and claims to Governor Patrick Henry, who is lying ill; urges upon the governor the pressing needs of Kentucky; and claims the protection of Virginia's strong arm. Virginia has nearly as much as she can do to care for herself; but the heart of Henry is touched by the representations of the chivalric young man, and he gives him a letter to the Representative Council of the State. These gentlemen say they can do nothing for him, because the Kentuckians are not yet recognized by the legislature as citizens. They, however say, "You shall have five hundred pounds of gunpowder for the Kentuckians, as a loan from friends, provided you will enter into personal recognizances for the value of the same." "No," he replies, "I cannot accept it. It is unjust to demand individual security from me, when I ask the powder for the service of the country." "But," they say, "it cannot be had otherwise." "Very well," he says, "a country that is not worth defending is not worth claiming. Kentucky will take care of itself." Mr. Jefferson, Mr. Wye, and other members of the Council, much impressed by the lofty, decided tone of the young man, at last procure him an order for the powder, to be delivered to him at Pittsburg. Receiving it there, he embarks it in a keel-boat, and, with the little guard of seven men, they hasten down the river, hotly pursued by the Indians; until, gaining the mouth of Limestone Creek, the site of Maysville, they ascend it a little way, scatter the precious cargo in various places of concealment in the woods, set their boat adrift, hasten to Harrod's station, and returning with a sufficient escort, bring the ammunition in safety home, and supply the scattered forts with the means of defence against the now increasing waves of Indian incursion from north of the Ohio. Nor is the powder the only good gift he brings. Against the strenuous opposition of Col. Campbell and the great land speculator Col. Henderson, he and his colleague succeeded in inducing the Virginia legislature to erect Kentucky into a county; and thus he brought back to his adopted home its first political organization, entitling it to representation in the

Virginia Assembly, and to the benefits of a regular judicial and military establishment.

And now is in full activity that fearful torrent of savage invasion which surged so furiously in upon the scattered stations and settlements of Kentucky during the revolutionary years. British soldiers, French Canadians, Indian warriors, either in separate or allied hosts, beleaguer the rude log forts, haunt the settlements, waylay hunter and woodsman, peaceful laborer, and innocent child. One after another, the best and bravest of the Kentuckians are picked off by the lurking foe; blood flows like water; and this infernal league of pretended Christians with savages little less than fiends in ferocity and cruelty, seems likely to waste away the sparse and feeble white settlements, by a slow and bloody but sure process of exhaustion. For a year and more, George Rogers Clark ranges the woods, commonly alone in the midst of all the war and all the danger, keenly enjoying a long series of desperate adventures, and participating in many hardy frontier fights, of which no detailed record remains. But his profound and penetrating genius soon awoke to the important truth—which the Virginian authorities had not apprehended—that the true field for opposing this bitter, cruel contest, was not so much within the devastated fields and haunted forests of bleeding Kentucky, as afar within the distant forests of the

North; at the great Indian towns where the warriors recruited their forces, where their squaws labored and their children played; and still more, at the British posts of Detroit, Vincennes and Kaskaskia, the unfailing fountain of succor to the tribes; where arms and clothing and gay ornaments were sold by British officers with white skins, but hearts black and vile with inhuman, supersavage ferocity, to the red warriors for scalps; or given freely away to them, if only they would earn them by a foray in the American settlements.

Clark resolves to attack these posts, profoundly convinced that thus he will strike a fatal stroke at the heart of the war; and in 1777, he already sends two spies to examine the ground, whose report of the activity and efficiency of the English garrisons in maintaining the savage war stimulate his resolve still more. In December of the same year, he lays before Governor Henry the plan of a bold, sudden and secret blow at the enemy, which that officer and his council quickly approve. With two sets of instructions, a public one authorizing him to go and defend Kentucky, and a secret one directing him to organize a force and take Kaskaskia, he returns, raises four companies instead of the authorized number of seven—for the women will not let so many men leave their homes undefended—then sifts these, after the fashion of Gideon, until he has a hundred and fifty-three men; and with a military chest containing twelve hundred pounds in depreciated paper money, and reinforcing this small amount by a bounty of three hundred acres of land for each soldier, he sets out. They descend the Ohio until within forty miles of its mouth, disembark, sink their boats to hide them, and then, each man carrying his baggage and stores, himself foremost in the march and partaking of every exposure, they plunge into the howling wilderness of marshes and forests—a tangled, hopeless labyrinth in which their veteran guides even lose their way. After a most toilsome march of one hundred and twenty miles, they reach the neighborhood of the fort unperceived, on the evening of July 4th, 1778. Waiting until midnight, Clark makes a brief, stirring address to his men, then sends Capt. Helm with a detachment across the Kaskaskia River to secure and guard the town, and himself advances against the fort. A lonely light burns in a small house outside the stockade. A corporal's guard silently secures the party within; and a Pennsylvanian among them, not much a lover of England, willingly volunteers to guide the assault, and shows them an entrance through a postern gate. Colonel Clark, with his main body, takes possession of the various defences of the fort; and the fearless Simon Kenton, with a file of men, stepping softly into the bedroom of the commander, Lieutenant

Rocheblanc, governor of the Illinois country, quietly asleep by the side of his wife, touches him. He wakes, is informed that he is a prisoner, and is forced to make unconditional surrender of the fort and garrison. But Mrs. Rocheblanc, a bold and shrewish dame, springs out of bed in her night-gear, seizes her husband's papers and disposes them about her person, railing in good set terms at the ungallant intrusion into a lady's bed-chamber. And so delicately over-polite are the rough sons of the woods that they will not lay hands on a woman; and thus the scold gains time to secrete or destroy all the documents. Clark now proceed to strike a wholesome fear of the "Bostonais,"—as the French called all the American colonists—into the bosoms of the simple Frenchmen; and the measures he takes for a day or two are well calculated to maintain the horrible apprehensions which the British have diligently instilled into them of the ferocious and bloodthirsty brutality of the "Long-Knives." Surrounding the town, he orders the troops to whoop and yell all night, as the Indians do; sends runners throughout the town to proclaim in French that any enemy found in the streets will be instantly shot down; that all the inhabitants must observe profound silence; and that no intercourse will be permitted between houses. Then he sends a sergeant's guard, who completely disarm the town in a couple of hours. When daylight returns, having gained abundant intelligence respecting the posts and defences in the vicinity, and having secured his prisoners and sundry suspicious persons, and even ironed certain militia officers in the British service, he draws off his troops behind a hill, prohibits all intercourse between them and any doubtful characters, and places the town under martial law. In all things he acts with an air of stern promptness and cold severity, using but few words, and those of a menacing character.

This threatening demeanor soon becomes intolerably fearful to the simple-minded French. They deputed six principal citizens, with the priest, Father Gibault, at their head, to beg this terrible commander to mitigate a little the mysterious vengeance thus delaying to fall. The priest and his fellows are admitted to the quarters of the American general, and find him seated with his officers. The almost gigantic forms of the dreaded Bostonais, their sordid apparel, all torn and begrimed from thicket and swamp, their rough, grim features and wild fierce looks, appall the very souls of the unwarlike French, and for a short season they stand speechless in their terror. At length the priest finds voice to prefer, he says, one small request. Evidently the townsmen were expecting a repetition of the inhuman Acadian tragedy. He says, that as his people expect to be torn from each other probably forever, they beg leave to assembly once more in their little church, to take leave of each other. Colonel Clark briefly and austerely grants the request, but warns them against attempting to leave the town. Something more the deputies would have said, but Clark, with a stern gesture, intimates that he has no time for further conversation, and they retire. The sad congregation assembles at church, and indulges in the melancholy pleasure of a last farewell; and again the little embassy waits on the conqueror. They humbly thank him for the favor received; and add, that although they know they must submit to the fate of war, and can endure the loss of their property, they would pray not to be separated from their wives and children, and to be allowed some small means of support; and they say something further of the submissive ignorance in which they have obeyed their commandants; of their total unacquaintance with the causes of the war; and hint at good inclination toward the United States.

Clark turns sternly to the priestly spokesman—"Do you take us for savages and cannibals?" he asks. "We disdain to war upon the innocent and the helpless. We are defending ourselves against the Indians—not attacking you. The French king is leagued with us; the victory will soon be ours; we only desire to transfer your allegiance from Great Britain to the United States; and, to prove my words, take home the news that your friends shall be released. Your townsmen may go where they please, safe in persons and property."

The astounded deputies would now have apologized for their mistaken estimate of American character, but are prevented, and desired to communicate their information to the inhabitants. The most unbounded joy instantly takes the place of the terrified gloom that had darked the town; the bells ring out; and crowding into their well-beloved church again, the devout little flock offer heartfelt thanks to God for this unexpected release.

Clark now sent a detachment which secured Cahokia; and the inhabitants of Vincennes, a little afterward, themselves expelled the British garrison, and declared themselves citizens of the United States and of the State of Virginia. After considerable negotiation, in which he exhibited great judgment and still more remarkable knowledge of the Indian character, he succeeded, before the end of September of the same year, in impressing all the tribes of the Illinois and upper Mississippi with a great respect for the American character and name, and in concluding treaties with all of them.

Before the end of the year, however, Hamilton "the hair-buyer," governor at Detroit, both alarmed and ashamed at the brilliant success of Clark, learning that many of the Virginians had returned home, mustered a force of eighty soldiers, together with some Canadian militia, and, making a rapid march down the Wabash, reached Vincennes, now garrisoned by Capt. Helm with one soldier and a little squad of volunteer militia. Hamilton, informed that the garrison was feeble, was already advancing to the attack at the head of his forces, when Helm, springing upon a bastion, near a six-pounder trained upon the British column, and waving his lighted match in the air, hailed them with the stern command, "Halt! or I will blow you to atoms!" A little doubtful whether this bold defender would not fulfill his threat, Hamilton actually obeyed the order, beat a parley, and made a formal demand for the surrender of the fort; to which Helm replied that he would capitulate if allowed all the honors of war, but otherwise he would hold out the fort as long as a man was left alive to shoulder a rifle. Hamilton consented to the terms, and was violently disgusted when, the gates being thrown open, the bold Kentuckian marched out with all possible formalities, and laid down his arms, together with a force of five men, all told! The lateness of the season preventing him from further movements, Hamilton occupied the fort at Vincennes, and while he prepared to complete his re-conquest of Illinois in the spring, launched war-party after war-party upon the frontiers of Virginia and Pennsylvania, thus keeping his Indian allies employed until his projected combination of movements in the spring.

Col. Clark was informed, in the end of January, 1779, that Hamilton had now but eighty soldiers at Vincennes; and preferring to take him rather than be taken by him, prepared for a winter march against Vincennes. He set out on the 7th of February, with one hundred and thirty men; having sent a detachment in an armed keel-boat, to await orders in the Wabash below the mouth of White River, and to permit no passage upon that stream. For one hundred and fifty miles the little army pursued an Indian trail, through dense forests and low prairies, soaked and flooded with the long rains of an uncommonly wet season; across creeks commonly fordable with care, but now presenting lagoons miles broad, knee-deep, waist-deep, even arm-pit deep, so that they must carry provisions, arms, and ammunition on their heads, to keep them dry. Thus they labor on, through forest and low land, through mud and mire, through flood stream and falling rain, and in six days have advanced a hundred miles, to the crossing of the Little Wabash. Wading two feet deep, and often over four, they proceed through a similar dreadful country seventeen days more, and on the 18th encamp at evening on Embarrass River, within nine miles of the fort, and within hearing of the morning and evening gun. After waiting two days, they succeed in capturing a boat and getting across the river. There however still remains a broad and deep sheet of water, upon reaching which the detachment—which indeed could not possibly have sustained the hardships of this extraordinary march so long, had not the weather been remarkably mild—showed evident signs of alarm and despair. Col. Clark, observing this, quietly put some powder in his hand, wet it with water, blacked his face, raised an Indian war-whoop, and marched into the water. Electrified and amused, the weary troops forgot their discouragement, plunged in after their stout-hearted leader, and, singing in chorus, waded, most of the time up to their arm-pits, for miles and miles, until at last they reached the opposite highlands, so utterly worn out that many of the men fell as they touched the shore, letting their bodies lie half in the water, rather than take the two or three additional steps to higher ground.

Having sent a message to the inhabitants of the town, who thought the expedition was from Kentucky and never dreamed of it coming from Illinois, Clark, after resting a day or two, set out for Vincennes; marched up and down among some hills, showing different colors, that his force might look three or four times as large as it was; drew up his men back of the village, and sent fourteen riflemen to pepper the fort. So complete was the surprise, that the crack of the rifle was Hair-buyer Hamilton's first intimation of the siege. He was at the moment —it was evening—amusing himself sociably with his prisoner Capt. Helm, over a game at cards and a glass of apple-toddy. As the report struck his ear, Helm sprang up, as if inspired, and cried out, in his rough delight, "It's Clark, by ——, and we shall all be his prisoners!" The town at once surrendered. The riflemen gathered about the fort, and shot down every man who showed himself over the wall. After the moon went down, Clark had a deep ditch dug within ninety feet of the fort; and early next day the marksmen, posting themselves in it and thus sheltered from the guns of the fort, blazed away by dozens at every port-hole, silencing two pieces of cannon in fifteen minutes, by shooting every man who touched them, until the terrified gunners refused to man the batteries, and the fort lay silent and unresisting beneath the unerring aim of the hunters. After eighteen hours' firing Clark summoned the fort, which Hamilton, after considerable negotiation, surrendered. Clark lost only one man before the walls; and during the siege, he also surprised and routed a party of Indians, just returned from an attack on Kentucky, and took a convoy of goods and military supplies sent from Detroit, worth about fifty thousand dollars. He sent Hamilton and some of his officers to Virginia, where, along with Rocheblanc from Kaskaskia, they were, with extreme propriety, put in close prison in irons, in retaliation for the horrid cruelties perpetrated under their command on the frontier, and for their barbarous treatment of the American prisoners.

In 1780 Col. Clark called on Kentucky for volunteers for an inroad into the Indian country, to retaliate for Byrd's expedition. So ready was the response that in a short time he found himself at the head of a noble force of a thousand riflemen, with whom, using the speed and secrecy so characteristic of his military movements, he surprised an Indian town in Ohio, slew seventeen of the savages, burned their dwellings, and destroyed their crops. The Indians were thus obliged to hunt for a living all summer, and could not send their accustomed war-parties against the settlements.

With his usual penetrating breadth of view, Clark had long considered a scheme for taking the British post at Detroit; and in December, 1780, he induced the government of Virginia to coöperate with him in his design. But the invasion of Arnold interrupting the plan, he served under Steuben against him; and then resuming it, succeeded so far that two thousand troops were to rendezvous at Louisville for the expedition, in March, 1781, and he himself was commissioned brigadier-general.

But many unforeseen difficulties prevented the

army from marching; and the bold and active Clark, who had dreamed so long of extirpating the British power in the Northwest by thus striking at its centre, was obliged to remain almost in idleness, defending the frontier against a few scattered bands of Indian marauders. Thus chafing in unwelcome restraint, he grew discontented; and then, resorting to a greater evil to cure the less, fell into habits of drinking; and as thus his high spirit preyed upon itself, and his unhappy vice sapped strength of mind and body together, his great powers showed signs of failure. The shrewd, observant backwoodsman, who then, as now, judged men as men, and thought them neither less nor more for titles, prerogatives, or pretensions, saw his lack of that passive endurance which marks the loftiest grade of heroism; saw that he was less a soldier and less a man; and as mind and body failed, his influence went down too.

Yet, in that period of stupid, terrified dejection, which followed the great calamity of the defeat at Blue Licks in 1782, where the furious, reckless rashness of one man—Hugh McGary—cost Kentucky a confounding defeat, and the lives of sixty of her best and bravest men, Gen. Clark showed himself still a ready and active soldier. He proclaimed that he would lead his regiment upon a retaliatory expedition into Ohio, and called again for volunteers, 'o gathered to his standard with the old-time promptitude. Again a thousand riflemen assembled on the Ohio, and marched upon the Indian towns. The savages fled so fast before this powerful and vengeful force, that not only did they nowhere offer to resist, but only twelve in all were either killed or taken. Five of their towns were burned, and a vast quantity of their provisions, being all their crops, were destroyed; and so severe was this lesson to the Indians, that from that time they dared no longer invade Kentucky, except in sly, small war-parties.

Once more, in 1786, General Clark headed an army destined against the Indian towns on the Wabash River; but the expedition was unsuccessful, and returned without reaching its destination. After this, Clark's name appears no more in public transactions, except as temporary holder of a major-general's commission from France in that force which the frantic visionary and revolutionary democrat, Genet, would fain have raised in Kentucky to bring Spanish Louisiana under the dominion of the French republic. After long suffering from infirmities, his powerful frame succumbed to a paralysis growing out of rheumatic disorders. He died at Locust Grove, near Louisville, in February, 1818, and was buried there.

This brief and unsatisfactory sketch is all that my space allows me to devote to the great qualities and bold deeds of "the Washington of the West"—

unquestionably the greatest military genius ever produced by Virginia, notwithstanding that the only area for his operations was the pathless wilderness beyond the mountain; and unequalled among all the western pioneers, not only for military ability and daring, speed and secrecy, but for practical statesmanship, political foresight, judgment in combining plans, and energy in executing them; and a quality still higher, which points him out yet more clearly as a born ruler and a statesman, namely, the power of controlling men. His genius was sufficiently shown in the success with which he led his hardy little band, through unparalleled sufferings, against Vincennes, and in the complete obedience and subordination which he so easily obtained from the rude, reckless, and utterly independent hunters and fighters of the forest; but it appears still more in the influence and admiration which he gained among the wild savage tribes of the Northwest, who feared and wondered at him almost as at a superhuman being.

To give one more touch to the sketch I have attempted to draw, of life in the cabin homes of the wilderness during the Revolution—for no single lecture gives space for more than a sketch—let me briefly narrate a single achievement, which story has been often told before, but which has not yet lost its romantic freshness; a story which nobly illustrates the generous daring and military abilities of the sons of the western woods—the story of the battle of King's Mountain.

I will first briefly sketch the deeds of the mountain men before their gallant attack on Ferguson. Col. John Sevier, chief militia officer of the eastern part of the State of Tennessee—then Washington County in North Carolina—received in March, 1780, a requisition from General Rutherford, of North Carolina, for one hundred men to be sent to the aid of South Carolina. Colonel Isaac Shelby, of Sullivan County, also then in North Carolina, received a similar requisition. They each raised two hundred mounted riflemen; but were fortunately too late to reach Rutherford, and suffer in the fatal battle of Camden. They, however, reached the camp of Colonel McDowell, Rutherford's second in command, in July, and were presently sent to attack Colonel Moore, who had been raising the tories in the western Carolinas for the king, and now occupied a strong fort on the Pacolet River. With six hundred men more under Colonel Clark of Georgia, the riflemen, a thousand in all, set off at sunset, marched twenty miles that night, and at dawn had surrounded the fort, which, after some parley, surrendered.

Cornwallis, irritated at this bold stroke, detached Col. Patrick Ferguson with one hundred picked men, to gather and train the tories of the western counties of South Carolina, and to take and hold the strongest positions there. Ferguson was a bold, experienced and successful soldier, himself a trained and skillful rifle shot, and a ready and ingenious man. He had already invented, to oppose the fatal skill of the mountain rifles so much feared by regulars and lowland tories, a breech-loading rifle, capable of being discharged seven times in a minute. He soon raised so many loyalists as put him at the head of two thousand men, and a small body of horse. Col. McDowell detached Shelby and Col. Clark with six hundred men to watch his movements and cut off his foragers. These Ferguson repeatedly but vainly endeavored to surprise. It would have been strange indeed if the regulars could have surprised those sly Indian-fighters! He did once, it is true, come up with them; but when he did come up, the Americans, who were sharply engaged with his advanced guard, rode off with twenty prisoners, two of them officers, whom they had just taken; so that Col. Ferguson only lost by his haste.

Col. McDowell soon sent Shelby and Clark, together with Col. Williams of South Carolina and six hundred men, to surprise a party of some five hundred tories at Musgrove's Mill on the Ennoree, about forty miles distant, and in a line directly beyond Ferguson's camp. Again the hardy riders, setting out at dusk, riding hard all night long, and skirting round Ferguson's camp four or five miles off, met at dawn a strong patrol, about half a mile from the tory camp. These they drove in, and at the same time learned that instead of five hundred, the enemy in front numbered more than twice as many, having just received a reinforcement of six hundred regulars. Evidently they could neither attack double their number, wearied as they were by their long night ride; nor could they for the same reason safely retreat. They therefore determined to hold their ground and receive the enemy's attack. Sending forward an advanced party to skirmish, fire and retire at discretion, they speedily threw up a slight breastwork of logs and brushwood, and lay down behind it. The tory drums and bugles soon announced their advance with horse and foot; they drove in the scattered advanced guard, and thinking that all the Americans were retreating, advanced hastily and in disorderly array, until they were greeted, at seventy yards from the breastwork, with a destructive fire. Undismayed, they attacked with spirit, but for a whole hour could make no impression upon the feeble but stoutly defended line of the riflemen. Just as part of the Americans were beginning to give way, Col. Innes, the British commander, was wounded. Every one of his subalterns but one was already killed or wounded; Captain Hawsey, a notorious tory leader, in command of the loyalists, was shot; the whole British line wavered, and a furious charge from the riflemen drove them in disorder over the Ennoree. The tories fled first, and of the regulars, who fought like brave men, more than two hundred were made prisoners.

The indefatigable mountain men, without waiting to rest, remounted their horses, which had been reposing during the battle, and prepared to swoop down upon the British fort at Ninety-Six, thirty miles further. As they were in the act of starting, an express came up with a letter which he gave to Col. Shelby. It was forwarded by McDowell; was from Governor Caswell of North Carolina, dated on the battle-field of Camden, bringing the news of that fatal field; and advised McDowell to "get out of the way," for that the enemy would now endeavor to cut off in detail all detached parties of Americans. So much false and erroneous intelligence was abroad in those days of treachery and peril that none would have known whether to believe this sad letter, had not Col. Shelby been familiar with Gov. Caswell's hand-writing. Instant decision was necessary, and was made. It was probable that Ferguson was now informed of the defeat on the Ennoree, and would instantly push to cut them off from McDowell. Nor would their weary horses and wearier selves admit of the further advance on Ninety-Six, through regions swarming with tories now encouraged by the British successes over Gates and Sumptei It was not safe to delay even an hour, lest the energetic Ferguson should be upon them. The prisoners were instantly distributed, one to each three horsemen, to take turns in riding behind them; and the whole force, facing westward, rode straight for the mountains. Weary as they were, they pushed on all that day, all the night, and all the next day until late in the evening, without a single halt. This prompt retreat and desperate speed saved them; for it afterward appeared that Ferguson's second in command, Captain Dupoister, had ridden hard after them with a strong force of horse, until at the end of the second day his men broke down under the fatigue and heat. Shelby passed the mountain; Clark and Williams carried the prisoners northward. McDowell's army disbanded, and he and many of his men also crossed the mountain to the hospitable settlements of Watauga and Nollichucky, whence had come many of the bold riflemen who fought so well against Moore and Innes.

Thus disappeared the last remnant of an American army south of the Potomac, except the dispirited and broken band that remained with Gates at Hillsboro'. Congress was penniless and bankrupt; the States were little better; the army unfed, unpaid, and miserable; the whole country distressed and discouraged; the British triumphant, their forces ravaging and rioting at will up and down the land, and their tory allies waging an inhuman and monstrous warfare upon their whig neighbors and countrymen. Large numbers of the Carolina whigs sent their families across the mountains for safety, themselves remaining in the extremest peril to protect their property. Earl Cornwallis, having occupied his time until the arrival of provisions from Charleston, in putting into operation a rigorous system of military tyranny—not hesitating to murder and banish the whigs and rob them of their property, to uphold his authority in South Carolina—advanced from Camden toward Virginia, on the 18th of September, 1780.

Col. Ferguson, at the head of his force of regulars and loyalists, had been diligently at work among the tories in the western counties. He had followed close after Dupoister in the fruitless chase of Shelby and his mountain men; but failing in this, had now posted himself at Gilbert Town, near Rutherfordton, in North Carolina, not far from the foot of the mountains. Here he delivered to one Phillips, a prisoner on parole, a haughty message to the people west of the mountains: that if they did not cease opposing the British arms, he would come across, lay the country waste, and hang their chiefs.

This message Phillips brought to Shelby in the end of August. That leader, mounting in haste, rode fifty miles and more to his brother colonel, Sevier, and on consulting, they determined to raise as large a force of riflemen as possible, make a forced march through the mountain, and surprise Ferguson, or, at least, weaken him and render him unable to fulfill his threat.

The rendezvous was fixed for the twenty-fifth of September, at Sycamore Shoals, in Watauga. Here, on the appointed day, gathered more than a thousand men, many of them armed and equipped with money obtained on the personal security of Shelby and Sevier; all well mounted; almost every man carrying a Deckhard rifle—a choice weapon for true aim and long range, named from its maker, a famous gunsmith of Lancaster, in Pennsylvania. Nearly all wore the hunting-shirt of the backwoods, leggins and moccasins; a few appearing in their usual citizens' dress. Volunteers for the defence of their hearth-stones, they needed neither uniform nor *esprit de corps*, except what common danger and common patriotism inspired.

Early next morning, after prayer by a clergyman present, the riflemen mounted and took up the line of march, following trading and pioneer paths. Unencumbered with the staff and baggage of a regular army, they moved so rapidly that on the second day they abandoned some cattle which they had undertaken to drive along for provisions. Light-armed, with rifle, shot-pouch, knife, tomahawk, knapsack and blanket, they hunted as they went, for food, and drank the water of the mountain streams, until after passing the mountains, when they quartered themselves on the tories.

On the day after starting, two men were missing. They had deserted to the enemy. To render their information useless, the army descended the eastern slope of the Alleghany by remote and unfrequented paths; and on reaching the foot, fell in with a party of several hundred whigs, waiting there in the woods for an opportunity to act against the British. These gladly joined them. And from all the settlements small daily additions were made to the force of brave men eager to reach the foe.

October 3d a council was held, within eighteen miles of Ferguson's post at Gilbert Town. After some discussion, a messenger was sent to Gates for a general officer to command the force, and Colonel Campbell, who had led four hundred men to the rendezvous at Watauga, was chosen commander in the interim. Next day the mountain army advanced to Gilbert Town; but Ferguson was gone. He had heard of the vengeful storm gathering along the western mountains, and after exhausting the language of entreaty and reproach upon the intimidated loyalists—who feared it too—in endeavors to assemble them about his standard, he unwillingly retreated toward Cornwallis, sending him an urgent request for a reinforcement, and marching in several directions among loyalist neighborhoods, to keep out of the way of the riflemen.

But Col. Campbell and his hardy riders understand Ferguson's movements. A council is held, and a still more rapid pursuit resolved on. All that night the commanders pick the best men, horses and rifles, and at dawn set out again with nine hundred and ten of the flower of the army, leaving the rest to follow more leisurely. They hear, as they hasten along, of one and another large gathering of tories, but on they go; they are striking for Ferguson, and will turn aside for no meaner game. Four hundred and sixty more men, under Col. Hambright and Col. Williams, join them at the Cow Pens, where they halt and alight for an hour to refresh. Except this delay, the indefatigable riflemen never once stopped during the last thirty-six hours of the pursuit.

It is the morning of the 7th of October, 1780. The determined mountain men are still sternly hastening upon the hourly freshening traces of the fleeing Ferguson. They ride on through a rain so heavy that they are fain to keep the locks of their rifles dry by wrapping them with blankets and hunting shirts, even at the expense of exposing themselves to the storm. The advanced guard comes up with some unarmed men, who report themselves just from Ferguson's camp. A brief halt is made, and a close examination discovers the facts, that Ferguson is in camp three miles in front; that next day he proposes to march to Cornwallis's headquarters; and that certain roads will lead directly to his camp, which is pitched on ground which Col. Williams declares, on description, that he and some of his men know well. Brief consultation suffices. Ferguson must never reach the camp of the haughty British earl. The storm has cleared away. They resolve to march at once, to complete their work first, and rest and refresh afterward. The command is at once given to put the rifles in fighting condition and prime anew; the order of battle is the well-known hereditary manœuvre of the Indians and of these veteran Indian fighters: to surround the enemy and attack him at once from all sides; and remounting, the little army is again in motion. Within one mile of the enemy an express to Cornwallis is taken; on his person is found an urgent letter to the earl, stating Ferguson's force—the number of which, eleven hundred and twenty-five men, is prudently concealed from the Americans by their officers—demanding instant reinforcements, and informing his commander-in-chief that he is securely encamped on the top of a hill which he had named King's Mountain, in honor of his majesty; and that "if all the rebels out of hell should attack him, they could not drive him from it." All these items, except his force, are communicated to the Americans; and spurring on, they advance at a gallop to a point within sight of Ferguson's stronghold. Arriving within view of the field of battle, it is at once evident that the right plan has been adopted. Ferguson and his regulars and tories hold the crest of the mountain, in a line about a quarter of a mile long—an isolated height rising from the general level of the country, and covered and crowned with open woods. The final orders for the battle are given, while yet out of rifle-shot: Campbell, Shelby, Sevier, McDowell and Winston, with their men, are to file to the right, round the mountain; Hambright and Chronicle are to pass round the other way and meet them; and Cleveland and Williams to fill the remainder of the line in front. When in position, each division is to front face, raise the war-whoop and charge. They advance again, dismount about a third of a mile from the hilltop, tie their horses, and the detachments separate for their places. Before they are quite ready, the enemy, hitherto silent and watchful, open fire and wound some of Shelby's men. Shelby and McDowell, on this, face at once toward the foe, and return their fire with effect; while Campbell's column, coming up, charges fiercely up the mountain and commences a fatal fire on the tories who hold that end of the line. Ferguson, hearing the firing, sends a force of regulars from the other end of his line, and with levelled bayonets they charge upon the advancing columns of McDowell,

Shelby and Sevier. So furious is their assault, that those three columns are driven headlong down the hill. But at this very moment, the four columns on the left, having pushed up the hill and driven in the pickets, begin a close and heavy fire upon the regulars, who have here a slight breastwork of wagons, and are under the command of Ferguson himself. Capt. Dupoister, who had headed the charge on Shelby, is at once recalled, receiving as he comes a severe fire from Col. Williams' column, and is ordered to charge again with all the regulars upon their new adversaries. Again the bayonets are levelled, and a desperate attack drives the riflemen to the foot of the hill, Major Chronicle being killed in the struggle.

It is of course, impossible for riflemen to withstand the shock of a bayonet charge. But the resolute mountain men, though they retreat, do it only to renew the fight; for the enemy dared not advance many rods from his vantage-ground above. As Dupoister returns from his charge on Shelby, to charge again on Cleveland and Chronicle, the columns of Shelby, Campbell and McDowell follow him up, rallying readily to the shout that the British are retreating; and pushing up almost to the British camp, they exchange a deadly fire with the tory riflemen at that end of the height. Again the bayonet is tried; but already the fatal rifle-bullet has thinned the ranks of Ferguson's scanty band of regulars until the British colonel is forced to have his tories' butcher-knives stuck into the muzzles of their rifles, for bayonets, before he can muster a line strong enough for the charge. Down they come, however, and again the riflemen retreat before them; but this time not so far, and after a comparatively feeble attack, Dupoister retired within his lines.

And now the American columns have surrounded the mountain, and closing in, a fatal ring of fire draws slowly and sternly up around the stubborn British colonel and his bold troops. While a fierce discharge is kept up at each end of the British position, Sevier's column now makes a powerful attack upon their centre. The British forces are partly concentrated to repel these obstinate assaults; and while a stubborn contest is maintained here, Shelby and Campbell, with one bold charge, reach the crest of the mountain at the end held by the tories, effect a lodgment, and slowly but surely drive their traitorous foes in toward the other extremity of the line.

Hotter and closer grows the ring of the fire; and still the levelled bayonets gleam on this side and on that, and the light-footed mountain men, vanishing before them, swarm back upon their footsteps the moment they halt, while the Americans on the opposite side seize the opportunity to advance again in their turn. But the charges of the wearied and fearfully diminished band of regulars grow less furious and shorter. And all the time Shelby and Campbell are creeping along the crest of the hill, driving the tories before them, crowding them in upon the regulars, the deadly mountain rifles picking them off with fearful rapidity. Ferguson, cool and daring as ever, still rides up and down his line, encouraging his men, supporting the weakest places, exposing himself to every danger, and carrying in one hand, which has been wounded, a silver whistle, whose loud and piercing sound, heard over the whole battle-field, enables him to signal instantaneously to all his men. He sends Dupoister with the regulars to reinforce a weak position. It is but one hundred yards away; but before he reaches it, the fatal Deckhard rifles have left him so few men that their aid is not worth counting.

Ferguson now orders his cavalry to mount; intending to head them, and sweep down in a resistless attack upon the Americans. But they cannot mount, or if they do, they fall out of their saddles as fast as they reach them; for lifted on the horses, they present a fairer mark for the rifles.

And still the ring of fire contracts; and now, driven in disorder, far in from the British left, the tories, who always blenched first when they fought beside the regulars, dismayed and hopeless, raise the white flag of surrender. But Ferguson gallops up and tears it down. Then the regulars at the other end of the line raise another, and the heroic commander, seemingly the only man left in the host, rides back again through the fire and cuts it down with his sabre. This second time his brave subordinate Dupoister, who had admonished him before that further resistance was hopeless, and that he ought to surrender, admonishes him again. But he declares in the bitterness of his soul that he "will never surrender to such a damned set of banditti." And still riding desperately to and fro, he encourages and strengthens the wavering ranks, and alone restores the battle; for whenever his voice or his whistle is heard, the enemy rallies again, and fights bravely. But the riflemen, seeing that his resistance will end only with his life, after having seemingly spared him for his bravery for a long time, now forced to make an end of the contest, aim their fatal weapons at him. He falls, and dies at once.

Dupoister, now left in command, seeing that his men, few in number, crowded in disorder together, and falling rapidly under the dreadful concentrated fire of the Americans, could no longer hope for success or safety, almost immediately raised the white flag again, and called out for quarter. The fire of the Americans ceased, except from a few young men, who either did not know what the flag meant, or supposed it would come down again as before. Shelby called out to the British to throw down their arms, which they did; when all firing ceased, and the Americans, after one hour's hard fighting, were completely victorious.

Ferguson's force was annihilated; for two hundred and twenty-five were killed, nearly two hundred more disabled, and all the rest, more than seven hundred, prisoners. Not one man escaped. The Americans had lost about thirty killed, and sixty wounded. Encamping on the battle-field that night, they rose early, and at dawn—a peaceful Sabbath dawn—went forth and buried their dead. Then they burned the wagons of the enemy, and prepared to return to the mountains, with their seven hundred prisoners, fifteen hundred stands of arms, many horses, and a great mass of supplies and booty. In the midst of a tory neighborhood, near Cornwallis, and with more prisoners than they could sarely spare guards to watch, the mountaineers were seriously embarrassed with their success. Taking the flints out of the captured arms, however, they made the strongest of the prisoners carry them; marched all day at a "present," keeping close watch on the prisoners, and at sundown met the remainder of their own force, with whom they kept on westward until the fourteenth. Then, halting near the foot of the mountains, they held a court-martial upon sundry of the tory prisoners, atrocious violators of the laws of their country and of humanity; condemned thirty of them to the death which they had a thousand times richly deserved; but hung only nine of the worst, respiting the remainder. Justice thus executed, Sevier and his force crossed the mountains, and put themselve in readiness to defend their homes, if necessary; while Campbell, Shelby and Cleveland guarded their prisoners northward to secure captivity.

This bold and splendid achievement was the turn of the tide in the affairs of the war. Without it, it is difficult to see what limits could have been set to Cornwallis's victorious progress northward, unopposed as he was by any embodied force, and daily reinforced in camp by tory levies, while other gangs of those ignoble banditti, starting up everywhere, were daily riveting the chains of the hateful British authority over all the South behind them.

But the destruction of Ferguson and his host exploded in the midst of Earl Cornwallis's plans like a thunderbolt in a powder magazine. It scattered them to the four winds of heaven; the few fragments left for reconstruction formed only a frustrated and strengthless plan; and the pause of astonished terror that followed afforded time for the dispirited Americans to rally again, and enter upon that series of operations so gloriously consummated at Yorktown.

When Cornwallis heard the news, magnified by its journey into the startling story that the victorious host of riflemen, three thousand strong, were in full march toward his camp, he instantly gave up, for the time, his northward march, struck his tents, marched back toward the south all night in the greatest confusion, crossed the Catawba, and never stopped until he reached Winnsboro', a hundred miles away, where he remained, quiet and frightened, for three months. During this respite, the North Carolina whigs rallied and gathered in considerable force. General Smallwood, with his veteran and celebrated Maryland corps, and Morgan's riflemen, strengthened them. Gates soon joined them, with the sad remains of the Southern army. From Hillsboro', a thousand Virginians came down. General Nathaniel Greene assumed the command of this new force in December, and America was again in a condition at least to face the foe, and maintain, with renewed courage, the contest which seemed to have been decided upon the terrible field of Camden. To those hardy sons of the wilderness, the mountain men of eastern Tennessee and western Virginia, in all probability, is due the glory and the praise of having decided the question of the acquirement of our national independence.

Lecture VII.

SKETCHES OF

CHARACTER AND ADVENTURE

IN THE WEST,

TO THE FAILURE OF BURR'S EXPEDITION, 1806.

SKETCHES OF

CHARACTER AND ADVENTURE

IN THE WEST,

TO THE FAILURE OF BURR'S EXPEDITION, 1806.

The close of the Revolutionary struggle left our ancestors weak and well-nigh disabled by their long, unequal contest, and torn by internal dissensions and broils. Threatened by external force, the government impoverished to the last degree and as creditless as a notorious spendthrift, the currency depreciated as far as depreciation was possible, all things seemed to portend dismemberment and anarchy; a state far worse than that in which the commencement of the struggle found them. But the boundless recuperative energies peculiar to our people, came to their rescue, and out of the wild chaos of inharmonious elements, there arose in course of time the magnificent fabric of civic order, symmetry, and splendor, beneath whose protection we and our children sit.

I have spoken of the depreciation of the currency. In Virginia, at the close of the Revolution, a bowl of rum punch cost five hundred dollars, in the ordinary currency of the time; in New England, a mug of cider was once bought for one hundred dollars. "Part of an old shirt" was valued, in an inventory of an estate, at three pounds. Gen. Green Clay, an eminent surveyor and citizen of the State—or rather, at that time, the District—of Kentucky, riding a spirited horse from the west side of the mountains to the east, disposed of him to one of the French officers attached to the army which aided Washington in the taking of Cornwallis, for the moderate sum of twenty-seven thousand dollars, which he invested in wild western lands; and these, forty years ago, were worth half a million of dollars.

The bond which held the colonies together was of the slightest imaginable description. The old Congress had limited powers, and was afraid to use what it had; rarely daring to assume any responsibility.

What was to be done? How should the treasury be replenished? How should the credit of the country be established? Virginia, always the readiest of the sisters of the confederacy to do what in her lay to speed any good work, assigned to the general government that magnificent domain which belonged to her in virtue of conquest; which the perseverance and heroism of her sons, inspired and guided by the indomitable energy of George Rogers Clark, had wrested from the power of Britain and made her own property.

All that vast and splendid country, afterward known as the Northwestern Territory, was thus given freely to the general government, in order that by the sale of its lands to emigrants and settlers at such a moderate price as their resources would justify, the coffers of the Republic might be filled. Massachusetts had a partial claim to what is now the State of Ohio; but always desiring to look before she leaped, always keeping a sharp eye on the main chance, she waited to see what should be the end of the matter; so that it was not until 1786, two years after Virginia had given to the United States what formed afterward the States of Illinois, Indiana, Michigan, and the greater portion of Ohio, that Massachusetts surrendered her claim to the western country, by cession to the general government. Last of all, old Connecticut, who held with a still more unrelaxing grasp to her reserved territory in the northeastern corner of Ohio, at length became convinced of the propriety and justice of ceding her claim, and did so.

Thus, the whole of that wide domain passed into possession of the federal government. At first, however, it was of comparatively slight use to the people. The Indians held most of it; and although hostilities upon their part were suspended for a short time immediately after the close of the Revolution, yet, as their late ally, the government of Great Britain, made no terms for them in the treaty of 1783, but left them to care for themselves, and as the United States claimed that territory by right of conquest, without stipulation or provision for compensation to them, granting them only slight reserves for residence and hunting-grounds, their ire was again awakened, and their vengeance was ready to descend upon the frontiers.

Further, Spain and France had aided our country in the struggle against our mother; but after that struggle was ended, and we had achieved our independence, they asked to be remembered and compensated for their expenditure in our behalf. Both were in quest of territory. Both were jealous of the predicted power and greatness of the new nation. Both desired, in common with Great Britain, to restrict our fathers within certain predetermined limits. France and England joining, desired to make the Ohio River our northern boundary. Spain, on another side, desired to keep them east of the Mississippi and north of the Yazoo, that she might remain in possession of all the district lying south and west of those rivers, for her own occupancy. One difficulty after another was thrown in the way of our national diplomacy. The old confederated Congress found itself incapable of the task it had shouldered; unequal to the difficulties of the emergency. It is not my province to detail to you the history of the convention for the formation of the Constitution; the theory or powers of the new government; nor the policy of the cabinet of George Washington, with its two poles of dissimilar character and creed, by way of equipoise — Thomas Jefferson representing the Republican or Democratic, and Alexander Hamilton the Federal principle. The great diplomatist of this administration was John Jay—for intellect, patriotism, clear-sighted subtlety, nobility of purpose and force of character, and lofty purity of morals, one of the proudest names which our annals can boast. Jay, at this time, charged with the duty of negotiating treaties with England and Spain, found himself in a most perplexing situation. Spain claimed the right of ownership to the Mississippi River; denied the right of the western people to navigate that river, and was about to close all the ports upon the Gulf against our commerce, and thus cut off the people west of the mountains from all opportunity for foreign exchanges. Enormous crops of all kinds grew up in their fertile and exuberant fields, but there was no market in which they could sell. They had pressing needs, but there was no market where they could buy. Their only opportunities for obtaining the most necessary merchandise were by mule tracks and pathways across the Alleghany Mountains, from Baltimore and Frederick. Long trains of these animals, with pack-saddles laden with salt, iron, and lead, and whatever else was in demand among the emigrants and settlers of the West, were daily travelling the mountain roads, at all seasons of the year.

But this meagre system of exchange offered no prospect either of speedy wealth to those engaged in it, or of present or future adequacy to the wants of the western settlements, now beginning to increase so vigorously.

Already the feeling had become definite and universal among the western settlers, that the free navigation of the Mississippi must be secured; when, in 1784, an assembly of the people of Kentucky was summoned at Danville, by Col. Logan, one of their oldest and ablest pioneers, to consult upon measures for opposing an invasion by the southern Indians, which he had learned was in contemplation. This rumor proved to be incorrect; but the assembly, which contained a large number of influential and intelligent citizens, who had come together under the impression that it was intended to wage an energetic warfare upon the northwestern Indians, took occasion to examine the existing laws applicable to the raising of a military force; when, to the common surprise and chagrin, it plainly appeared that since the end of the war, there was no existing authority to call out men for any expedition against Indians or any other enemy, nor even to assemble volunteers or militia for the defence of their own homes and hearths. Open on three sides to the incursions of a ferocious and active enemy, their hands were effectually tied, and no defence left them except such purely voluntary aid as might be given without the countenance of laws. Such a state of things was unendurable; and even in time of safety, the growing and high-spirited District of Kentucky, now composed of three large counties, could not but be restive under the tardy and difficult administration of a government acting at Richmond, and separated from the western settlements by so many hundred miles of mountain and forest. The assembly was unanimously and earnestly of opinion that Kentucky should have a government independent of Virginia; but having no legal authority, recommended a convention of delegates, one to be chosen from each militia company, to assemble in December of the same year, to consider the question of separation from Virginia.

This convention assembled, and was the first of a series of nine, successively called by the Kentuckians—unused to the management of representative machinery—or required by the Assembly of Virginia or by Congress, in the course of the long series of legislation and negotiation that lasted for seven tedious and wearisome years, before the final act of 1791 constituted Kentucky a State. During all this long period, the feeble and disorganized community beyond the mountains was vexed by a seemingly interminable series of conventions; by uncertainty and fear respecting its fate; by incessant and cruel hostilities from Indians and English; by party spirit of the violent and reckless type which so commonly curses newly-settled States; and by the artful and secret intrigues of agents and partisans of the court of Spain.

In 1784, while all these disturbing influences were actively at work, there crossed the mountains, from Maryland, a distinguished citizen and soldier of that State, who had played a conspicuous part in the Revolution, General James Wilkinson; a man long afterward intimately connected with all the principal political movements in the West. He had been aid-de-camp to General Gates; had figured, with considerable credit, in many of the struggles of the Revolution; and, at the conclusion, finding his fortunes impaired and his finances in so complicated a condition that, with his present means, there were no hopes of remedy, he directed a sagacious eye to the growing West; and deciding promptly upon a removal, came with a stock of goods to what is now Lexington, in Kentucky, for the purpose of establishing himself in trade. His fine personal appearance, winning manners, agreeable and dignified address—his tact and ingenuity, knowledge of and adaptation to human nature, and subtlety of speech—his powers of insinuation, and plausibility—his eloquence, whether spoken or written, equally adapted to the popular level—all these endowments placed him at once in the highest position in the country. He was elected a member of several of the organizing conventions; became a prominent political character at once; and when the question of the navigation of the Mississippi absorbed a large portion of the attention of the Kentuckians, this bold man embarked upon a hazardous adventure. He procured a flat-boat, loaded it with tobacco, descended the Ohio, and then the Mississippi, and depositing his cargo in New Orleans, opened negotiations with the Spanish government. The secret portion of his correspondence with Baron de Carondelet, the Spanish governor at New Orleans, has never been made public; but General Wilkinson returned to Kentucky and informed the inhabitants that he had made certain overtures to Carondelet; that he had acquired for himself, by judicious negotiation, the right of deposit for all his merchandise, be it of what sort soever, in the government warehouses of the capital of Louisiana; and that he had secured a permission to trade there for a given number of years. He began at once to purchase all the products of Kentucky for the purpose of prosecuting this trade. He hinted furthermore that Carondelet had informed him, under proper instructions from the Spanish government, that if the people of Kentucky, would sever their relations with the older States and erect themselves into an independent territory or State, Spain would treat or negotiate with them making such treaties as should be most desirable and agreeable to them, relative to outlets for trade or otherwise.

This was the first hint the people of Kentucky received in regard to this matter. Wilkinson for some time continued his trade with New Orleans, and began to lay the foundation of an immense fortune. Carondelet, not satisfied with his negotiations with Wilkinson, sent one Power to approach some of the other distinguished citizens of the District—for a district it still remained. This man came to Benjamin Sebastian, a prominent lawyer, and afterward a distinguished judge, and laid before him certain schemes for the furtherance of the plan which had been already submitted to Wilkinson; and which insured to the people of Kentucky the free navigation of the Mississippi, and the right of deposit at New Orleans for any number of years that they might desire. At the same time, Mr. Guardoqui, the Spanish minister accredited to our government, then in New York, entered into treaty stipulations, with a similar object, and in a secret manner, with Mr. Brown, territorial delegate to Congress from Kentucky and subsequently its representative when admitted as a State.

And while the uneasy excitement about the secret plans of Spain is spreading in Kentucky, and the more open propositions of Guardoqui are almost published by Brown—while the people are also vexed and harassed with their interminable series of conventions to no purpose—the object of the Spanish court is nearly gained by Mr. Jay. This negotiator lays before the confederate Congress a proposal, not to give up the principle of the right to navigate the Mississippi, but to cede the exercise of it for twenty years, in consideration of certain advantages offered in return. The seven northeastern States earnestly favor the scheme; but nine States being required to adopt it, it fails. While it is in agitation, however, the wrath of the Kentuckians becomes so hot against the New Englanders, for this selfish disregard of the interests of the West, that they become almost ready to sever all connection with the Union, and to set up an independent sovereignty within the great valley.

Had this project prevailed in Congress, it is exceedingly probable that the after-progress of this country would have been much hampered and entangled by the indefinite complications which would have sprung from the establishment of a rival commonwealth beyond the mountains. As it was, the bitter feelings which the scheme engendered toward New England remained strong for many years, and the name of Jay was for a long time almost infamous in the popular mind of Kentucky, as having been connected with what they apprehended to be a treacherous and unscrupulously selfish scheme to sacrifice them and their future for the advantage of a distant section of the country. Yet Jay had never for a moment contemplated the resignation of the right to navigate the Mississippi. Indeed he would have been the very last man in the nation to yield a single jot of principle or of justice, to inflict a wrong, or to distribute benefits unfairly. His sole error was the universal one of under-estimating the prospective growth of the commonwealths of the Valley. So far was he from any improper pliancy on this point, that he had steadfastly supported the right to the river navigation, both during the war and after it, in defiance of all the tortuosities and intrigues which European diplomacy could bring to bear upon him, and of the large offers of pecuniary assistance and threats of alternative desertion which were constantly presented by the court of Spain as inducements toward the granting of what we sought. But the masses of the people, however sure their "sober second thought," are little competent to judge of the conduct of a negotiator in a foreign land, in difficult times, who must look at the needs and rights, not of one section of his country, but of all; and though Jay, now a historical character, has long justly held a lofty and honored place among our Revolutionary heroes, in the hearts of Kentuckians, as well as all others of his countrymen, his spotless name was long a by-word and a hissing among them.

So guarded were the words and actions of the advocates of an independent government in Kentucky, that even now it cannot be demonstratively proved that they had actually agreed with Spain to establish it. Still it is known that one or two of them received Spanish pensions; and there can be no reasonable doubt that Wilkinson, Brown, Sebastian, Innis, and a few more, did earnestly desire such an independent government, probably from the double desire for political power and position for themselves, and whatever pecuniary gains they could extort from the Spanish government. It is certain that they pushed their plan to the furthest point possible, without instant ruin to their own prospects in Kentucky.

I proceed with the story of the Spanish intrigues, though out of strict chronological order. Carondelet's negotiation with Judge Sebastian through Thomas Power, was brought to an end in 1795, by the treaty of October of that year, with Spain, which secured the navigation of the Mississippi. Two years afterward Power came again to Kentucky with a plan from Carondelet for forming an independent government west of the mountains. The public mind was to be prepared by newspaper articles; the scheme aided by Spain with men and arms. This proposition was submitted to Sebastian, to Innis, to Nicholas, and to Wilkinson, and was decidedly discouraged by all; not as treasonable or unpatriotic, but merely as impracticable under the circumstances. Wilkinson, however, intimated that if he should be appointed governor of Natchez, for Spain, he might be able to proceed in some plan of the kind. Power returned to New Orleans with this answer; and thus ended, as far as is now known, any actual attempts by Spain to dismember our Union. Sebastian, however, received a Spanish pension of two thousand dollars a year, until 1806.

The story of the West after the Revolution would not be complete without some reference to the meddlesome and impertinent endeavors of revolutionary France to reap in her turn some advantage among the hardy and excitable population of the new trans-Alleghanian State. There was no part of the United States where the French nation received more love or sympathy than in Kentucky. Her generous aid in the dark days of our own contest with England were gratefully remembered; and her magnificent attitude of successful defiance to the banded powers of Europe who sought to beat down her newly-established republican government, was enthusiastically admired. That crazy democat Genet, the French ambassador, deluded by the triumphant progress which he made through the country, believing that he could wield the moral and physical power of the United States in aid of France in the contest between herself and England and Spain, sent four emissaries into Kentucky, to raise two thousand men, and appoint a general, descend the Ohio and Mississippi in boats, attack the Spaniards in Louisiana, and bring them under French authority. General George Rogers Clark, the hero of Kaskaskia and Vincennes, now considerably fallen in social and political position, was so imprudent as to consent to receive the supreme command of this chimerical army, with the long-tailed title of "Major General in the armies of France, and Commander-in-Chief of the French Revolutionary Legions on the Mississippi." The work of enlistment went vigorously forward. Democratic clubs, humble imitations of the Jacobin clubs of France, were established over Kentucky, and grew rampant with denunciations of the federal government; of the Spanish treachery in closing the Mississippi; of the vile tricks which Washington and Jay were contriving to unite this country and England againt France; of the tyrannical excise act. The new State was in a perfect ferment of disloyal and fanatic excitement. There was much correspondence amongst the Federal and State officers respecting these military schemes. President Washington, Governor Shelby, and General Wayne wrote backward and forward. Depeau, one of the French agents, wrote an extraordinary letter to Gov. Shelby, in very French English, intended as a courteous announcement of his business, and an invitation to join in it. Shelby was even so much swayed from his usual straight-forward common-sense as to write to Gen. Wayne, in substance, that he had great doubts whether he could consistently endeavor to stop any Kentuckian or Kentuckians who should merely set out to leave the State with arms and provisions. Washington, who could not see the force of such reasoning, laconically ordered Wayne to garrison Fort Massac, on the Ohio, and to do what else might be necessary to stop this muster of fools. The Democrats, on this, grew more excited than ever. They called a convention and passed some resolutions full of bitter enmity to the general government; and this convention took measures to call another, which squinted hard in the old direction of separation from the Union. But just in the nick of time the news came that the French Republic had recalled Genet, and disapproved and disavowed his acts. This pricked the bubble. Lachaise and Depeau, the chief French agents, instantly lost their authority, and disappeared. Gen. Clark lost his long title and his military command. The officers and soldiers of the intended army lost the generous grants which their French friends had lavishly promised them, of lands which they did not own. And the public mind, losing so many and promising subjects for excitement, grew at once quite calm.

While Carondelet's intrigues were still proceeding, and while the democratic and federal quarrel was yet hot and fierce in Kentucky, the unpopular administration of Washington was succeeded by the actually hateful one of Adams. In the new government the people of Kentucky had little confidence, and entertained for it still less respect; for they were convinced that it was unfriendly to them. Nevertheless, Kentucky had been admitted as a State; and a treaty had been formed with Spain, by which the right of navigating the Mississippi for three years had been obtained, as well as the right to deposit merchandise in New Orleans for purposes of commerce. But before this period expired, the Spanish governor of New Orleans shut the port, and refused the permission agreed upon by the treaty. For even after the organization of the new State, the scheme of wooing her from her attachment to the confederacy was still contemplated. Then came the alien and sedition laws, ill-judged and oppressive enactments, which awakened tumult and confusion throughout the country, especially in Kentucky and Virginia. The former, irritated by their enactment, took the first step in that system of nullification, afterward so strangely put forward again by South Carolina. By a series of resolutions passed by her legislature, in 1798–9, she denied the right of the general government to interfere in matters of private State rights and authority. No State of all the country was so addicted to the principles of Jefferson, perhaps; it might be said, no people ever worshipped a demagogue in the form of a politician as did the Kentuckians Jefferson. And accordingly, they repudiated the doctrine of Adams and his congress, and passed a set of resolutions, drawn up by Jefferson with his own hand for the purpose. Thus did Kentucky defile its statute book with a direful blot; a stain which it has taken long years of fealty to the Union, to the federal authority, the united central power of the Republic, to wipe out. And no lapse of time will remove the spot from her history. The written word remaineth. The resolution in the book will forever tell of the folly that placed it there. Let us hope that the lesson will not be lost upon her sister States.

Thus goes on the muddy, crooked stream of politics; Spain intriguing still; England dispatching her emissaries from the North with the hope of harassing the Kentucky people—and they yet retaining, though not without doubt and difficulty, integrity toward the confederacy. It is time for me now to pass from this political part of my subject, and to return and trace downward another line of history.

As I have said, the Indians suspended their hostilities for a brief period after the close of the Revolutionary struggle. Finding that England had made no provision for them in her treaty with the colonies, they resumed hostilities after a more fearful sort than had ever been seen before. By the treaty between England and the United States, the former was to relinquish all fortresses within our territory after the boundary line had been run—the line which is now the northern boundary of the Union. But there was also another stipulation: that English merchants were to be allowed to collect their dues and debts in this country precisely as before the Revolution. Virginia, indignant at the carrying away of slaves by the British fleet, "nullified" this provision of the treaty, and prohibited by law the collection of British debts. England seized upon this pretext to retain her hold of the fortresses upon the northern border. So that her troops were yet stationed in certain forts in Michigan, northern Ohio, and Indiana; and from these centres of operation and influence, the Indians were constantly supplied with arms and provisions, sometimes with advice and encouragement; and were continually making descents upon the border settlements, hindering and almost absolutely preventing the settlement of the Northwestern Territory.

Thus the people of Kentucky must be still on the war-path; their cabins and block-houses burned; their wives and children tomahawked and butchered as before. Let us pause a moment to recount some of the incidents of this period, which may be said to reach from about 1784 to the battle of the Fallen Timber, in 1794.

A man named Davis walks out one morning, and has only got a few steps from the door, when he turns round and finds an Indian between him and the threshold. Thinking to elude the savage, he runs round the house so as to enter before him; but on returning finds that the cabin is filled with Indians, and he himself is hotly pursued by the one whom he had first seen. He rushes to a cornfield and succeeds in concealing himself. Hearing no noise, and no shouts or screams from the cabin, and knowing that without arms he can do nothing for the rescue of his family, he runs at the top of his speed for five miles to a block-house occupied by his brother and some other settlers. These quickly sally out, return to Davis's house, find that no blood has been spilled; and after great difficulty—for the Indians have taken every means to obliterate their traces—succeed in getting upon the trail. Following this with all speed, after a number of hours they succeed in overtaking the savages, who have still the wife and children of Davis with them. One of the children, a boy of eleven, is instantly thrown to the ground, as the Indians see his father and friends approaching, and the hair and skin from the top of his head skillfully removed by that surgical process called scalping. The rest of the Indians, frightened at the crack of the rifles, take to their heels, leaving the remainder of the family in a sink hole by the side of the trail. The boy, springup, his head streaming with blood, cries out at the top of his voice: "Father! after them! Cuss those redskins—they've got my *har!*" This is an illustration of the spirit of the boys of that period.

There was a redoubtable hunter and Indian-fighter of the name of Hart, whose quickness and keenness in the warfare of the woods had obtained him the name of Sharp-Eye from his Indian enemies. This man had performed a number of feats which had won him the unenviable distinction of the special hatred of these red people. Making a descent upon his neighborhood, secreting themselves over night, they attack his family as they are sitting at their breakfast one morning. An Indian levels his rifle and shoots Hart dead. The son, a boy of twelve years of age, grasps his father's rifle and sends a bullet through the Indian's heart. The other savages rush at the door in a body. The brave boy hurls a tomahawk and splits the skull of a second; drives his scalping-knife to the hilt in the heart of a third, and then—the party is a large one, and the contest is too unequal—they carry him off with his mother, rather proud of the achievements of the lad. A sister was killed on the journey; but the boy and his mother, after being captives for some time, were ransomed, and returned home.

The spirit of the women of the country was of the same indomitable sort. The house of a settler was attacked just before the break of day. Hearing a noise outside, he incautiously opened the door and stepped out on the threshold, when he received the contents of six or seven Indian rifles. Falling across the entry, mortally wounded, his wife hastily pulled the body in, and closed the door, just in season to prevent the Indians from entering. They immediately, with clubs and tomahawks, commenced to cut away the door. There were no firearms in the house, the settler having been so reckless as to be without them. They succeeded in breaking down one of the puncheons of the door and were pressing in. The bold wife had nothing but an axe; but as one savage after another crawled through, she hewed him down with the axe, and drew him inside; until four were dispatched. The other three, thinking almost any other plan more promising, now climb the roof and seek to descend the chimney. But female ingenuity is fertile in resources. There is only one feather bed in the house, and quick as thought she empties it into the bed of glowing coals in the fireplace. Two more of the Indians, suffocated by the pungent fumes, fall into the fire, and as they grovel in the live coals, she splits their skulls with her axe. The last of the party tries the broken door again. As he is crawling through, the valiant woman gives him also a death-wound with her heavy weapon, and is left safe for a time and alone with her great sorrow and her brave revenge, and with a ghastly company of eight bloody corpses—her husband and his seven murderers.

There was for many years resident in the North-western Territory, in what became afterward the State of Illinois, a French creole woman, born at the post of St. Joseph's, upon Lake Michigan. She was fortunate enough, during her singular life, to have three husbands, two of them Frenchmen and one American. She was known as Madame Lecompte, the name of her second husband, for that of the third she did not choose to keep; a very vigorous, clear-minded person, capable of adapting herself to circumstances, and well experienced in the customs of her Indian neighbors. Born in 1735, she sojourned some time in Michigan, and afterward descended to the French settlements in Illinois, and here took up her residence at Kahohia. Many times, when the Indians were making descents upon the French at the instigation of the English, this woman, who was much beloved by the savages, received previous information from them that they were about to attack the settlements, in order that she might escape before the onslaught. The message always came in the night-time; but instead of escaping, the bold-hearted woman would instantly set out for the Indian camp, approach as day was breaking, and freely enter amongst their host, secure of respectful treatment. Sometimes she would stop with them one, two, or three days; protesting, urging, reasoning with them, and inducing them at length to give up their foray. Returning to the settlement, with three or four hundred savage warriors, who had come out to burn and slay, she brought them, in friendly guise, to make their humble acknowledgments to the settlers, and to partake of their hospitality. Thus, in a dozen cases at least, did this brave woman, at Kahokia and Kaskaskia, prevent the destruction of the French and American inhabitants. She lived till 1843, reaching the astonishing age of a hundred and nine years; and the old chronicler, Governor Reynolds, whom I am so fortunate as to number among my personal friends, says, that to the last she was active in body and mind, and possessed her faculties and functions, intellectual and physical, at that advanced period, better than women of forty or fifty do now. She was accustomed to go out in all weathers, walking on the ice and snow, and in the open air, and health, longevity, beauty of complexion, were more certainly secured by this means, says Governor Reynolds, than by making pilgrimages "on fine, rich carpets, between the piano and the air-tight stove."

William Whiteside, a soldier of the Revolution,

who had fought bravely and well at the battle of King's Mountain, a strong athletic woodsman, of Irish blood, was in 1795 settled in the American Bottom, between Kaskaskia and Kahokia. Getting intelligence that a party of Indians was encamped in the neighborhood, with the design of stealing his horses, the fiery old warrior summoned a little band of fourteen men, his tried companions in many a combat with the savages, and set out to surprise them in camp. Surrounding them just before day, a furious charge was made, and after a severe combat, all the Indians were killed but one, who fled, and who was killed when he got home, by his tribesmen, for his cowardice. In this battle, Capt. Whiteside received a wound which he thought mortal, and which brought him to the ground. But he neither flinched nor feared; and he lay there exhorting his men to fight bravely, not to retreat an inch, and never to permit the enemy to touch him after he was dead. One of his sons, who was unable to use his gun, being wounded in the arm, now came up, and on examining his father's wound, discovered that the ball had merely glanced from a rib, and passing round, had lodged under the skin near the spine. He quietly drew his butcher-knife and cut out the ball, as he would out of a tree, merely remarking in a dry way, "Father, you're not dead yet!" The old man, on reflection, thought so too; and jumping to his feet, cried out, "Boys, I can fight the Indians yet!" and rushed again into the fight.

I shall not delay to give details of the incessant border barbarities of the Indians; nor of the expeditions which, one after another, went forth against them. After a considerable period, the general government undertook the defence of the western settlements. I need not detail the adventures, the sufferings, the defeats and degradation of the hapless hosts of Harmor and St. Clair; nor the splendid triumphal progress of Anthony Wayne; nor the decisive victory gained by him in the great battle of the Fallen Timber, which reduced the belligerent tribes to a condition of humble, though unwilling submission. But I will take time to narrate a few circumstances of individual adventure in Wayne's army, which will serve as additional illustrations of the character of western woodsmen of that day.

Attached to Wayne's army was a small body of scouts, whose business it was to range up and down the woods in front and flank of the line of march, familiarize themselves with the movements of the savages, and every now and then to arrest some Indian and bring him to the camp, that the general might get his news at first hand. The head of these scouts was Captain William Wells, who had associated with him a man named Miller, another named McLennan, and three others. These, while in camp, were gentlemen at large, and no duties devolved upon them; but when they were on the war-path their occupations were of a sufficiently hazardous description to make up for former ease. In 1793, Wayne had sent out Wells, with Miller and McLennan, for the purpose of catching an Indian. They proceeded northward in the direction of some Indian towns. When yet at a distance, they heard a sound of merry-making; and approaching an open glade in the wood, found three Indians seated near its centre, cooking venison, laughing and talking at leisure. The three spies were too distant to rush in upon them; and it was necessary to take one of them alive. They therefore skirted along the timber till they came opposite to the point from which they had first discovered the savages. Here there was a fallen tree; and creeping along this until they were safely ensconced between the branches, it was arranged that the spy on the right should shoot the Indian on the right; he on the left should pick his man in the same way, while McLennan, who was in the middle, and the fleetest man in the party, was to run after the third Indian, and seize him. The fire was given, the two Indians fell dead, and, as was expected, the middle one took to his heels with all dispatch, McLennan after him. The smoke had not cleared away before the two men were seen bounding along at the top of their speed. Near at hand was a stream of water. The Indian, seeing McLennan gaining on him, ran to the river, and plunging over a bluff, twenty feet high, landed in a deep quagmire. McLennan, without pausing, sprang over him; and up to their breasts, as they stood, both mired fast, but within reach of each other, a desperate struggle ensued. The knife and tomahawk were drawn, and the two foes were on the point of a bloody conflict, when the other two spies came up, and burst into a hearty laugh at the absurd phase of the spectacle. The Indian, seeing that there was no chance for him, dropped his weapons and surrendered. The others extricated them from their embarrassing attitude; and while the two who had been in the morass were washing off the dirt, it was discovered that the man who had thus been seized, was not really an Indian, though burned and browned so as to be almost of their tawny complexion; but that he bore indubitable marks of white origin. Miller had himself been a prisoner with the Indians many years, having been captured in his early youth; and had left a brother, Christopher Miller, in their hands. A strange suspicion flashed upon him. It was years since he had seen his brother. The white Indian, however, was sulky, and refused to answer any questions, until Miller, riding up—for they had placed him upon a horse—called him by his Indian name. The man flushed, turned crimson, and asked, "How do you know my name?" Here was the truth revealed as by a miracle. The brothers' hands had been providentially stayed from shedding each other's blood; and after long and urgent entreaty, pleading even with tears in his eyes, Miller succeeded in winning Christopher from his wild Indian ways; and at length induced him to join their scouting and foraging party, of which he became one of the most reso lute and indomitable members.

Thus reinforced, and with two other men, they were sent on a subsequent occasion, by General Wayne, to take other prisoners. They had proceeded thirty-five miles from Fort Defiance, in the direction of Maumee. This was in the year 1794, just before the great battle in which Wayne was victorious. Arriving within two miles of the English post, they rode boldly into an Indian town near to where Fort Meigs was afterward built, as if they had come from the British fort; and being painted and decorated with feathers in Indian style, although they met Indians constantly, as some of them could speak the language, they were supposed to be none other than a party of Indians. In an out-of-the-way place, beyond the town, they seize an Indian warrior with his squaw, gag and handcuff them, tie them upon the saddle, and turn toward the American camp. Presently they reach the neighborhood of a large Indian encampment; and now these seven reckless men make a detour, and gain the brush at some distance, where they conceal their prisoners, and then resolve to return and have a bout with the Indians in camp. It is understood by previous arrangement that they are to ride in as if they were all Indians, and enter into an amicable conversation with any parties about the fires, in order that they may gain all the information possible. Sitting quietly on their saddles, every man with his hand on the trigger of his rifle, they coolly ride into the camp as agreed. They have an agreeable chat of fifteen or twenty minutes with the Indian warriors, who are loitering around the fires; when an old chief sitting upon a log, whispers to his friends that there is something suspicious about these men; they don't seem Indians. Wells overhears the remark; the spies discharge their rifles each into the breast of an Indian, and then putting spurs to their horses, and lying down on their necks so as to present less mark for their enemy's fire, they ride full speed into the forest, whooping and hallooing as if they were demons. The Indians however, grasp their rifles and deliver their fire, in confusion and bewilderment. Yet before the spies have got beyond the circle of the firelight McLennan is shot shrough the shoulder, and Wells, receiving a bullet in his arm, loses his rifle. May, a third man, was taken prisoner; the others, after a dangerous and fatiguing journey, arrived safely at camp. And this was a funny freak; an amusing adventure; a specimen of the sport relished by the rugged Borderers of that old day.

McLennan was the fleetest runner in Wayne's army; doubtless one of the fleetest that ever lived. It is told of him on good authority, that when the army was encamped at Greenville, he took a short run, and sprang over a camp wagon which rose, with its cover on, just nine feet from the ground.

Captain Wells, the chief of this band of daring men, met an appropriate fate in a characteristic manner. Long after Wayne's expedition, during the Indian hostilities in 1812, he held the official position of interpreter to the Miami nation. The Pottawatomies had surrounded the American garrison of Fort Dearborn, where Chicago now stands; and Wells, whose niece was wife to the commander, Major Heald, had gone thither with the intention of aiding the troops to escape to Fort Wayne. But he was excessively obnoxious to the Pottawatomies, who were also much enraged at finding that the garrison of Fort Dearborn had destroyed their powder, instead of delivering it up as was agreed. A little after the garrison, according to a sort of capitulation between the officers and chiefs, had set out on their journey to Fort Wayne, the irritated Pottawatomies attacked them. Wells, seeing instantly that there was no hope, and knowing that if he were taken prisoner, he would be subjected to long and dreadful tortures, wetted powder and blackened his face in token of defiance, and mounting his horse, began to pour out on the Indians all the abusive and insulting terms he was master of. This, as he had intended, soon irritated them to such a pitch that one of them shot him down from his horse, and then springing upon him like a beast, cut him open, tore out his heart and ate it.

And now I come to the last portion of my subject. In the early years of the present century there suddenly arose from the midst of peace and security, a danger that threatened anew the existence of the country, by aiming at the disruption of its territory. This was the result of certain plans of a man who had served with credit in the Revolutionary war, rising to the rank of colonel; of a singularly acute, and shrewd intellect, fascinating address, perfect courtesy of manner, profoundly acquainted with human nature, a quick reader of the faults and follies of all about him, as haughtily and unscrupulously ambitious as Lucifer himself; long a most able and successful politician; once Vice-President, after failing of the Presidency itself only by a few votes; fallen however, in consequence of that failure in the esteem of his party; the deliberate and delighted murderer of the greatest statesman our country ever boasted; but now an outlaw by proclammation, quite bankrupt in fortune and in political hopes, and ready for any design, how bad or desperate soever, which exhibited any chance of regaining wealth and power. For between fame and notoriety, Aaron Burr seems to have no choice.

Burr's plans were masked by a pretended enterprise for colonizing a large tract of wild lands among the distant rivers and marshes of upper Louisiana, in which he held a nominal interest under the Spanish grant to the Baron de Bastrop. His actual design he most probably never fully revealed to any person. But the common belief is well founded that he intended to attack the Spanish possessions, and to carve out for himself some principality or magnificent estate somewhere in the West, between the Mississippi River and the Isthmus of Darien. Whether his empire was to be Mexico, Texas, or Louisiana, and how far his scheme included the territory of the United States, will probably never be known.

Burr visited the West in two successive years, 1805 and 1806; winning friends and partisans everywhere, and by that strange personal magnetism which was, perhaps, his most remarkable characteristic, becoming especially a favorite among the ladies. Upon his second visit, however, he was arrested at the suit of Col. Joseph Hamilton Daviess, then U. S. attorney; who, almost alone among the whole population of Kentucky, was profoundly convinced of the treasonableness of Burr's designs. Daviess is famous as an orator; but far more deserving of renown, it seems to me, is the impregnable moral courage and lofty rock-like steadfastness to his convictions which he showed in the series of vigorous endeavors he made under circumstances the most discouraging, to insure the trial of a man whom he believed a criminal. He was one of the very few federalists in Kentucky; and as such, all his public acts were of course bitterly censured, and his motives continually questioned. In the present instance, however, the bold attorney had not only to stand up under the weight of this political odium, which his powerful shoulders had already easily supported for years, but under the accumulated storm of obloquy, indignation, and ridicule, which was liberally hurled against him from all sides, for his persevering attacks upon a man of national reputation, whose personal and political friends filled Kentucky, and who numbered among those who were either his very partners in crime, or his zealous followers in a supposed justifiable political enterprise, numbers of the influential citizens of the District.

Did the occasion permit, an interesting account might be given of the exciting legal contest which began on the third of November, 1806, before the United States District Court, of which Harry Innis, previously a fellow-intriguer of Benjamin Sebastian with the Spaniards, was judge. A motion by Daviess, for process to bring Burr up to answer a charge of misdemeanor in organizing a military expedition within the United States, against a friendly power, opened the case. The motion was denied, but was granted a short time afterward, at Burr's own request. Twice, a day was fixed for the trial, and each time the resolute attorney found himself, to his keen mortification, obliged to ask an adjournment on account of the absence of an essential witness. The second time Daviess requested the Court to keep the jury impannelled until he could bring up the recusant by *capias;* and while Burr, who had, on the former occasion made a dignified and most telling address to the Court, remained silent, Daviess was opposed by Henry Clay, Burr's counsel; and for hours together these celebrated orators battled with each other upon the legal question, but illuminated and pointed their arguments with brilliant rhetoric and sharp and personal assaults and rejoinders, which held the crowded court-room in the profoundest silence.

Innis refused to keep the jury without business; and Daviess, to gain a little time, sent to them an indictment against the absent witness, John Adair, which they found not a true bill. He then moved to compel his attendance by attachment, but was again baffled; and the case going to the grand jury, with the witnesses then present, Burr was triumphantly acquitted by the throwing out of Daviess' bill. The friends of the victorious plotter gave a splendid ball in Frankfort in honor of the occasion, and Daviess' friends, rallying, followed it by another in his honor.

Burr had only secured the services of Clay by a most sweeping and enormous falsehood. He assured him in the strongest and broadest terms that he neither entertained views, nor possessed friends nor means intended or calculated to disturb the government in any manner whatever; and that he had signed no military commission, and owned no military stores or weapons; and to this vast lie he pledged his honor. The tremendous impudence of the fabrication will appear, when it is remembered that his military preparations had begun four months before, and that at the very moment of making it, the advance of his army, organized, armed, and provisioned, was on Blennerhassett's island, on the frontiers of Kentucky; or even descending the Ohio.

It was not long before the delusion which had so long obscured the Kentuckians, was thoroughly dispelled, and they did justice to the penetration and resolute perseverance of Daviess, whose reputation throughout the West rose to a higher pitch than ever. There are few public men who are not, at some period of life, called to pass through a similar ordeal of misunderstanding, perhaps almost ignominy. But to him who is in the right, the time of recompense always comes. The clouds do not always tarry about the mountain's side. They roll themselves up and shrink away in the sunshine, and the everlasting peak stands out in its grandeur, lifted high in the heavens, uninjured by the darkness that is past, and seeming even more magnificent at the withdrawal of its transient veil.

Burr, leaving Frankfort at the conclusion of the trial, joined his forces, descended the Ohio and Mississippi, and was arrested and his men dispersed near Natchez. He was taken to Washington, the capital of the Mississippi Territory, and without difficulty found friends who gave bail in ten thousand dollars for his appearance at court. He appeared, moved unsuccessfully for a discharge, and apprehensive of the consequences of a removal before a higher court, fled away eastward by night.

On the 18th of February, 1807, late at night, Nicholas Perkins, register, and Thomas Malone, clerk of the court, are playing backgammon in their cabin, in the little village of Wakefield, on the western verge of Alabama, when a knock is heard at the door, and on opening it, two travellers inquire of Perkins the route to Col. Hinson's. While he answers that it is seven miles away, by a difficult path and over a dangerous creek, his companion throws more pine-wood on the fire, and the blaze now enables the inquisitive register to observe that the speaker has a keen, striking face, and eyes that flash and sparkle with wonderful brilliancy; that he wears an old hat and coarse clothes, but remarkably handsome boots. The travellers ride on, and Perkins instantly assures his companion that the inquirer is Aaron Burr, and urges him to go with himself at once to Hinson's and procure his arrest. Malone declines. The register, hurrying off to the sheriff, one Brightwell, awakens him; and they set out at once for Hinson's, which they reach after a severe journey. Perkins thinks best to stay in the woods, lest Burr should recognize him, and sends Brightwell into the house, who satisfies himself that they are right, but, for some reason, delays to take any steps for the capture. Perkins, after waiting shivering in the woods until he is tired, and hearing nothing of the sheriff, now makes the best of his way to Fort Stoddart, on the Tombigbee, commanded by Captain Edmund P. Gaines, where he arrives at sunrise. Gaines, on learning the news, at once sets out with a file of men, and about nine o'clock meets Burr, with his companion, together with Brightwell, the recreant sheriff, who seems to have been fascinated by Burr, and now to have been guiding him on the road to Pensacola; from which port he would have sailed for Europe, to endeavor there to obtain new means for his intended expedition. Notwithstanding the vehement eloquence with which Burr denounced the proclamations and proceedings for his arrest, and the ingenious mode in which he enlarged upon the responsibility of stopping travellers, the straightforward young soldier marches him to the fort, and retains him there for some time, while he prepares to send him prisoner to Virginia. During this time, Burr makes himself a favorite with an invalid brother of the commander, with Mrs. Captain Gaines, an accomplished and lovely woman, daughter of Judge Harry Toulmin, and with every one he meets.

After some weeks, Gaines succeeds in forming an escort to his mind, consisting of Colonel Nicholas Perkins, who had caused the arrest, two United States soldiers, and seven or eight men chosen by Perkins as especially reliable, energetic, and unseducible; and after a long and most fatiguing journey, all the hardships and dangers of which Burr endured without a complaint, they reached the settled country of the Atlantic seaboard. While passing through South Carolina, where Burr was still popular, and of which his son-in-law, Alston, was governor, he attempted to escape, leaping from his horse and appealing to the citizens whom he found assembled at a merry-making at one of the towns on the road. But Perkins, a tall and athletic man, seized Burr and flung him bodily into the saddle, and with one guard holding his horse's bridle, and others urging the beast from behind, they hurried him onward out of reach. In the revulsion of his disappointment at this failure, Burr, ordinarily so inaccessible to fear or sorrow, for once gave way to a violent outburst of grief, and even wept like a child; and one of his guards, a kind-hearted man, wept with him. Burr was safely conveyed the remainder of the distance to Richmond; the story of his trial there, and his subsequent varying fortunes, his obscure and evil life, his unhappy death, is sufficiently familiar to you. The moral of his career has often been recited, but it will bear a repetition. The lesson is simple, but fearfully important; and its weight is not lessened by any circumstance in the manners or the morals of our times. Burr was a man of splendid intellect, and of powerful passions. He had both the magnificent machine, and vast motive power. But he was destitute of moral sentiment, or of religious feeling. He lacked the guiding and controlling hand that must measure the application of the force, and direct the working of the enginery. And without this, without the wise and just hand on engine and on helm, the magnificence of the vessel only makes her ruin the sadder; the power and speed of her movements only drive her with a more fearful crash upon the fatal rocks. Head without heart tends straight and fast to destruction, and brings the awful fate of Aaron Burr.

Lecture VIII.

MANNA IN THE WILDERNESS;

OR,

THE OLD PREACHERS AND THEIR PREACHING.

MANNA IN THE WILDERNESS;

OR,

THE OLD PREACHERS AND THEIR PREACHING.

After the defeat of the English forces before Fort Duquesne under the ill-fated Braddock, it was desired still to wrest that strong position from the grasp of the French, and General Forbes was placed at the head of an expedition to effect that object. It was thought fit, however, that he should be preceded by some person sufficiently able and experienced to bring over the minds of the indomitable inhabitants of the wilderness from the cause of the French to that of the English. The person selected for this hazardous enterprise was a Moravian missionary, Christian Frederick Post. He had long been laboring among the Delawares on the Susquehanna, and had acquired a thorough knowledge of the Indian languages, and of their habits and customs. He was calm, simple-hearted, intrepid, and accustomed to all the perils he had now to face. Confiding himself and his cause to the hands of his Great Master, he betook himself to the forest, attended by a little company of savages. His negotiation was eminently successful; and though his life was threatened again and again, he succeeded in returning safely to the settlements. By the wise and skillful efforts of this man, the Indians were completely won over to the cause of the English. The fall of Fort Duquesne was the consequence; and the arms of the English were crowned with triumph.

After the close of the war, in 1761, Post returned to his labor among the Indians, crossed the Alleghany River, and found himself upon the Muskingum, in the now State of Ohio. Here he settled among the Delawares, whose language he knew, and among whose brethren he had already labored for many years. But the tribe among whom he now found himself, while a part of them were inclined to a peacable disposition toward the English, were still in part exceedingly hostile; and he found great difficulties in his way. These, however, he serenely met and overcame. Having taken possession of a piece of ground allotted him, he proposed to erect a cabin, for the double purpose of a home and a school-house, that he might instruct the savages and their children. As he commenced clearing the timber from this ground, some of the Indians inquired his intentions. He told them that a missionary must live, and in order to eat, he must raise corn.

"Nay," said the Indians; "the French priests with whom we are acquainted, to whose labors we have been accustomed, look fat and comely, and they raise no corn; and if you be the servant of God, as you say you are, and as they say they are, your God will feed you, as he feeds them; you can therefore have no large tract of ground to till. If you have a farm, other English will come and open farms, and then a fort must be built to defend you; and then our lands will be taken away from us, and we shall be driven toward the setting sun." The logic of the Indians was excellent, and their power sufficient to sustain it, if it was not; Post had, therefore, to content himself with a small patch sufficient for a vegetable garden. Here, then, in company with the celebrated Heckewelder, he commenced his labors.

The war of Pontiac beginning in the following year, the two missionaries, warned of their danger by the simple-hearted Indian children of the forest, returned east of the mountains, and there remained for six years, when, together with David Zeisberger, they came back to the Muskingum, and laid the foundations of the town of Gnadenhutten, a memorable settlement of the good Moravians and their Indians. This was the first establishment of those devout and useful missionaries west of the mountains. Many an Indian's heart was won to the cause of the truth by their patience, constancy, and judicious humble instructions; and flourishing out-stations began to grow up all around them. During all the Revolutionary struggle, the Moravians were successfully laboring toward the conversion of the Delaware Indians. But the towns they occupied were unfortunately just upon the frontier, between the whites upon the one side, and the Indians upon the other. The Wyandots and Shawnees, fiercest of all the hostile tribes of the Northwest, in making incursions upon the frontiers of Virginia and Pennsylvania, must needs pass through the settlements of these Christian Indians; and the settlers in the western parts of those States, in attempting to make reprisals for the outrages perpetrated upon them, must also take the same road. They were thus feared and suspected by both parties; and the British in the neighborhood of Detroit, at length determined that their settlements should be broken up, and, with or against their will, they must now be removed to the neighborhood of Sandusky. This they were loath to do, and would not voluntarily abandon their peaceful homes and firesides, their pleasant maize fields, and the sunny clearings around their comfortable residences. But they were forcibly taken away by command of the British officers. Nearly a hundred of them perished in the winter of 1781–2, in the neighborhood of Sandusky; and the survivors resolved to return to their old settlements, and there gather in their corn, which had been allowed to remain out during the winter.

A company of settlers from the western part of Pennsylvania about this time resolved on an excursion into the Indian territory for the purpose of punishing the Wyandots, who had been committing outrages within that State. About ninety of these men, under the command of one Col. Williamson, after two or three days' march from Fort Pitt, reached the peaceful settlements of our Christian Indians. The converts were abroad in the fields, men, women, and children, gathering in their corn. Seeing the white men approaching, and supposing them friendly, they came forward to meet them courteously, and cordially invited them to their homes. The whites told them that they had come for the purpose of conveying them for safe keeping to Fort Pitt. Some of the Indians had been there the preceding year, and had been treated with remarkable kindness by the commandant. To this proposition of the whites they therefore readily acceded, and collected themselves in the village. All the remaining Indians, who were scattered in various localities within a circuit of four or five miles, were also brought in. When they were all gathered together, they were put under a guard, and the question was then put by the colonel, "Shall these Indians be put to death or marched to Pittsburg?" All in favor of sparing their lives were ordered to step out two paces in advance of the line as the detachment stood. Only sixteen men of the whole ninety took the requisite step. The vote was for death. The intelligence was communicated to those humble and simple-minded people, now imprisoned and helpless within their own dwellings, and they were told that with the morrow's dawn they must all perish. They begged for life, but their prayer was unheeded, save by that Ear which is ever open to the prayers of all. The white men were deaf to their pleadings, and even to the wailings of women and the innocent entreaties of little children. And on the morrow that company of men, with your blood and mine in their veins, Anglo-Saxon men, took those people, five and thirty men, four and thirty women, five and forty little children, laid them out on blocks of wood, and standing over them with their axes, clove their skulls in sunder; one of the most atrocious, horrible, devilish deeds that was ever perpetrated upon the face of God Almighty's earth!

Fearfully enough was this black-hearted murder avenged by Him who watches the deeds of his recreant children. Next year these same volunteers fitted out another expedition. They marched this time five hundred strong, intending not only to burn and lay waste the territory of the hostile Indians, but also to destroy those of the inoffensive Christian Indians who yet remained. I am glad to say that most of them, diabolical miscreants as they were, fell victims either to the tomahawks of the hostile savages, or to the silent and unrelenting power of the wilderness. Col. Crawford, who had been an old friend and agent of George Washington, and was unwillingly and unwittingly made commandant of this last party, was burnt alive with peculiarly frightful torments, by the Wyandots, by whom he was taken prisoner.

The Moravian brethren were the first to bring the Word of Life and Truth into the vast region of the Mississippi Valley; always of course excepting the old Jesuit Fathers and other Catholic missionaries who came with the French. There are yet, in the western country, and have been ever since the time of those atrocious murders, descendants of the Christian Indians, the converts of the Moravian brethren; and I believe there are yet some white Moravians in the eastern part of the State of Ohio.

South of the Ohio, the earliest Christian denomination to enter Kentucky as a field of labor, were the Baptists—a large and exceedingly influential sect in Virginia and North Carolina, from which States most of the early settlers of Kentucky came. While there were few preachers who came with the single purpose of preaching the Word, there were a good many who were licensed to administer the sacraments, or whose object was to instruct the young, or like their secular companions, to take possession of the country, and to secure for themselves farms and estates. These were not long after followed by Presbyterian ministers and missionaries, who came here expressly for the purpose of preaching the Gospel. It is not my desire here to assume a sectional or denominational position. Nevertheless, it is necessary to call special attention to the characteristics, peculiarities, lives, manners, customs, names, and reputations of some of the preachers of my own church, the Methodist. I am not to detract in the slightest degree from either the Baptists or Presbyterians, the two other pioneer churches in the wilderness. Their case has been presented in literature. But the Methodist church has had comparatively little advocacy before the people at large. But little is known, outside of its own limits, of its operations, movements, or men; or of their agency in the promotion of civilization and Christianity. And it is with these men that I am more familiarly acquainted, and as, for the major part of this lecture, I am to rely upon my own personal observation and acquaintance with living men, and with and of those who have passed away from the scene of action within the last twenty years, it is both natural and necessary that I should principally speak of them.

The Baptists did a noble and excellent work, as did also the Presbyterians, in the early times of the

West. The Methodist church was a younger church than these—its first regular preachers having landed on this continent in 1770. Fourteen years after their first teacher, sent out by Wesley, set foot in America—seven years after the first Baptist minister in Kentucky—and three years after the first Presbyterian—they commenced penetrating the wilds of the Far West, and their pioneer missionaries, James Haw and Benjamin Ogden, crossed the Alleghanies and entered the boundless tracts of Kentucky. Others rapidly followed him. At first there was much antagonism—a sort of pugnacious rivalry or "free fight" between these various denominations out in the West—nor has this yet quite passed away. There is an active, rough, resolute courage, independence, and pluck about the western people, which inclines them to close scuffling and grappling, a sort of knock-down attitude visible through all the moods of their life; and their clergy are not free from the same peculiarities. They were therefore great controversialists; and there was an immense din about Baptism and Pedobaptism; Free Grace and Predestination; Falling from Grace and the Perseverance of the Saints, etc., etc. Brethren of different denominations often held what they called discussions or debates; where one of one denomination challenged one of another. Meeting together before the people, occupying a temporary pulpit in a grove, they would thus treat—and maltreat—the doctrines and views of each other, to the eminent edification, and oftentimes the entertainment of the assembled multitude. The people, nevertheless, were somewhat insensible to the preached Word during the first twenty years of its dispensation. They were absorbed by Indian wars, and by the pressing demands upon their labor, necessary to maintain physical existence in a new country. Soon afterward came in French infidelity with French politics; and deism and atheism were openly avowed on every hand. Many of the principal citizens of the West were not afraid or ashamed to own themselves skeptical or infidels in regard to the old system of Revelation. Thus the field which these pioneer preachers were called to till was a hard and stony one; and they had much difficulty in pushing their way.

The Presbyterians and Methodists found it necessary, toward the close of the last century, to conjoin their efforts and unite for the furtherance of the common cause. This was in the southern part of the State of Kentucky. They held "union meetings;" sacramental meetings, where the two denominations worked together, kindly and efficient yoke-fellows. Under these efforts the people at length became much excited on the subject of religion, and there then broke out, in the spring of 1800, the most extraordinary revival of religion that ever happened on this continent, or perhaps in the history the church since the

Day of Pentecost. It was called the Cumberland Revival, or the Great Revival. It broke out at one of these sacramental occasions, when the Methodist and Presbyterian ministers were holding a two or three days' meeting, for the purpose of stimulating the attention of the people to the all-important subject of personal holiness. At this, there were strange manifestations. The people were seized as by a sort of superhuman power ; their physical energy was lost; their senses refused to perform their functions; all forms of manifesting consciousness were for the time annulled. Strong men fell upon the ground, utterly helpless; women were taken with a strange spasmodic motion, so that they were heaved to and fro, sometimes falling at length upon the floor, their hair dishevelled, and throwing their heads about with a quickness and violence so great as to make their hair crack against the floor as if it were a teamster's whip. Then they would rise up again under this strange power, fall on their faces, and the same violent movements and cracking noise would ensue. Such peculiarities characterized this first meeting.

The meetings went on, and at length there was a grand convocation at Cane Ridge, Kentucky, where the leading Presbyterian minister was Barton W. Stone, afterward renowned in the ecclesiastical annals of the West, as the father and head of those "New Lights" who became subsequently followers of Alexander Campbell, and a section of that body now called "Christian." Stone was then the Presbyterian minister of Concord and Cane Ridge meeting-house. He appointed a sacramental meeting. The report of these peculiar doings spread so rapidly through Tennessee, Kentucky, Virginia, and what is now Indiana, that people came sixty, seventy, a hundred, even three hundred miles to attend this meeting, and it is said that on one night there were not less than thirty thousand people present at the Cane Ridge ground. There were present eight or ten preachers of different denominations, standing up on the stumps of trees, fallen logs, or temporary pulpits, all of them holding forth in their loudest tone—and that was a very loud tone, for the lungs of the backwoods preachers were of the strongest. They roared like lions—their tones were absolutely like peals of thunder. The celebrated William Burke, who died in Cincinnati only a short time ago, was one of the principal orators on that occasion. He had not been treated, he thought, with courtesy by his Presbyterian brethren. He had arrived on the ground on Friday night, and was not asked to participate in any of the exercises on Saturday. Sunday morning came, and many friends crowded around him to know if he were going to preach. He said that if he were invited he would, but that he had not been invited. Brother Stone wanted him to get up, and make an *exposé* of his doctrines. "My doctrines," said Burke, "I preach every day," —this he said with a good deal of *vim*—"they are in the books—go and read. If I am to make an *exposé* of Methodist views, then you might be called upon for yours." Mr. Stone said he was satisfied; that that would do. Burke, however, was not satisfied, and as he was not asked to preach by the authorities of the ground, he took a stand on his own hook, a fallen log, and here, having rigged up an umbrella as a temporary shelter, a brother standing by to see that it performed its functions properly, he gave out a hymn, and by the time that he had mentioned his text, there were some ten thousand persons about him. Although his voice when he began was like a crash of thunder, after three-quarters of an hour or an hour, it was like an infant's.

It is said that all these people, the whole ten thousand of men and women standing about the preacher, were from time to time shaken as a forest by a tornado, and five hundred were at once prostrated to the earth, like the trees in a "windfall," by some invisible agency. Some were agitated by violent whirling motions, some by fearful contortions; and then came "the jerks." Scoffers, doubters, deniers, men who came to ridicule and sneer at the supernatural agency, were taken up in the air, whirled over upon their heads, coiled up so as to spin about like cart-wheels, catching hold, meantime, of saplings, endeavoring to clasp the trunks of trees in their arms, but still going headlong and helplessly on. These motions were called the "jerks;" a name which was current in the West for many a year after; and many an old preacher has described these things accurately to me. It was not the men who were already members of the church, but the scoffing, the blasphemous, the profane, who were taken in this way. Here is one example: A man rode into what was called the "Ring Circle," where five hundred people were standing in a ring, and another set inside. Those inside were on their knees, crying, shouting, praying, all mixed up in heterogeneous style. This man comes riding up at the top of his speed, yelling like a demon, cursing and blaspheming. On reaching the edge of the ring, he falls from his horse, seemingly lifeless, and lies in an apparently unconscious condition for thirty hours; his pulse at about forty, or less. When he opens his eyes and recovers his senses, he says he has retained his consciousness all the time—that he has been aware of what has been passing around—but was seized with some agency which he could not define. I fancy that neither physiology, nor pyschology, nor biology, nor any of the ologies or isms, have, thus far, given any satisfactory explanation of the singular manifestations that attended this great revival.

These meetings taking place in open woods, and attracting such immense multitudes, no provision could possibly be made for them by the surrounding neighborhood. People came in their carriages, in wagons, in ox-carts, on horses, and, themselves accustomed to pioneer habits and lives, they brought their own food, commonly jerked meat and corn dodgers, and pitched their tents upon the ground.

Such was the origin of camp-meetings. The first camp-meeting ever seen, after the Feast of Tabernacles, was that upon the Cane Ridge, where the people came without the design of encamping, but where necessity required it. These meetings proceeded for two or three years, and great was the overthrow which resulted to all forms of infidelity. Of course there also ensued great divisions and heart-burnings among the different denominations. The Baptist, as well as the Presbyterian and Methodist churches largely participated; and all these churches were split up more or less after the abatement of the first great excitement. A good many of the people converted in these meetings became Shakers. A body of Shakers who came from Philadelphia and settled in Kentucky, received large recruits. One man, who had gathered about him what he call the twelve apostles, set off in search of the Holy Land, and died miserably of starvation on an island in the Mississippi. And various were the other fancies. One said he held converse with the angels and spirits, not after the modern use of rapping on tables, but orally and immediately; and that physical food was not absolutely indispensable to sustain his life. He also starved to death; and then his church broke up. As I say, there were various opinions as to these fruits and consequences; but I have been told by old men who have watched the current of affairs since then, for these fifty-five years, that the good results of that meeting were not to be calculated.

I now come to a more particular consideration of some of the men concerned in this movement. The ministry of the Methodist church of the wilderness assumed the position and the responsibility of their calling, under the confident belief that each man of them was specially called, designated, and sent forth by the Holy Spirit of peace and power as an ambassador for Christ. The churches decided upon the gifts and graces of the men; settled, according to their best belief and conviction, whether the call be a real call. If their opinion coincided with his, he was then set apart for the sacred office of the ministry, and sent forth. At the time of which I speak, he was sent forth to an office which was no sinecure. His field of labor was the world. The allowance, the limit of the salary which the discipline of the church allowed him to receive, was sixty-four dollars per annum, and that was to include all presents he might receive of yarn stockings, woollen vests, and homespun coats, together with wedding-fees. Whatever he might receive, from whatsoever quarter, was to be counted up in this allowance of four-and-sixty dollars, and if the amount exceeded this, the surplus must be handed over to the church authorities for the use of the *poorer* brethren. Out of these sixty-four dollars, he must provide a horse, saddle, wearing apparel, and books. West of the mountains sixty-four dollars was a sum hardly to be expected, either in silver coin of the realm, or in presents of any description. Nothing more was allowed a man with a wife than without a wife, for it was understood among the ministers of the old church, that a preacher had no business with a wife, and that he was a deal better without one. The practice in that respect has sadly changed. Mr. Wesley had such an experience of his own in the wife line, that he discouraged marrying among the brethren; and Francis Asbury, who was the master-spirit of Methodism on this continent, was so absorbed in his work, so engrossed by it, that he discountenanced matrimony. He said, nevertheless, that it was the business of every living man, to support a living woman. He therefore gave one-half or two-thirds of his entire income, which was very small, to the support of an old woman, a distant cousin in England; and when she died, he appropriated the sum to the support of some other woman. Further than that, in the direction of matrimony, he never went. When one of the young brethren was so unfortunate or so absurd as to link himself in matrimonial bonds, it was understood that he had better "locate," in the language of the church, still retaining authority to preach, but pursuing some other calling as a means of support, and deriving none from the church. He retired from regular itinerant work, and became a local preacher. Thus did brother Asbury set the example to the younger brethren. McKendree, who was his successor in the episcopate, in the same way discountenanced all interesting relations with the sisterhood.

There was thus small encouragement, indeed, in the way of pecuniary support, which these men had to look forward to. They were coming to the wilderness to face perils, want, weariness, unkindness, cold, and hunger; to hear the crack of the Indian rifle from some neighboring thicket, to feel the ball cutting the air as it whizzed past their ear, and perhaps to fall from the unerring shot of some skillful redskin. And if their lives were spared, by the guardianship of a good Providence, or the interposition of his special care in their behalf, the bare earth in winter and summer was three-fourths of the time to be their bed, their saddle their pillow, and the sky their coverlet. They labored without pecuniary compensation or support, preaching the Gospel often at their own cost and charges; and when applying for victuals or a shelter, often and often were they sternly or rudely denied it by a brother of some other denomination, so bitter were the prevailing feelings of party denominationalism. Thus they worked on, with no provision for their advancing years except the guardianship of the Master who had called them —with no prospective suushine of affluence to cheer their downward path to the grave—with none of the comforts of this world, save the approval of their own consciences and the indwelling testimony of God's Spirit. Surely such an office was not a sinecure; and men who could make a respectable living in the craft of blacksmithing, farming, carpentry, or masonry, could hardly have gone into this work, if they had not felt the irresistible impulse of a special call. They were not, as a general thing, men of what we now call education. Book knowledge was very scant with them. They were thorough students of their Bibles; and their Bibles they generally read upon their knees. It was a common habit with them to read the Good Book in the shelter of a thicket, or out upon the lonely prairie. When the snow was on the ground, the travelling preacher, awaking from his night's slumber as the first rays of daylight were breaking through the eastern sky, giving just enough light to see the page of the Sacred Book, would seldom saddle and mount his horse till he had performed his private devotions, kneeling there in the midst of the snow and ice where he had been sleeping; would seldom proceed upon his journey till he had committed his way and commended his soul to God, and had studied, at least three or four chapters of his constant companion and manual. They were diligent students of the holy Scriptures, and they were learned in hymns. They studied the hymnbook nearly as devoutly and constantly as the Bible; and with these two, they had an arsenal from which they could bring forth weapons adapted to every emergency. There was another supplement to their Scriptures. This third volume, one which they constantly, carefully, devoutly perused, profoundly studied, was the ever-open volume of Human Nature. They were well acquainted with men; they read their eyes, their countenances, their hearts, their consciences.

From this analysis, you will readily conclude what was their style of preaching. They were earnest and forcible speakers. They felt that great issues were at stake, standing, as they so often did, before a congregation of three or four thousand. They felt that all this great company of men and women in a little time must be dead; that perhaps this was the last time they should ever have the opportunity of speaking to them. The weight of souls was on them;

they felt that the blood of these people might rest on their own souls, unless their full and immediate duty was done to them; therefore, most earnestly, and even passionately to warn, to counsel, to entreat, to admonish, to reprove, to win them by the love of Christ to be reconciled to God—this was the burden of their preaching. They were men of quick, intense, and profound emotions, of lively fancy, and vivid imaginations; and before their inward eye was ever clearly pictured their expected final haven of repose and joy, the antithesis to this their present painful life of weariness and labor. And, upon the other hand, the dark and unfathomable abyss of perdition was open to them.

They were thorough students of other books than the Bible, when they had opportunity; and these were frequently, and even generally, of an imaginative description. Young and Milton were singularly intimate companions of these old wayfarers. Miltonic descriptions of perdition abounded in their preaching; and the Judgment, with all the solemn array of the last Assize, was vividly delineated before them. And while to our sober, cold, and calculating criticism, it might seem that their descriptions of the the good and bad world savored too much of a topographical character—as if they had been travelling through certain countries, and were now giving a vivid detail of all they had experienced—while it might seem so to us, it did not to the people who listened to them. They were rude and ignorant like them; unversed in books. They were stern in their denunciation of what they did not believe; and rose-water sentimentalism, agreeable metaphysical disquisitions, a profoundly elaborate exegesis upon particular passages of Scripture, would have gone but little way in influencing those congregations of backwoodsmen. I have read of a certain bishop who, on a text concerning the miracles at the Pool of Bethesda, said: "My beloved hearers, I shall in the first place speak to you of the things which you know, and I do not know; second, of what I know, and you do not know; third, of the things that neither of us know." There was another eminent prelate, who, upon reading his text, said: "I shall first speak of the chronology of the subject, then its topography, and then its psychology." Neither of these styles of preaching would have gone far with the backwoods people. Their earnest life, filled with necessities, and arduous struggles to supply them, must have appropriate religious food; and these simple-hearted, firmly-believing preachers were just the ones to give it to them. And give it they did, with right hearty good will.

There was an immense deal of *vim* and stamina in their method. They spoke loudly and with their whole body; their feet and hands were put in requisition as well as their tongues and eyes. It was a very fierce, cutting, and demonstrative style of preaching, as you may fancy. With little opportunities to get up splendid discourses—for they had no studies but the woods, and no libraries but those of which I have told you—they had to make their sermons as they were travelling along the way—and a hard and rugged way it often was.

Such a man was Bishop Asbury, to my mind one of the most important, if not the most important personage in the ecclesiastical history of this continent. With all respect to Jonathan Edwards, Dr. Dwight, Dr. Channing, and all the other eminent and pre-eminent men of New England—I have read them, and knew some of them—I think that Francis Asbury, that first superintendent and bishop of our Methodist church, was the most renowned and redoubtable soldier of the cross that ever advanced the standard of the Lord upon this continent. Yet you will not find his name in a single history of the United States that I know of; and it is a burning shame that it is so. He travelled for fifty years, on horseback, from Maine to Georgia, and from Massachusetts to the Far West, as population extended; journeying in that time, as was computed, about three hundred thousand miles. He had the care of all the churches; was preaching instant in season and out of season; was laboring indefatigably with the young men to inspire and stimulate them; winning back the lost and bringing amorphous elements into harmony, in a church which, when he began with it, in 1771, numbered probably not fifty members; and which, when he was an old man—he died in 1816—numbered, white and black, from Maine to California, and from far northwestern Oregon to sunny southern Florida, nearly a million of members. So vast a church did Francis Asbury build, almost solely by his own profound wisdom, untiring effort, and ceaseless devotion; and he did as much for building school-houses and colleges, erecting churches, establishing sound views of morality, and lofty purity in the forms of life; for gathering and establishing in doctrine and discipline this immense body of Christians, now the most numerous in the country, having more by one-third of stated ministers, and more colleges; than any other two denominations in the land. That one who has done this should not have had his name even so much as named in a single school history in the United States, I say is a shame.

This man was surrounded by men much akin to him; for he seemed to infuse his spirit into all with whom he came in contact. One of his associates and friends, one of the young men whom he raised up, was afterward a famous preacher of eastern Tennessee—James Axley, a very renowned man in his day; and another was James Craven. Many of those old preachers were bitterly opposed to whisky and slavery. Old brother Craven, when once preaching in the heart of Virginia, said, "Now here are a great many of you professors of religion; you are sleek, fat, good-looking, yet there is something the matter with you—you are not the thing you ought to be. Now you have seen wheat"—most of his hearers were farmers—"wheat which was very plump, round, and good-looking to the eye; but when you weighed it you found it only came to forty-five or forty-eight pounds to the bushel. There was something the matter. It should be from sixty to sixty three pounds. Take a grain of that wheat between your thumb and your finger; squeeze it, and out pops a weevil. Now, you good-looking Christian people only weigh, like the wheat, forty-five or forty-eight pounds to the bushel. What is the matter? When you are squeezed between the thumb of the law and the finger of the Gospel, out pops the negro and the whisky bottle." Old father Axley, preaching on one occasion, cried out, "Ah, yes! you sisters here at church look as sweet and smiling as if you were angels; and one of you says to me, 'Come to dinner,' and I go; and when I go, you say 'Sit down, brother Axley awhile, while I go about the dinner;' and you go to the kitchen, and I hear something crying out, "Don't, Missus," and I hear the sound of slaps, and the poor girl screaming, and the sister whaling and trouncing Sally in the kitchen as hard as she can. And when she has performed this office, she comes back looking as sweet and smiling as a summer's day, as if she had been saying her prayers. That is what you call Christianity, is it?" It was in this way that these old preachers preached. The style was adapted to the people. They understood this, where they could not have understood profound disquisitions respecting original sin. This old brother Axley was sent in 1806–7 into Attakapas County, Louisiana, to travel there as a missionary. He was about five feet eight inches in height, strong and sinewy, accustomed to all manner of exposure and suffering. Among this rude border populace, of whom a large component are French Catholics, he had not much to expect in the way of comfort. He had no money, was very hungry, and indeed reduced nearly to starvation, when he came riding up to a plantation. They knew him by his coat to be a preacher, and they wanted none such in their houses. The old gentleman entered and asked if he could have a dinner and supper and night's lodging.

"No."

The only persons present were a widow lady and some children and black people.

"No," said the woman, "you cannot; we don't want any such cattle here."

Here, then, was a prospect of sleeping another night out in the cold. He had nothing to eat, and perhaps he ran an actual risk of perishing by starvation. He thought of the lonely journey, and of the perils that compassed it. Then his faith lifted him to the better, brighter world of heaven, its rest and reward for the wayfarer; and he thought of the good Father, and of the angels that are sent to succor and minister, and his heart presently filled with overflowing gladness; and he struck up a hymn, for he was a great singer. These men were all great singers, and when they could not carry a point by speech, they often fell back upon a song:

"Peace, my soul! Thou needst not fear
Thy great Provider still is near,
Who fed thee last will feed thee still!
Be still, and sink into his will."

He went on with his song, and, looking about him, saw that he was gaining ground. He sang three hymns, and by that time the woman and all the children and negroes were crowding to hear him, with tears in their eyes.

As he concluded, the old lady shouted, "Pete, put up the gentleman's horse! Girls, have a good supper for the preacher!" And thus the preacher was lodged and fed for a song.

Axley came to Baltimore to attend a general conference in 1820. There was a dispute about a technical question—whether presiding elders should be elected by preachers or not; and there had been a great deal of warm, not to say hot discussion about it. Brother Axley was silent. He did not say a word, until at the end of the session, the bishop called upon him to offer a prayer. He knelt to lead the devotions, and began thus: "Now, O Lord, thou knowest what a time we have had discussing, arguing, about this elder question; and thou knowest what our feelings are; we do not care what becomes of the team—it is only who drives the oxen."

He used the directest mode of getting to the centre of a subject. He preached among a people who were sharpshooters, and who practised driving a nail with their rifles at fifty yards. And as they practised close and sharp-shooting with the rifle, so did he with his tongue.

There is an old friend of mine, my first presiding elder, yet living in Illinois—Peter Cartwright—who was one of those old preachers in the West, and has many of their peculiarities. I may give you one incident of this man's life, as a specimen of their physical courage and prowess; for it was sometimes necessary for them to fight with carnal weapons, and many of them had obstinate combats with the rough pioneer people—and commonly came off victorious. Cartwright, in common with most of those early old preachers, was a strong opponent of slavery. Now the question was being canvassed in Illinois, between 1818 and 1823, whether this institution should be ingrafted upon the Constitution, when the State was applying for admission into the Union. The old gentleman resolved to remove to Illinois, and take a hand in the quarrel. He had been living in Kentucky and Tennessee, and had preached there for a quarter of a century, when he was appointed to Illinois as presiding elder, and had a circuit from Galena on the northwest, to Shawnee-town on the south—a district nearly as great as the entire country of England. Around this he was to travel once in three months, at a time when there were no roads, scarcely a bridge or ferry—and keep his regular appointments to preach, Sunday after Sunday, besides attending love-feasts, and administering the sacraments. Then, after preaching on the Sunday, he would generally announce a stump speech for the Monday, and call upon his fellow-citizens to come and hear the question discussed, whether slavery should be admitted or not. Of course, taking a political side, he was regarded as a politician, and there was a good deal of angry feeling about the old preacher. On one occasion, he rode to a ferry upon the Sangamon River; the country about was rather thickly populated, and he found a crowd of people about the ferry, which seemed to be a sort of gathering place for discussing politics. The ferryman, a great herculean fellow, was holding forth at the top of his voice about an old renegade, one Peter Cartwright, prefixing a good many adjectives to his name and declaring that if he ever came that way he would drown him in the river.

Cartwright, who was unknown to any one there, now coming up, said: "I want you to put me across."

"You can wait till I am ready," said the ferryman.

Cartwright knew it was of no use to complain; and the ferryman, when he had got through his speech, signified his readiness to take him over. The preacher rode his horse into the boat, and the ferryman commenced to row across. All Cartwright wanted was fair play; he wished to make a public exhibition of this man, and, moreover, was glad of an opportunity to state his principles. About half way over, therefore, throwing his bridle over the stake on one side of the boat, he told the ferryman to lay down his pole.

"What's the matter?" asked the man.

"Well," said he, "you have just been using my name improper, and saying that if I ever came this way, you would drown me in the river. I'm going to give you a chance."

"Are you Peter Cartwright?"

"Yes."

And the ferryman, nothing loath, pulls in his pole, and at it they go. They grapple in a minute, and Cartwright being very agile as well as athletic, succeeds in catching him by the nape of the neck and the slack of the breeches, and whirls him over. He souses him down under the tide, while the companions of the vanquished ferryman look on, the distance insuring fair play. Cartwright souses him under again, and raising him, says: "I baptize thee in the name of the Devil, whose child thou art." He thus immerses him thrice, and then drawing him up again, inquires: "Did you ever pray?"

"No," answered the ferryman, strangling and choking and dripping in a pitiful manner.

"Then it's time you did," says Cartwright; "I'll teach you: say 'Our Father who art in Heaven.'"

"I won't," says the ferryman.

Down he goes under water again, for quite a time. Then lifting him out, "Will you pray, now?"

The poor ferryman, nearly strangled to death, wanted to gain time, and to consider the terrors.

"Let me breathe and think," he said.

"No," answers the relentless preacher, "I won't; I'll make you," and he immerses him again. At length he draws him out, and asks a third time, "Will you pray now?"

"I will do anything," was the subservient answer. So Cartwright made him repeat the Lord's Prayer.

"Now let me up," demanded this unwilling convert.

"No," says Cartwright, "not yet. Make me three promises: that you will repeat that prayer every morning and night; that you will put every Methodist preacher across this ferry free of expense; and that you will go to hear every one that preaches within five miles, henceforth."

The ferryman, all helpless, barely alive and thoroughly cowed, promised; and Cartwright went on his way.

That ferryman joined the church afterward, and became quite an eminent and useful member.

Peter Cartwright, I say, was my own presiding elder. This is a veracious story; and I might go on for pages giving you anecdotes of these Methodists, their peculiar powers, their odd original ways, their methods, their perils, and their success. They were an urgent sort of people: very pressing, deadly in earnest—their souls were firmly convinced of the truth of what they were saying—there was no evasion, equivocation, or doubt about it; they therefore spoke straight to the mark, and did what they had to do. They had their faults and their defects, no doubt. Who has not? Doubtless they may have been lacking in niceties and elegances—the refinements and beauties of civilized society; but they were adapted to their condition and exactly filled their station. It is much the practice to ridicule ministers of the Gospel; to treat them decently as it were out of pity, as debilitated beings, half-way between women and children—with a kind of condescension and patronage. And the question is often asked, with what is meant to be tremendous emphasis and overpowering sarcasm, "What have the ministers done; and what are they doing now?" I beg leave to say in their behalf that they ask neither patronage nor condescension; neither compassion nor pity. They are able to do their own work, and have done it; and if your country along this Atlantic seaboard fails to furnish abundant and superabundant evidence of their possession of the noblest elements of the ministerial character—sublime courage, indomitable energy, daring self-forgetfulness, lofty, ardent, absorbing, and efficient Christian piety—then I say go west of the mountains, and in those noble pioneers who bore to the starving and perishing multitudes in the wilderness the means of grace—who hastened when most need was, not waiting for mere human helps, bringing manna, such as was at hand, and amply sufficient for spiritual food, here and hereafter—go and find among them some of the sublimest elements of human character that this or any other country ever furnished. These constitute a most complete and unanswerable refutation of the mean, and base, and slanderous insinuations which are so unhappily current throughout a large portion of our society.

Perhaps I cannot more appropriately conclude this lecture than by giving a hasty summary of the life and character of one of the more prominent of the early western preachers; and for the same natural reason already alleged, my instance will be taken from among those of the Methodist denomination.

Of Bishop Asbury I have barely spoken, and of his abundant labors. That mere mention must on this occasion suffice.

Peter Cartwright, also already alluded to, a man yet enjoying a green and vigorous and useful old age, and one of the most characteristic and efficient of the western pioneer preachers, was born in Amherst County, Virginia, in 1785, the son of a Revolutionary soldier; was taken to Kentucky by his parents a few years afterward, when they settled there; and was brought up in Logan County, a district so wild, wicked, and infested with desperadoes and refugee criminals, as to be popularly known in that region as "Rogues' Harbor." A strong, active, sharp-witted, jovial young fellow, he grew up a horse-racer and gambler, in embryo at least, and went on until he was sixteen, in the high road to all the vices of that rude and lawless period and community. Then he was suddenly converted, with one of the inexplicable convulsive changes which we hardly dare consider or seek to analyze, lest on one hand we find delusion, or on the other prove deficient in reverence for the operations of the Holy Spirit. He sold his race-horse, burned his cards, fasted and prayed, read the Bible, and after laboring under fearful anguish for months, at last, at one of the numerous camp-meetings held in consequence of the great gathering at Cane Ridge, found peace in believing, by another revulsion as sudden as that which had plunged him into an agony of remorse and dread three months before. He joined the Methodist church in 1801; that body then numbering, in the Mississippi Valley, about two thousand five hundred souls, all told. It contained in 1787 just about ninety-five souls. Now it contains, within the same territorial limits, not less than three quarters of a million.

Cartwright was licensed as an exhorter in 1802, and as a preacher six years afterward. From that time until this, for more than fifty years, he has been a steadfast and most efficient laborer in his chosen field. The brief summary which he gives in his autobiography—one of the most entertaining books ever written—of the totals of his work, may be condensed somewhat as follows: His entire loss by non-receipt of the regular Methodist allowance—formerly eighty dollars a year, all over that sum to be handed over to the church—and by robbery, casualties, etc., $6,000; extras received to offset against this, $2,000; amount of money given in charity, etc., $2,300; number received into the church, 10,000; number baptized, children and adults, 12,000; funeral sermons preached, 500; total number of sermons preached, at least 14,600.

The crowded years of this long and busy life were marked from week to week with the strangest occurrences, the natural results of the wild unfettered thoughts and life of the West; often most grotesque and at first sight coarse, and even ridiculous, silly or absurd to an eastern man; and yet requiring but a brief consideration to discover how peculiarly fit and proper were the rough repartees and even the comical tricks, practical jokes, and ready physical force with which this hardy soldier of the church militant upheld his authority, or silenced his opponents at camp-meetings, or in controversy with the ignorant fanatics, the deceivers, and the rabid sectarians of his rugged field.

When a Baptist preacher was drawing off his converts, he drove him away by joining his band of believers in character of a Christian, and then at the place of immersion confounding him by suddenly leaving him the alternative of admitting him into the church unimmersed, or taking the responsibility of denying him Christian fellowship unless rebaptized.

His old-fashioned Methodist hatred for fashionable ornaments comes quaintly out in his story of a rich man, who could not find peace in believing until he had torn off his shirt-ruffles and thrown them down in the straw at the camp-meeting; after which, "in less than two minutes God blessed his soul, and he sprang to his feet, loudly praising God!"

A "book-learned" minister once tried to confound him by addressing him in Greek. With ready wit he listened, as if intelligently, and replied at some length in the backwoods German, which he had learned in his youth, which the other took for Hebrew, and was confounded. And the old man proceeds to compare the educated preachers he had seen to a "gosling with the straddles."

The camp-meetings were almost always infested by rowdies, who often organized under a captain and did all in their power to break up the exercises by noise, personal violence, liquor-selling and drinking, riotous conduct, stealing horses and wagons, and all manner of annoyances. Once Cartwright blocked their game by appointing their captain himself to the business of preserving order. Again, the captain of the rowdies was struck down among the "mourners" just as he had come quietly up to hang a string of frogs round the preacher's neck. Once he confronted their chief with a club, knocked him off his horse, and as his discouraged companions fled, secured him and had him fined fifty dollars. Once he captured the whisky which the rowdies were drinking, and when they came up at night to stone the the preacher's tent, he had already been among them in disguise and learned their plan, and singly drove them all off with a sudden sharp volley of pebbles.

Again, he sent a liquor-seller to jail for selling on the camp-ground, had himself and four bold friends summoned by the timid officer as a posse, and never left the culprit until he had paid fine and costs; and when the enraged rowdies undertook to beat up the preacher's quarters at night, he drove off one of their leaders by hitting him a violent blow with a "chunk of fire," and another with a smart stroke on the head with a club, which drove out his "dispensation of mischief." At another time, he had himself and five stout men summoned by a frightened peace-officer, secured a whisky-seller who had been rescued by his fellows, then took the deputy-sheriff, who would have ordered the prisoner released, and seizing thirteen more of the mob, had them all fined, or made to give security on an appeal. One more whisky-dealer, who kept a loaded musket by him, the shrewd and fearless Cartwright secured by night in his own wagon, scared him handsomely, fired off his musket, threw away his powder, and drove him away, beaten and ashamed.

Discussing doctrines with a boastful Baptist presbyter, he silenced him with a question witty and ingenious, whether its implication is true or not, viz.: "If there are no children in hell, and all young children who die go to heaven, is not that church which has no children in it more like hell than heaven?"

Coming to a new circuit, he found at his first appointment but one solitary hearer, and he a one-eyed man; but preached his very best to him for three-quarters of an hour. At his next coming, this hearer had so sounded his praises that he had a large attendance, and a great revival followed.

When a certain woman used to disturb his class-meetings, he hoisted her out of doors by main force, and then held the door shut by standing inside with his back to it, while he went on with the exercises. When a fat and unbelieving old lady troubled him at camp-meeting by kicking her daughters as they knelt to pray among the "mourners," he caught her dexterously by the foot and tipped her over backward among the benches, where she bustled about a long time to get up, because of her size, while the victorious preacher went straight on with his exhorting. There was a dance at an inn where he stopped, and no room to sit in but the ball-room. A young girl politely asked him to dance with her. He led her out on the floor, and as the fiddler was about to strike up, said to the company that it was his custom to ask God's blessing on all undertakings, and he would do this now. Instantly dropping on his knees, he pulled his partner down too, and prayed until the fiddler fled in fright, and some of the dancers wept or cried for mercy; then proceeded to exhort and sing hymns, and did not cease his labors until he he had organized a Methodist church of thirty-two members, and made the landlord class-leader.

A grey-haired old man, a Baptist, whose custom it was to do so, once interrupted the amusing stories he was dealing out to his congregation, by calling out sternly, "Make us cry, make us cry; don't make us laugh!" With equal sternness, and turning short and sharp upon him, Cartwright instantly answered, "I don't hold the puckering strings of your mouths, and I want you to mind the negro's eleventh commandment, and that is, 'Every man mind his own business.'" The abashed old man was silent.

While Cartwright was candidate for the Legislature of Illinois, he sought out a man who had spread a slanderous story that he had tried to escape paying a note, by perjury. Finding him in a public place in a crowd, he told him to acknowledge his falsehood there and then, or he would "sweep the streets with him to his heart's content." The coward acknowledged his lie; and if he had not, the fearless preacher would surely have chastised him as he promised. While he was in the House, afterward, an enraged opponent threatened to knock him down if he finished a certain course of remark. Cartwright finished it, and when the House adjourned, marched straight up to him and asked him if he was for peace or war?

"Oh, for peace," was the answer; "come home and take tea with me." So they went, arm in arm; and when the company, including the governor and his wife, were about to eat without asking a blessing, Cartwright said plainly, "Governor, ask a blessing." The official blushed, apologized, and requested the preacher to do it, which he did.

He once had a discussion with an infidel, who ruled the Bible out of evidence; to which Cartwright submitted, and in his turn would have ruled Tom Paine out. And when his adversary flew into a rage at this, and cursed and blasphemed, the preacher in his turn filled with righteous wrath, seized him by the head and jaw, and rattled his teeth together like so many pebbles. The angry man would have struck him, but was prevented, and afterward became his friend.

But the time would fail me to relate the innumerable singular experiences of this wonderful old man. Such as he are the real pioneers of Methodism in the Mississippi Valley; strong, fearless, active, ready, quick-witted, jovial, even humorous and jocular, rough, as able as the best in a free fight, yet kindly, pure, sensible, fatherly, benevolent, unwearied in self-sacrifice and well-doing; wise in counsel, thoroughly practical, yet the personification of idealists in their prompt appreciation of whatever was proper for their use, whether fashionable or not; often set in some narrow prejudice and bitterly sectarian, yet broad and liberal in views of church government, and showing and wielding with effect all the qualities which constitute rulers of men. And above all, filled and overflowing with the love of Christ and the ardent desire to save souls. Such were Peter Cartwright and his noble brethren of the early church of the wilderness.

I might occupy pages in commemorating the noble and admirable qualities of others of the great Methodist leaders; of Henry B. Bascom, the young Apollo of the West, the lofty orator, and noble useful Christian and minister; of the veteran preacher James B. Finley; of many others of the great army of devoted men, some now gone to their last account, some yet living and laboring among us—still at work within my own beloved church. But I must close. Whole volumes have already been written upon the lives of Cartwright, Bascom, Finley, and others. It would be presumptuous and useless to attempt more in this place than this passing allusion.

Lecture IX.

WESTERN MIND;

ITS MANIFESTATIONS,

ELOQUENCE AND HUMOR.

WESTERN MIND:

ITS MANIFESTATIONS, ELOQUENCE AND HUMOR.

The query was propounded in the "Edinburgh Review" more than a quarter of a century ago, "Who reads an American book?" The question has been often asked, both on this and on the other side of the Atlantic, why have we not an American literature? I should now hardly be willing to concede that we have not. It would be a strangely ignorant or prejudiced Englishman who would pretend that we had not. And yet it would not be strange if we had not. The demands upon American mind have been of too pressing and urgent a character to allow it to devote much time or attention to the specific pursuit of letters. Here was a continent to subdue; a wilderness to be reclaimed; mountains to be scaled; lakes, oceans and gulfs to be joined together; and meantime the supplies for daily necessity and daily consumption to be raised, and conveyed to market. Men must have bread before books. Men must build barns before they establish colleges. Men must learn the language of the rifle, the axe and the plough, before they learn the lessons of Grecian and Roman philosophy and history; and to those pursuits was the early American intellect obliged to devote itself, by a sort of simple and hearty and constant consecration. There was no possibility of escape; no freedom or exemption from this obligation. The early settlers had to solve the imperative instant questions of present want; problems that were urging themselves upon their attention with every day, and with every recurring season. When the forest is felled, and the soil is turned, and the granaries are established, and the mouths of wives and little ones filled, and their bodies clad, then may American intellect betake itself to the study and making of books.

These remarks apply to the sea-board here, as much as to the interior. We are comparatively a young people. Agriculture, commerce, manufactures—the earliest practical problems of society—though now in somewhat more developed forms, must still be studied. And if this is true of the country east of the mountains, how much more emphatically and peculiarly is it true of that west of the mountains! The former is an old country in comparison with the latter. The earliest settlers of our race established themselves there only in 1770—only ninety years ago—a brief space in a nation's life. And how vast and various were the tasks which at once presented themselves to the few settlers, demanding instant and constant fulfillment, and threatening death if neglected. A boundless territory, to which the land lying east of the mountains is scarce more than a drop in the bucket, was to be wrested by sturdy and long-continued labor from the dominion of nature, freed from savage beasts, and made the cultivated fruitful home of civilized society. Tillable and arable fields, homes, gardens, towns, were all to be acquired by a series of laborious victories over the unresisting, yet opposing forces of nature.

Again: the men who did this must also maintain and cultivate and protect the structure of social life, by framing something—whether rude or elaborate matters not so much—but something in the nature of a body of laws, and a system of government. The crude and scanty means of educating the young and preaching the Gospel were also to be afforded; but I need only mention them.

And still further: all this had to be done in the presence of a class of perils dreadful beyond anything conceivable by the citizens who now dwelt so securely under the shadow of strong municipal and State organizations, and whose very recital makes the flesh creep, and the blood run cold. I mean the Indian and British hostilities, which were so long such a terrible and incessant drain upon the vigor and the very life-blood of the infant western commonwealths. Such requirements drew heavily upon all the functions of body, mind and heart; chiefly however upon the first. For the first task of a new nation, as I have shown, is for the muscles and sinews. Only when this is fulfilled comes the demand upon the brain and upon the soul.

But the western people have been steadily rising in the path thus indicated, for many years. In common with the older communities east of the mountains, they have been rising and advancing in the pilgrimage of humanity, up from the region of muscular development and animal activity, to that of intellectual and moral culture. Such progress can never be rapid. Life's great tasks are not achieved in a hurry. Personal culture is the work of time; and it is only in him who descends from a line of cultivated ancestors, that the highest exhibition of human attainments, ordinarily speaking, is possible. Much more is this true of a race—of a nation.

Around the early settler lay the broad shadows of the primeval forests. Beneath him was the rich turf that had never been disturbed by a coulter; and around him the solemn primeval groves that had never reverberated to the sound of the axe—where only the deafening yell of the savage war-whoop had disturbed the silence, and where only the dreadful carnage of savage warfare had discolored the soil. He possessed broad streams, matchless in beauty, and a soil rich beyond measure; vacant; only awaiting occupancy; and returning the largest product and profit to the tiller's energy and industry. In this lovely country, cabin homes were to be erected, and the forms of social and civil organization to be established.

These things were rapidly done. And is this a little thing? Do you call this an insignificant product of a nation's brains; a trifling net result of a nation's activity? The erection of such a government as that whose blessings we now enjoy, where every man, the humblest, the poorest — where every child, though an outcast and alien, sits secure beneath the broad and certain ægis of our national liberties, our national freedom, our national jurisprudence and police—do you call this, indeed, a small result? We have whittled out, amongst us, constitutions for one-and-thirty confederated States. The vast genius and learning, the still vaster skill and talent, all the combined energies of France, month after month, and year after year, endeavored to construct a constitution; and how has it failed! It failed first, a little after our own Constitution went into successful operation; and it has been failing almost ever since. But what we have to show is a noble result of the labor of a nation's brains. If we had never written a book, if we had never penned a line save those which are found in our Congressional debates, and statute-books and Constitutions, I take it that we have nevertheless built one of the grandest intellectual pyramids the sun ever yet shone upon. This is not a tribute to national vanity; it is a just statement of a nation's claims.

And now these settlers, hardy, intrepid, unkempt, unwashed backwoodsmen, betake themselves to their business as law-makers. And in this, as in every other business they proceed with a certain eager earnestness, a kind of rapt enthusiasm. If they are to be law-makers, they will be law-makers in deed and in truth; and there shall be no shilly-shally, no child's play, no trifling about it. The laws may be simple, and even seasoned with a spice of grim comicality; but they are stringent, direct, and effective. There was one, for example, at an early day in the West, that no man should be allowed to remain in that region who had not some visible and honorable means of support. Every man must have work to do, and must be doing it, sufficient to procure him the money, or the money's worth, which is necessary in order to live. There came into one of the new States where this law was in force, a young man who seemed to have no employment. His hands were in his pockets, and his mouth puckered to a whistle, and that seemed his business in this life. Some of the old gentlemen of the vicinity informed him that they had a statute of this description on their books, and that he must find some occupation, or he had better go to some other and idler country. But he fancied, as some of our young folks to-day are apt to do, that they were a set of incapable old fogies, who set an absurd over-value upon their laws and constitution, and that they were not to be heeded. In his coat pocket was the secret of his living—a pack of greasy cards, intc the mystery of the manipulation of which he proposed to initiate all the young men of the place; winning their money, corrupting their morals, and debauching their dispositions; and then to "gang his gate" as a missionary of the devil, onward to other regions, to repeat the same operation. At the expiration, however, of the notice served by the old fogy gentlemen, a writ was, to his astonishment, served upon him by an officer, and he was carried to the "jug," as they metaphorically called the jail, putting the end for the means, I fancy, because they saw clearly enough that the jug generally brings people there. Having deposited him here for safe keeping, due advertisement was made, and the young man, in pursuance of the quaint penalty attached to this law, was marched out into the middle of the public square, and set up on the horse block, where the sheriff, as auctioneer, knocked him down to the highest bidder. This fortunate person was the village blacksmith, who forthwith put a chain round his leg and took him to his smithy, where for three months, from six o'clock in the morning till six in the evening our young friend was inducted, with some exertion on the blacksmith's part, and much more on his own, into the whole art and mystery of blowing and striking; and was deposited for safe keeping every night in the jail. At the expiration of his time, the young man, liberated from his confinement, shook off the dust of that town from his shoes, and as he turned his back to the place, swore it was the meanest country that a white man ever got into.

Their laws, I say, may have been strict, and the execution of them may have been stringent and swift enough; for oftentimes the only sheriff was the ready rifle, resting upon the pummel of the saddle, and the only judge, the awful Judge Lynch, who held his dread tribunal under the shadow of the first tree, and whose decrees were executed without appeal, bill of exceptions, new trial, recommitment, respite or pardon, by stalwart men, who swung the culprit up by a rope led over the branch of a tree, instantly after judgment given.

The law of these new countries, whether codified and written by select wise men, or dictated by the clear but rough conclusions of the untutored shrewd conscience and commonsense of the community, must be enforced, and judgments under it executed. For laws not enforced are hotbeds of crime. The case here was urgent, the pressure instant; and the conduct of such courts of "Regulators" as very commonly administered this prompt rude justice, though it seems, compared to our civilized and refined notions, harsh and barbarous in the extreme, was, in truth, the only possible means of securing any legal sanctions, any punishment for guilt or protection for innocence. For these new settlements were an Alsatia to which there gathered all the vagabonds, ruffians, swindlers, thieves, criminals of every name, whose evil deeds had made the older settlements too hot to hold them, and who trusted to renew a safer course of guilt among the wild forests and thinly scattered settlements. Society must and will protect itself; and until better means are provided, it will use those which are at hand. It has always been so since Cain, the murderer, felt that every man that found him would slay him, and since the hand of every man was against the first outlaw, Ishmael. It has always been so, down to the day when we have seen great cities rid, only by such rude and lamentable means, of bands of villians impregnable to their laws. It will be well for our own great Republic to remember this; for precisely as our voters cease to consider thoughtfully, decide carefully, vote wisely, and act decisively—precisely as they shall fail in their great political duty of making good laws, choosing good men to enforce them, and then watching sharply over the good laws and the good men too—just in that same measure, for every neglect do we take a step backward toward the law of the strong hand, social dismemberment, and barbarism.

Besides the law-making or law-enforcing assemblies of these rude foresters, whether more or less formal, the militia musters afforded another favorite opportunity for these social and genial people to gather themselves together. There was fighting, and desperate fighting too, in their midst or on their borders, for half a century and more after their first settlements. This long experience resulted in a decided tendency to military organizations and amusements; and these drills and gatherings were punctually attended, and all the exercises of the occasion strictly and earnestly obeyed, both on account of their vast practical importance, and as a gratification of their military instincts. Such "public bandings," as they were called by a local synonym of the "trainings" and "musters" of other States and all similar gatherings, were eagerly made use of by politicians; a class of men who very early became numerous and active in the West.

Perhaps this circumstance may be said to have produced the first manifestations of western mind, and one of its most prominent and characteristic ones,—viz.: oral political addresses—stump speeches, so called. This name was derived from the platform most commonly used by the orators of the back woods, whose actual or intended constituents, as the case might be, could not be troubled with the elaborate niceties of desks or boarded rostrums, and who, by a most natural ascent, usually occupied a stump, the convenient Pnyx of every country square or court-house green. These ambitious aspirants, commonly not much if at all more learned than their rugged auditory, and superior to them only in shrewdness, or desire of office, or impudence, or all, neither needed nor could use any subtle trains of reasoning or lofty sublimities of thought. Any excessive tumefactions of speech often collapsed ignominiously at the prick of some stinging joke, probably bearing no particular relation to the speaker's speech, and applicable only because successful. Thus, a well-known anecdote of one of these windy gentlemen relates that he was quite overthrown at the summit of a gorgeous flight of eloquence, and left to slink dumbfounded from the stage, because an unscrupulous adversary of tropes and figures bawled out at his back, "Guess he wouldn't talk quite so hifalutenatin' if he knowed how his breeches was torn out behind!" The horrified orator, deceived for an instant, clapped a hand to the part indicated, and was destroyed—overwhelmed in inextinguishable laughter.

But a trifling misadventure did not always upset the speaker. Thus, one of them who had let fly that favorite fowl of orators, the American eagle, was tracing his magnificent flight into the uppermost empyrean. He followed the wondrous bird with ecstatic eye and finger raised; and as he cried out, "Don't you see him, fellow-citizens, a risin' higher and higher?"—an unsophisticated "fellow-citizen," in his immense simplicity, confiding that there was a real eagle, and gazing intently in vain to behold him, sung out, "Well, d—d if I can see him!" "Hoss!" exclaimed the speaker, transfixing the matter-of-fact man with his gaze and his gesture, and speaking in the same oratorical magnificence of tone—"Hoss! I was a speakin' in a figger!" And off he went again with his eagle; his promptness and seriousness in the two transitions effectually shutting out any ridicule.

This audience was of men whose physique had been cultivated at the expense of much of their intellect; whose sense was not proper but common; whose knowledge had not come from books, but from the hard necessities and incessant exertions of a laborious and perilous life. The speaker, then, must use their vernacular—a vernacular which we should think vulgar—and his metaphors and similes, if he used them at all, must be such as would readily penetrate beneath their tangled hair, and find lodgment in their intellects. And he must, at the same time, appeal to their feelings; for the feelings exercise a much quicker and surer power over the intellect, than the intellect over the feelings. He could not, accordingly, stand still and merely emit his words as a fountain passively pours out water, for he who would move his audience must be moved himself. It would never do for him to stand and read off a written paper, first looking at the audience and then back to his manuscript. It is the eye which wields the speaker's power over an assembly. If you would affect any man, your eyes must meet his. If you would transfuse into him your thought, your feeling, your passion, your imagination, your poetry, —if, in a word, you would transfuse your life into him, your eye must meet his; in the forcible old Scripture phrase, you must "see eye to eye." And, as it is with one man, so it is with many. For the manner of the word is powerful, much more than the word itself. It is not the brains which produce results, it is the individual, the being, the self, the I, behind them; the manner of the speaking clothes the spoken words with whatever of power or beauty is exerted or shown by the speaker. It is the power of the orator accordingly, his earnestness, his profound conviction, his intense realization of his truth, his yearning desire to transfer his conciousness of it to the hearers, which, as it were, throws it red-hot into their minds and hearts. They receive it; and the sensation or emotion which spreads among them as he speaks, flashes back to him from their kindling eyes; and his strength, which he has sent out to them, comes back to him, grown gigantic with the strength of thousands; and now he speaks in the power of a thousand souls instead of one; and the flux and reflux of mutual influence, as managed for his purposes by the intellect of the speaker, thus become the means and the measure of his power over himself and them. Thus it is, that the rude fellow upon the barbarous backwoods hustings, who overflows with language ungrammatical and unrhetorical, whose address fairly bristles with odd phrases and border lingo, becomes a prophet clothed in garments of supernatural power, and leads his audience, willing captives, whithersoever he lists, till, like the ancient Franks when they made a king, they bear him on their shoulders to his triumph.

Such a people, not trained to logic nor disciplined in reasoning; who proceed by common sense, practical prudence, ordinary business forecast, and acquaintance with the men and things and principles of everyday life, yet of excitable passions and feelings, and who are only to be effectully appealed to by a speaker of the kind I have attempted to describe, and who is, in their phrase, "dead in earnest," are passing through a mental discipline preliminary to the higher walks of literature, and to the development of the nobler moral faculties.

And this first manifestation of western mind—in their peculiar spoken eloquence, is always the same; whether before a jury, on the stump, at the camp-meeting, at a militia muster, a barbacue, a corn-husking, a house-raising, a log-rolling, a wedding or a quilting—for the constituency is always the same—is unvarying and universal. The man who would move them, would fuse their minds into one homogeneous subjection to his will, no matter what his other subordinate or collateral attainments, must always have these elementary primal powers; the power to say whatever he has to say clearly and forcibly, and the power of saying it with the strength of conviction, earnestness and intense enthusiasm.

The men of the East, trained to a colder style of speech, who demand a reason for every thought submitted to them; who have had the discipline of two studious and orderly centuries this side the Atlantic; who are under the organic influence of so many generations dwelling among churches and school-houses and printing-presses—a discipline which is a great privilege, a benign heritage, yea, even a benediction from above upon them—can scarcely conceive and could not at all comprehend the influence which one of these western orators exerts upon his audience, or its gladdening and rejoicing effect upon his own nature; nor how the people gather and throng around him and revel in his speech as an unbought, unpurchaseable pleasure, one of the rarest of life.

This rough people, born and bred in the wilderness, has, after the universal human fashion, expressed a characteristic and interesting representation of its traits and tendencies in its language. For there is, so to speak, a western Anglo-American language, corresponding singularly and strictly with the western style of thought, and the character of western men. This language is thickly studded with rude proverbial forms, all redundant with wild untrained metaphors, some of which, if you please, we will call cant and slang. But all these phrases have a meaning, often quaintly and curiously expressed; and they have usually sprung spontaneously out of the associations or necessities of the speakers' lives. Or, again, they are as freely and naturally the outgrowth of the minds that produce them, as is the luxuriant cane of the strong deep rich soil of the brakes; not drawn or pressed forth by forces from outside, but the free fantastic blossoms of untaught spontaneous thoughts.

To this western language, as well as to the thought that threw it out, fun and humor gave a color almost predominant. Even in the hardest and sternest periods of their history, when the crack of the rifle and whiz of the tomahawk were constantly in their ears, they relished fun to the last and most exquisite degree. A vein of humor runs through all the nature of this people. They may seem stern, even savage; sombre, and even sorrowful; self-possessed and quiet; and all these they are, at times, perhaps often. But not constantly; they are moved by the influence of the occasion, and carried out from these serious frames of mind. But they are jovial and fun-loving, always; and whatever their circumstances, they will have, from time to time, a season of such utter heart-felt relaxation as sometimes to border on license; where the most uproarious jollity and glee is the order of the day. There is a curious entry in the diary of George Rogers Clark, made during a visit to Kentucky at a time when the whites were suffering greatly from the attacks of the savages, showing how this characteristic struck the hardy soldier: "25th July, 1776. Lieut. Lynn was married this day at Harrod's Station"—remember that in all that year there was not a day when the neighborhood of Harrod's Station was free from the presence of hostile savages—"and the merry-making was absolutely marvellous." Old Bishop Asbury, who made a journey into the same region in 1783 or 1784, while the Indian fighting was still going on, and the people were pressed to the uttermost, says, "It is marvellous to see how the desire for matrimony reigneth in this country." The entrances upon these matrimonial speculations, so heartily ventured upon by the young people—by the girls generally at fifteen and the boys at seventeen—were invariably made the occasions for the jolliest and most thoroughgoing fun.

The negroes were *ex officio*, as ever, lovers of jokes and fun, and even in time of war were as cool and as inclined to jollity as their reckless masters. One of them, who was out along with his master and a band of foresters in hot pursuit of a party of Indians, who had committed an outrage upon some lonely cabin or blockhouse, made an observation which still remains on record; a simple speech enough, but which may serve to illustrate my point. The pursuers gained sight of the Indians while descending a hill. As the foremost of the whites was hastening forward, closely followed by the warlike Sambo, the captain of the whites, observing that the Indians greatly outnumbered his force, gave the low whistle which was the signal of retreat. Sambo, however, heedless of the unwelcome order of recall, pressed on down the hill with his white companion, and taking shelter in a thicket, observed an immense Indian peering above the hill beyond, to reconnoitre the position of the pursuers, his head just visible from behind the trunk of a tree. Sambo raises his rifle and blazes away at him, singing out at the top of his voice, "Dar! Take dat to remember Sambo the black white man!" and then retraces his steps.

Even the Indians, usually reckoned so sombre and saturnine a race, were by no means destitute of a very peculiar dry and quaint humor. Indeed, it is beyond doubt that in the social security of their far and peaceful homes in the wilderness, they laughed and chatted and joked, and sung and told stories with as much glee, and careless, happy delight, as any civilized circles. But though the indications of their possession of wit and humor are equally well authenticated, they are much rarer. A good specimen of Indian humor, without any such intention on the part of the savage, was a remark made by one of them while the fearful earthquakes of 1811–12 were devastating the valleys of the Mississippi and Ohio, and the wildest and most terrific freaks of nature were being exhibited in many portions of that vast area. While New Madrid seemed sinking bodily into the abyss, and the bed of the vast Mississippi River was undergoing an absolute change of location, its great floods rushing through the monstrous chasms which opened a new and strange path for the waters, while the great trees were rocking to and fro, trembling and falling, and the earth gaped in bottomless rents, the savage stood cool and stoical, his arms folded upon his breast, gazing upon the scene. A white man addressed him with the inquiry, "What do you make of all this? What do these things mean?" The Indian, sorrowfully enough, and as if the last prop of all his hopes here and hereafter were gone, thus delivered a most original—and aboriginal

—theory of earthquakes: "Great Spirit got whisky too much!"

The wild life of the borderers naturally occasioned the coining of many singular words and phrases. These, like many of the idioms and modes of speech peculiar to the Indians, were the result not of imagination, but of a paucity of language. It is common to descant upon the poetry and eloquence of the Indians; and the celebrated speech of Logan is often mentioned—as Jefferson mentioned it—as almost unparalleled in the records of ancient or modern oratory. Yet, in the first place, it may well be questioned whether those words ever passed Logan's lips. And if they did, although it is very true that they are preëminent among specimens of Indian oratory, it is still true of that oratory in general, that its poetical phrases and ever recurring formulas and figures and personifications are singularly few in number, and monotonously repeated, and this for the reason that these wild and unreflecting and thoughtless people, ignorant of abstract thinking, destitute of abstract ideas, and circumscribed within a very narrow circle of mental action, are unable to convey any except a very small number of very ordinary and every-day ideas, without employing terms borrowed from material nature. Their language possessed no words—or almost none—for the expression of abstract ideas; nor did it contain words of high intellectual significance, or deep ethical meaning. Even for conceptions as ordinary among us as "prosperous circumstances," "affluence," or "a season of remarkable enjoyment," they had no better form of expression than "a sunshiny day;" or "a day as placid as the bosom of a lake." Such terms as these, or, for instance, those well-known figurative expressions of "burying the hatchet," "brightening the chain of friendship," and the like, although to those unacquainted with them seeming poetic enough, are in truth the meagre products of the barest and barrenest poverty.

It was this dry and meagre form of language which drove both Indians and Anglo-American borderers to the use of analogous terms, whose inappropriateness often renders them quaint or even witty, where no such effect was intended. There is in print a well-known writ, issued by an Indian justice of the peace, long ago in Massachusetts, which illustrates my point. It ran thus:—"I, Hihoudi. You, Peter Waterman. Jeremy Wicket. Quick you take him, fast you hold him, straight you bring him before me. Hihoudi." A singularly close parallel to this was the proclamation of the western sheriff, at the beginning and ending of court. As the ermined judge ascended the tribunal, this matter-of-fact functionary bawled out, "O yes, O yes, court am open!" and when the labors of the day were over, he proclaimed again with genuine western adherence to sense and logic, and disregard of form, the substance of the fact, thus: "O yes, O yes, court am shet!"

Thus, I repeat, many of the expressions of the western borderers which seem to us imaginative, humorous, or ludicrous, though in some cases, perhaps, derived from ancestors or ancestral peculiarities, were usually adopted as the first which came to hand when the new idea to be expressed came up asking for a word. The foresters had no training in language, and no habitude in abstract thought, or in modifying and distinguishing notions. But they had abundant readiness and self-reliance, and when they wanted a new word they either took an old one and modified it into a new one, much on the principle which forced their wives to make one utensil serve as wash-basin, kettle, dish, dish-pan, and swill-pail; or they manufactured one out of whole cloth, often in ridiculous exemplification of that figure of speech to which the grammarians have given the clumsy name of *onomatopœia*: namely, making the sound suggest the sense.

The former of these two methods made words like "spontanaceous" for spontaneous; "obfusticate" for obfuscate; "cantankerous" for cankerous; "rampagious" or "rampunctious" for rampant; "hifalutin" or "hifalutinatin" for high-flying; "tetotaciously" for totally; and the like. The latter resulted in terms having often a ludicrous general similarity to proper English words of the long Latin kind, but utterly unfounded in fact; the merest phantoms of a raw, absurd and unconscious fancy. Such are "sockdolager" for a knock-down blow; "Explatterate," to crush or smash; "explunctify," for the same; "honey-fuggle," to hang about one and flatter him for mean purposes; and so on.

Many of the figures of speech and forms of rhetoric which characterize western eloquence, partake of the same bombastic and unsound character; this, however, of course not being true of the best of the western orators. And all these, words and figures and sentences, while they possess a show of poetical or imaginative character, with more or less of its actual essence, are nevertheless as a whole the products of deplorable and extreme barrenness of mind and poverty of thought.

But with the gradual growth of population, wealth, refinement and education, there is of course a gradual change in these respects; the phraseology and the intellect of the people improve and develop together. This change is brought about at the West, in great measure, by means of the increasing frequency of public speaking. And we must not judge of the power exerted upon the people, nor the good done them, merely by estimating the amount of positive information furnished by the speaker, and his grade of intelligence. It is from the stimulation which their natures experience, from his pouring out and rendering up to them of the treasures of his own life and soul, that the abiding profit of his work is derived. Now the rude speeches and sermons of the West task and stimulate the intellects of the people, and set their minds in motion. The steam is turned on; and when that is done, the engine must move forward or backward, or else explode. It may be admitted—to carry out the figure—that an explosion has sometimes happened, but on the whole, the general result has been a movement ahead. As was naturally to be expected, there was undue emphasis, exaggeration, violence, and exceeding heat. All this was perfectly natural, and to be expected; but from this noisy fermentation has come out, after all, a style of eloquence which has become distinctively and emphatically American eloquence. The spoken eloquence of New England is for the most part from manuscript. Her first settlers brought old world forms and fashions from the old world with them. Their preachers were set at an appalling distance from their congregations. Between the pulpit, perched far up toward the ceiling, and the seats, was an awful abysmal depth. Above the lofty desk was dimly seen the white cravat, and above that the head of the preacher. His eye was averted and fastened downward upon his manuscript, and his discourse, or exercitation, or whatever it might be, was delivered in a monotonous, regular cadence, probably relieved from time to time by some quaint blunder, the result of indistinct penmanship, or dim religious light. It was not this preacher's business to arouse his audience. The theory of the worship of the period was opposed to that. His people did not wish excitement or stimulus, or astonishment, or agitation. They simply desired information; they wished to be instructed; to have their judgment informed, or their reason enlightened. Thus the preacher might safely remain perched up in his far distant unimpassioned eyrie.

But how would such a style of eloquence—if, indeed truth will permit the name of eloquence to be applied to the reading of matter from a preconcerted manuscript—how would such a style of delivery be received out in the wild West? Place your textual speaker out in the backwoods, on the stump, where a surging tide of humanity streams strongly around him, where the people press up toward him on every side, their keen eyes intently perusing his to see if he be in real earnest—"dead in earnest"—and where, as with a thousand darts, their contemptuous scorn would pierce him through if he were found playing a false game, trying to pump up tears by mere acting, or arousing an excitement without feeling it. Would such a style of oratory succeed there? By no means. The place is different, the hearers are different; the time, the thing required, all the circumstances are totally different. Here, in the vast unwalled church of nature, with the leafy tree-tops for a ceiling, their massy stems for columns; with the endless mysterious cadences of the forest for a choir; with the distant or nearer music and murmur of streams, and the ever-returning voice of birds sounding in their ears for the made-up music of a picked band of exclusive singers: here stand men whose ears are trained to catch the faintest foot-fall of the distant deer, or the rustle of their antlers against branch or bough of the forest track—whose eyes are skilled to discern the trail of savages, who leave scarce a track behind them; and who will follow upon that trail, utterly invisible to the untrained eye, as surely as a bloodhound follows the scent, ten or twenty, or a hundred miles—whose eye and hand are so well practised that they can drive a nail or snuff a candle with the long, heavy western rifle. Such men, educated for years, or even generations, in that hard school of necessity, where every one's hand and woodman's skill must keep his head; where incessant pressing necessities required ever a prompt and sufficient answer in deeds; and where words needed to be but few, and those the plainest and directest, required no delay nor preparation, nor oratorical coquetting, nor elaborate preliminary scribble; no hesitation nor doubts in deeds; no circumlocution in words. To restrain, influence, direct, govern, such a surging sea of life as this, required something very different from a written address. The effect of the New England manner of preaching upon a western man is illustrated by the broad and random criticism of that same rough old Peter Cartwright, of whom I have already written. All that he thought it worth while to say of the young clergyman who delivered a written sermon somewhere along his western track, was, that "it made him think of a gosling that had got the straddles by wading in the dew." What that eloquence is which can and does control such a constituency, can scarce be conceived, except by those who have heard it. Yet there is is, and of a lofty grade of power and beauty; and it has become distinctively American in method and style.

It would not be difficult to fill volumes with quotations illustrative of the eloquence and wit and humor of the West. But such quotations are too plentiful in our contemporary literature to make any such selection at all necessary; and I have preferred accordingly to present such an imperfect analysis as I might of the shaping causes which have waited on its birth and growth. The causes of the character of western mind, the nature and derivation of its constituents, have been too little examined to be understood or appreciated.

As I already quoted a negro as affording an instance of the grim and cool humor characteristic of his western home, if not of his own tropical blood, so I desire to cite another as having, in a brief and homely description, exemplified a very high order of rude natural eloquence. This was a preacher, who was endeavoring to set forth the attributes of the Almighty; and who summed up the mysterious and awful powers of the Unknown God in a single sentence, which, for terseness and telling force and beauty, it would be difficult to match. Using a common western and southern idiom, he thus said: "He *totes* the thunder in his fist, and flings the lightning from his fingers."

I well remember the impression produced upon me—a boy of twenty-two years of age, educated in the woods and prairies of the West—when I attended for the first time the session of Congress at Washington. I imagined that whatever eloquence I might have heard was, at least in some sense, deficient in the higher and sublimer qualities of oratory. I had heard and read much of the great men of our national legislature, and fully expected to be charmed beyond measure, in House and Senate, with new revelations of majesty and beauty; to be educated into a perfect passion for eloquence; to sit long happy days and nights in the halls of Congress, listening, a humble scholar, to those great men as they expounded or enforced the principles of the laws and the statesmanship of the land. The disappointment I experienced was inconceivable. I had expected a new kind of speech, something loftier and nobler than I had heard before; but, after hearing the most famous debaters, the world-renowned champions of that great arena, I went home to my boarding-house every evening with the mental exclamation, "Can it be possible that all these men have taken lessons in eloquence from the old Methodist preachers and exhorters of the West?" The most effective and successful of them were those who spoke loudest and with most passion, and thumped the desks the hardest, just as it was at the West. I have seen Adams and Webster thumping on the desks in front of them as if they had no knuckles at all, or wanted to knock them off. The western style of oratory has become American; it is extempore, the thoughts suggested by the occasion, and the words such as mustered upon the hasty call of the thoughts; often harsh, or rude, or ill-sounding words; but, nevertheless, words of force, every one effective in performing the service of the occasion.

A western writer, in a sketch of a trip into the State of Kentucky about 1806, has occasion to describe one who was an early and splendid master of the style of eloquence of which I have spoken. This writer had occasion to visit the lower or Green

River counties, and on arriving at a county town found the court just assembling, and a great concourse of people from all the region round, gathered together in expectation of a trial which had excited very great interest in all the neighborhood. He entered the court-house, an extempore affair—for all the appurtenances of justice, like the speeches of that day and place, were improvised. The abode of justice was a log-cabin. On one side sat the judge, and the sheriff, shouting out "Oyez, oyez," proclaimed the opening of the court. Business was begun, and the docket regularly called; and in process of time this case, so eagerly looked forward to, was put in course of trial; the witnesses were called and examined, and the pleadings commenced. The case was a civil suit for damages for slander, brought by a poor orphan girl, whose fair name, her only possession, had been defamed by the defendant, a wealthy man in that region. She had no kinsmen who could revenge this great wrong by personal prowess, by the strong hand, as the custom of the country would ordinarily have required; and the spirited young girl found herself perforce left to the slow resource of the law. The counsel for the plaintiff, as he appeared to my authority, was tall, straight, and rather slender; of dark, or at least, swarthy features. Long black locks fell over his face, an eagle-eye looked keenly from beneath his forehead, and his costume, as unjuridical a dress as could well be conceived, was that of a hunter in those woods: buckskin hunting-shirt, with fringed border leggins and moccasins. He rose and commenced his speech. As he proceeded, the wild backwoodsmen, who had gathered from their sports and antics about the court-house green, crowded around, and now breathless, their attention riveted by the eloquence of the speaker. Every niche of the little building was crowded, and every window and doorway filled wlth absorbed listeners. As with imperative and heart-touching power the speaker described the helpless loneliness of the orphaned maiden his client, her sad isolation within the broad and busy world, judge, and clerk, and jury, and audience, were subdued with irrepressible emotion. And again, as he assailed the man who attempted to defile her reputation, it seemed as if a tornado of fire were drying up all the streams. As the hot and scorching wind of his sarcasm and invective swept through the audience, their eyes flashed and their bosoms heaved; he carried their very souls captive, and every man of them made the orphan's cause his own. So utterly did the assembly pass beneath the influence and into the spirit of that indignant and terrible denunciation, that had the slanderer been on the spot it is very doubtful whether he would have left the place alive. And when the words of this backwoods counsel were ended, the jury, without retiring from their seats, brought in a verdict for heavy damages.

Some years thereafter, and just subsequently to the war of 1812, this same writer had occasion to be in the State of Indiana, and was near one of Harrison's battle-grounds. Early in the morning he rose and rode out to see the scene of the fight; and first he repaired to a spot where, underneath a broad and noble tree, was a little mound of earth without paling or defence, and with no stone to mark the head of him who rested there—for he had come to visit the grave of the eloquent advocate whom he had heard in southern Kentucky. Here lay the successful lawyer, the all-powerful orator, the brave soldier, the noble and upright man, the husband of the sister of Chief Justice Marshall, the man who had held Aaron Burr at bay, and who opposed and exposed the plots with which that arch seducer was wiling away honest citizens to treason and death; the equal antagonist of Henry Clay, and who, if instead of falling at the battle of Tippecanoe, he had lived as long as Clay, would have won as high, if not a higher place, than did even that great orator of the West. Such was he who is yet familiarly spoken of and cherished in memory throughout all the West as Jo Hamilton Daviess, one of the noblest, most lofty minded, loftily and daringly ambitious, and yet one of the most simple-hearted and truthful of all the eminent men that the fruitful border land has yet produced.

I have mentioned the name of him who was then the rival of Daviess. No two men are more perfect representatives and ideals of that western mind whose qualities and productions I have feebly endeavored to describe. They came from the people, and were rocked in the cradle of adversity. Their eyes were disciplined in the rights, and their ears to the sounds of the forest. They were the ready and sensitive and diligent students of nature, in all her stern and harsh and rugged forms, and in all her sweet sylvan beauties. Waterfalls and the quiet voice of placid streams, the vivid verdure of the spring and the warm luxurious breath of summer; the cold and the rigid frosts, the white still snow and the bitter furious storms of winter; the sound of the battle too, and the alarms and perils of war—all these had trained them. They bore throbbing fiery hearts, often vivid with excitement and wild with passion; and their audiences were men of like mold and hearts, and like passions with themselves. Thus they found congenial materials to be worked upon; free, open, sensitive and truthful souls, ready to receive the impress of their burning genius; and for men like them, starting in any professional career, either as lawyer, statesman or divine, no nobler or fitter materials could have been found.

Thus did Henry Clay embark upon the career of a lawyer's life, his heart in his hand; his nature in full and free sympathy with that of the masses; always true to freedom and justice, and no respecter of persons; enforcing as occasion served that perilous duty of the emancipation of the negro race; serving a writ for the keeper of a dram-shop, upon a distinguished lawyer, for drinks and liquor unpaid for, and so securing the undying hostility of an influential man. At one bound, he springs into the foremost rank of the legal talent of the day. He is little learned in books; he has not moved even in the graceful society of his own native Virginia; it must be the movements of the trees bending in the wind that have taught him his grace and dignity of attitude and gesture. He has spent little time over the great works of Greek and Roman orators; it is his own earnest convictions, his piercing intelligence, his true sympathies and keen perceptions and instincts, that reveal to him what are the thoughts required, and the words in which they should be clothed. Thus profoundly true, and wondrously adapted to that community, he becomes the master of the intellect of the West. Stepping by a transition so natural and common, from law into politics, he enters the United States Senate, and either there or in the House becomes the head of the party who advocated the last war with Great Britain; and boldly and deter minedly leads the van in upholding the government, in the face of many bitter adversaries and with many faint friends, and against the whole embodied opposition of New England. Sent to Europe as commissioner to conclude the treaty of Ghent, together with Adams, Bayard, Gallatin, and Russell, he is a controlling spirit in the negotiations; and Lord Castlereagh, one of the most polished and finished of the courtiers of Europe, from youth familiar with the most refined and aristocratic society of the old world, pronounces this untutored child of the wilderness the most elegant and accomplished gentleman he had ever seen. Returning home, he passes from one post of honor and distinction to another, receiving almost every office in the gift of the people except the highest; and links his name, together with one or two others, to every great event and epoch in our history from that date almost to the present. 1820, 1832, 1850, found Clay and Webster standing side by side; foremost in withstanding every storm. Against each onset, they stood, like some colossal monumental forms, breasting the full tempest and malignity of its fury, sometimes so utterly hidden in the darkness and rage of the elements, that they seem to be tottering and falling, to be ground to atoms far below. But they not only outlast, but govern the wild elements that assault them: they "ride the whirlwind and direct the storm." And as they thus stood so often, so shall stand for hundreds of years to come the names of the two great men, one from the West and one from the North; the graceful Ash of Kentucky, and the massive Granite Block of New Hampshire.

Henry Clay had not the culture, the profound legal lore, the thoroughly disciplined logical faculty, of Webster; nor his broad and dome-like brow, or the deep and cavernous eyes from which flashed forth such profound and mighty fires when he stood before Bench or Senate. But Henry Clay, graceful, agile, dextrous, full of fire and passion, yet with a will fixed as fate, a born commander of men—the joy and light of every social circle he entered; loved by women as no man on this continent has ever been; and for whose defeat in 1844 I suppose more women's tears were shed than for any single event before—stands before us as the illustrious type and representative of the eloquence of the western country. And, take him for all in all, as man of the people and orator of the people, whatever his short-comings or failings, it will be many a long year before we look upon his like again!

I cannot conclude without a brief reference to a few writers whose works embody most of the peculiar traits and oddities, fun, humor and wit, of the southwestern United States. These are, Col. T. B. Thorpe, now of New York, Johnson Hooper of Alabama, and Judge Longstreet of Mississippi. Thorpe's "Bee-Hunter" is an unrivalled sketch of the times of the first pioneers in Arkansas. Judge Longstreet, whom I am half sorry, half glad, to own as a fellow Methodist preacher, is the author of "Georgia Scenes;" and Johnson Hooper wrote that famous and most characteristic book, "The Adventures of Simon Suggs." These, and other works of these three gentlemen, contain the fullest and most characteristic delineations of the ways of thinking, acting and speaking in those distant regions, anywhere to be found in print.

Lecture X.

THE GREAT VALLEY;

ITS PAST, ITS PRESENT, AND ITS FUTURE.

THE GREAT VALLEY:

ITS PAST, ITS PRESENT, AND ITS FUTURE.

I HAVE now, in a series of isolated pictures, sketched the history of the Mississippi Valley, by a successive portraiture of its representative men and periods, during three centuries; from the first voyages of the hardy Spanish discoverers who skirted its coasts, and their bold and ill-fated endeavors to penetrate the hostile realms of its far interior, so long believed to blaze with unimaginable wealth of gold—so fearfully revealed as a fatal forest wilderness swarming with desperate and warlike defenders—down to that strange enterprise of Aaron Burr, which in so many points of wild and hopeless absurdity, of visionary hardihood, of unscrupulous, conscienceless wickedness, and disregard of rights human or divine, resembles the early inroads of the Spaniard;—and down to those other crusades, longer in continuance, scarcely less perilous for hardship and danger, and immeasurably loftier in spirit and in aim, the wandering self-denying missionary lives of the pioneer preachers—the worthy successors of Marquette, of Breboeuf and of Jaques.

It remains, in the concluding lecture, to sum up the whole in such a manner as may group into one single picture, the figures, the light and shade, the distance and the foreground of these several sketches —to treat what I will call the nation of the Great Valley, as one; to follow its history from the end of the series of delineations I have given, down to the present; and to essay the far more venturesome task of tracing some outline, or I should rather say of indulging in some dream—of its unknown future.

In thus attempting to fix the collective traits and total significance of the Valley and its people, let me ask the reader first to observe what that people is; what manner of race of men is that of the Valley. We have already studied them by classes, and by thought; but what are they historically—ethnologically?

It is a most ancient practice, to begin every history at the Creation—a practice honored by great votaries, from the times of the antique chroniclers of Germany, and the monkish Latin historians of the middle ages, down to that eminent authority, Herr Professor von Poddingkopf, so delightfully cited by the most eminent and the latest departed of all the American prose writers, the genial and beloved Irving. But I shall not go back so far; not quite back to the flood.

In Africa and in Asia, and in America too, there

have existed civilizations more or less exalted in grade, and lasting in endurance. But the works of the mound-builders of the West—for our cycle of allusions may begin at the very point whither it is at last to bring us—and the Aztecs of the south, the Egyptians and Ethopians, the Assyrians, Persians, Hindoos, Chinese—all the monuments of their arts and arms, their codes of laws and systems of thought, have passed either into utter oblivion, complete destruction, a stiff immovable catalepsy not deserving the name of life, or a superannuated and decrepit age.

But that race, whatever its earlier designations, which was the parent of the various European families of men, possessed higher qualities. It may not have been superior to others in stature, or strength, or beauty, in force or acuteness of intellect, perhaps not always in purity of morals or in religious truth. But in one thing it has demonstrated itself superior: in the capacity of unlimited and universal improvement. Through the vicissitudes of ages, under numberless phases of development, and despite many periods of torpidity and even of retrogression, one people has as it were evolved from within itself another, and always a better.

The genius of civilization, having done his utmost with Egyptains and Assyrians, led the Greeks and the Romans to far higher summits of intellectual achievement and of ethical knowledge. Then Christianity, in like manner, after experiment and failure in Asia, transferred the centres of her dominion to European soil. From the Christian Era, the history of Europe is the history of human progress. Among the nations of Europe, the Germanic civilization has been of a higher moral tone and a more deeply formed institutional character, than the Latin. And of the Germanic nations, that branch which became the Anglo-Saxon and then the English, stands this day foremost of all. And—now at last returning to this continent—the Anglo-American nation, a new nation, is evolved as it were from within the bosom of the English nation, by that strange process which, a long array of precedents assures us, places every such latest-born people upon a higher level of existence than that of its parent—there to exemplify some still greater principle, to teach some still loftier lesson of destiny and of progress. Last of all, there has arisen within this mighty Valley, streaming over the bordering Alleghanies, pushing westward by the side of the great northern Lakes, disembarking on the sandy shore of the Gulf, or struggling up the yellow flood of the Mississippi, yet one more nation within a nation; and now in the basin of the Great River is abiding and increasing a multitude already numerous enough to wield the political destinies of our land, and in possession of opportunities never before in reach of any human community on this earth, for achieving eminence in all that humanity desires of happiness, nobility and goodness.

In historic descent these are the foremost children of men; the youngest sons, the Benjamins of old mother earth; and truly they are planted in a heritage well worthy of a parent's or a brother's partial fondness. As Benjamin's mess was five times that of any of his brethren, so is the vast and fair domain of the Mississippi Valley—including as it naturally does the Gulf States—three times as extensive as the Atlantic slope, and somewhat less than twice as extensive as the third great natural division of our territory, the Pacific slope. I need not compare its wealth of soil and climate and rivers and metals, to theirs.

God reserved this goodly land for those who hold it now. Many were the bold voyagers of antiquity; but none until Columbus was directed across the western sea to America. Enough there were of hardy explorers among the sons of Spain, and enough of wise and strong men, able to found and to govern new kingdoms; but none of them were to establish themselves here. The traders and the soldiery of France were many and hardy and brave, and her Jesuits and Franciscans, with all the zeal that the love of souls and the desire of martyrdom could inspire, labored for years among the forest tribes; and the pliant genius and dextrous skill of her settlers almost fused the civilized and savage nations into one. But this splendid domain was not for France. Nor was it even to become a colony of the British empire; a possession of the resolute Anglo-Saxon men, who, if any of the European kingdoms, were fitted to hold and to govern it. All these claimants, one after another, sought to establish a title; but each and every claim was disallowed by him who ruleth both the affairs of the children of men and the armies of heaven. This land was not a land for Spain, nor France nor England. A separate race had been elected and consecrated to the sublime task of redeeming its vast expanse from solitude and barbarism; of conquering it for a cultivated humanity; of making it the home of happy multitudes; a broad foundation for God's church; a new field for the solution of man's threefold problem, his relations to God, to the earth, and to his neighbor. Neither the spirit of effete feudalism, nor the stronger spirit of a ceremonial church; neither the despotic power of a monarchy ruling under the civil law, nor the irresponsible destructive sway of any band of greedy traders, was to possess the new realm; but that strong off-shoot of the noble old Anglo-Saxon stem, which has well been called the Anglo-American, was to have and to rule it; and a long and severe discipline was that which had prepared it. The people of England, rising slowly and stubbornly upward from the slavery of the Norman conquest; helped unconsciously and unintentionally by the extorted gift of the Great Charter; beginning to control even the brutal bull-dog strength of the Tudor monarchs; then rising and slaying a senselessly oppressive king—a people taught by the sweet sounds of old Chaucer; around whose path had been thrown the strange and mystic imaginings of Spenser; who had listened to the "native wood-notes wild," of Shakspeare; and who had found even a nobler poet, and a fearless and mighty defender, in John Milton; who had learned wisdom of Francis Bacon; whose imaginations and consciences were at once entranced and convinced by the wondrous spiritual dream of Bunyan; and whose reason had been instructed by the clear understanding and acute philosophy of Locke: this people had here and there ripened to the point of capacity and desire for self-government, under the double and opposite stimulus of the lasting Puritan leaven which the Reformation had diffused in England, and of the grinding and intensifying tyranny of the Tudors and Stuarts.

Thus it came to pass that there went out from England that small body of strong men, who "builded wiser than they knew," and founded this nation. Well trained in cool self-reliance, iron courage, impregnable perseverance; strong and ready of hand and of heart, wise in thought, learned in that philosophy which is most readily transmuted into right and efficient action, and above all, clothed and penetrated and borne onward by a strength incredible to those not of them, the strength of Faith in God—they sailed away across the sea. With all these high and noble traits, unconsciously the greatest statesmen on earth, having prepared the iron pillars of their little nation of a hundred men in their ship, they landed in America, with the fabric of their church and State all ready prepared for erection.

And as in after years the posterity of these small colonies entered within the vast inland realm of which I am speaking—as the hostile savages faded away, and the forests began to fall, and the sunlight to work its wondrous chemistries upon the wealthy soil beneath, and bountiful mother Earth bared her bosom to the plough and hoe—how marvellously did that Providence which had planted them there, provide one aid after another, coördinate with the increasing needs of the increasing nation!

Small centres of inhabitants, feeble, unconnected, isolated, mere points of crystallization upon the vast expanse, lie like distant dots along the great rivers, or in the wide woods. It is intercourse that consolidates a nation. Life blood must circulate. A huge inert overgrown body dies of mere magnitude. But how shall this indispensable need be supplied? Antiquity hath no answer to the problem, or the Roman empire might have held together. Modern science has no suggestion to make: horses and men are the swiftest and strongest messengers, except the inconstant, treacherous winds. But James Watt studied the boiling of a teakettle, and as in the oriental tale there rose up from the thin vapor of a sealed jug a mighty giant, so did the genius of the Scotch mechanician evolve from the vapors of that mean vessel the superhuman might of the steam engine. Then one of our own countrymen, laying in turn his modifying hand upon the volatile essence of fire and water, constrains its giant strength into the service of the steamboat—and the wants of the nation of the valley are supplied! Again, as population thickens and wealth increases, and men begin more and more, after the mysterious word of the prophet, to go to and fro in the earth, Robert Stephenson invents the locomotive; and straightway the hurrying millions of the Valley, no longer confined to the channels of the rivers, flit over the mountains or through them and across the plain, on that stronger and closer network of civilization, and of interwoven civic strength, the railroad. And last of all, within these last years we have the electric telegraph, which may fitly be likened to that great system called the sympathetic nerve, which flashes hither and thither through the body the constant sustaining streams of unconscious life; which maintains the health and action of all the wondrous processes, and keeps all alive, but which the imperial, central, conscious will cannot reach. For so does the little telegraphic wire, flashing endless communication hither and thither all over the land, hold us, mind with mind, in a comprehensive, indissoluble unitary life. Ah, it is in such pecuniary enterprises as these, set up in the fervent worship of Mammon, that we shall find a power, all quiet and unrecognized, but with all the unimaginable strength of a truly Divine messenger, infinitely more potent against the rising yells of that infernal army of Disunion, this day thickening around us, than in any such old world fancies as patriotism and humanity, justice and forbearance!

Nor has less wisdom or kindness been shown in providing for the needs of the intellectual and religious faculties. I have already referred to the zeal and intrepid perseverance of the ancient Catholic missionaries, whose not unworthy successors, Father De Smet, Bishop Blanchet and their brethren are still faithfully and efficiently laboring among the fierce tribes of the distant Northwest. I have also spoken of the Protestant missionaries who quickly followed on over the mountains, to look after their small flocks in the wilderness. The minister and the schoolmaster were provided, as the rising generation began to need their aid. The fierce stern exigencies of their perilous life in the wilderness trained them in quickness of eye and readiness of hand, in prompt and lofty courage, in fruitfulness of resource and a hardy self-reliant perseverance that never yielded. While thus the hard school of necessity trained them, by rude, incessant, inevitable lessons, into a rough but noble strength, it was the duty of the teacher and of the missionary, not so much to excite the forces of nerve and soul—for that external stimulus so commonly needed elsewhere had here been supplied by nature and the wilderness and the savage, and mind and soul were here all awake, full of force and activity—but to direct, to moderate, to restrain. The work is prosperously in progress. The school-houses, log-built and humble though they were, have yet been the centres of a continual and increasing diffusion of knowledge and of goodness. In those obscure edifices, all the week, the teacher led his youthful charge in the paths of learning; and on the seventh day, the same lowly building became the sanctuary of the Most High, and the backwoods preacher expounded to the same children and to their parents also, the message of God, preparing them both for this life and for that which is to come.

But in thus seeking to sketch the characteristic elements of the people of the Great Valley, I must not omit to allude to one important feature, viz., the mingled currents of its blood. The main stock is Anglo-Saxon. Important infusions of Scotch and Irish blood were in the veins of very many of its best and bravest men. There has always been some small admixture from amongst the French of Illinois and Louisiana. Scarce a tinge of Spanish blood can be traced. On one of the outskirts or appendages of the Valley—the peninsula of Florida—a colony of fifteen hundred Greeks was once planted, whose blood still runs in the veins of some of the best families of St. Augustine. A somewhat more diffused intermixture may be followed, from those Huguenot French who settled along the Atlantic coast from Boston to Charleston. Great numbers of Germans have long contributed toward this miscellaneous national stock the solid or the graceful traits of the old Teutonic character. In the North may be traced colonies of Norwegians, of Dutch, a few Swedes and Danes. There has been no perceptible addition of Italian blood; nor of that of the Aborigines; for the border intercourse of centuries has been bloody and murderous, with a strange, sad uniformity. No modification is yet visible, and let us hope that none will be, from the last strange immigration of brutal Chinamen to our distant Pacific coast.

And thus we find the western people to-day, not one of those pure races whose uniform destiny seems to be to disappear, but a community of bloods rather than a race, one of those homogeneous mixtures of character not found except in these latter days of history, whose value and power amongst the great republic of nations no precedents enable us to ascertain, but for whom there are many reasons to anticipate a grand and noble future.

Having thus endeavored to represent the original and added constituents of the People of the Great Valley, let us next observe them and their landed commonwealths, at the point to which they have now attained.

Imagine, therefore, a spectator—yourself, if you will—with an ideal vision broad and keen enough to embrace and discern so much, and lifted high up in air, even so that you may look far abroad over all the Great Valley, and those adjuncts or appendixes which naturally and politically belong with it, namely the Gulf States and Michigan. And observe, being in spirit with this visionary beholder of mine, the multiplied features of power and grandeur presented to your eye. From the white and sunny sands of Floridian Cape Sable and the sea-washed little Wreck City of Key West, to the cold remote northwestern village of wintry log-built forest-circled Pembina and the improvised mining towns of Aurora and Denver, raised as it were in a night by the strong sorcery of Mammon on barren hill-sides all treeless and forlorn: from smoke-canopied Pittsburg, grimy dwelling of forges and mills, on the antique site of vanished Fort Du Quesne, to the struggling semi-prosperous frontier town of Brownsville, where Texans look with faces sour and contemptuous, yet eager and expectant, to the wide territories of Mexico, and where there seems to prevail a chronic border warfare, the frictional irritation between chafing races: from the skirting Alleghanies on the east to the interrupted but sufficient ramparts of the Rocky Mountains in the West, and from the warm blue of the salt Gulf to the cooler waters and hues of the great northern chain of fresh-water seas: over all this vast domain, grown up to its present level of magnificent power within three-quarters of a century —the lifetime of one man—how wonderful, how mighty, how complicated, are the masses and forms and movements of human life and labor!

Twelve millions of souls are fulfilling their destinies within the space of this great panorama; belonging to sixteen sovereign States, and five younger sisters—Territories, some of them already impatiently knocking at the doors of Congress for admission into the Union of their elder sisters; and if I do not add to this number that of their brethren beyond the western mountains, the half-million and more of California, and the thousands of Utah, and Oregon and Washington Territory, it is for the sake of geographical rather than logical correctness, for those Pacific States are most properly outskirts, suburbs, advanced posts of the great hive of men in the Valley.

Amid this vast and busy throng of men whose multiplied labors have already done so much to change the dark unbroken forest, and silent open prairie into a garden of God, are efficiently operating the manifold engineries of civilized life. To and fro, along the thousands of miles of the vast river system, are rushing a thousand steamers, from eleven hundred tons burden downward, in place of the little awkward *Orleans*, of a hundred tons, launched by Fulton and Livingston at Pittsburg, in 1812. The lake fleet, over and above this, is of twelve hundred vessels and more; and from the great southern marts of the Valley, another vast auxiliary ocean fleet brings in or bears away an annual mass of imports and exports of a hundred and twenty-five millions of dollars. The network of railroads has but barely begun to knit itself through and over a few portions of the Valley; but this beginning is a giant one. Over thirteen thousand miles of railroad, the more eager spirits of the Valley fly hither and thither on errands of business, or affection, or pleasure.

In 1776, the Baptist John Hickman first began to labor as a Protestant minister west of the Alleghanies. Now, in seventeen thousand churches, of twenty sects, the Word of God is statedly dispensed to an average of something like five millions of regular hearers.

When or where the first log school-house was erected, and the first little platoon of recruits of learning

> "Discharged their a-b ab's against the dame,"

—or master, I cannot say, except that it was within the last eighty years. But now, a hundred and fifty colleges crown woody heights, or shelter themselves in retired valleys; and in these, and in fifty thousand public and private schools, nearly two millions of youth are receiving a moral and intellectual training whose depth, and breadth, and thoroughness is yearly greater, and which yearly better prepares its graduates to plunge out into the great battle of life—to perform wisely and well his or her single duty as a citizen or a wife.

Once more: let me repeat a few similar statistics—dry kernels, but, to a reflective mind, nevertheless, the seeds of infinite conceptions of grandeur and beauty—relative to one section of the great domain of the Valley—the Northwest. This is the tract between the Ohio, the Lakes, and the Mississippi, which contains two hundred and sixty thousand square miles, and which Washington, who early owned lands within it, called a "western *world*."

A hundred years ago—in 1751—it contained five little French towns, with about one thousand inhabitants, all nestled down together, like a little group of timid lambs, within a hidden valley in the southwest of Illinois—and no other European settlements. The first State admitted into the Union from it was Ohio, in 1802. The earliest English settlements within Ohio were made in 1774, but none was of any importance until the settlement of Marietta, in 1788, when the English inhabitants may have numbered five thousand. Little more than three-quarters of a century has passed, and into what gigantic proportions has this section of the great Valley already grown! Five great States occupy its territory; not less than seven millions of people inhabit it; every year its farms produce not far from three hundred millions of dollars in value; its mines, eighty millions; its lumber, seventy millions; its twenty thousand and more of manufactories, a hundred and thirty millions; its fisheries, three millions. It has nine thousand miles and more of railroads; fourteen hundred miles of canals; seven thousand miles of telegraph. It contains two hundred banks, with twenty millions of capital. Its whole material extent, real and personal property together, is reckoned to be worth more than one and three-quarters *billions* of dollars.

But this startling expansion is not to be reckoned by business and statistics alone. The Northwest has built eight thousand churches, which will hold four millions of people; fifty colleges, and twenty-five thousand schools, where are studying a million and a half of pupils; and it supports a thousand newspapers, twelve hundred libraries more or less public, and scientific and literary societies innumerable.

Again, a yet more wondrous exemplification of the exuberant, gigantic vital strength of this great inland realm is afforded by the growth of its cities. In former ages of the world, many enormous cities were raised up by despotic power, or increased during centuries by a slow process of accretion. But in our great Valley it is as if the strong, rich soil gave birth to the sudden vastness of the marts, that rise almost like exhalations on lake-side and river-bank. A proud and glorious instance do they furnish of the superiority of the power of a free and enterprising people, over the spiritless, slavish obedience of Asiatic subjects, or of monarchical conservatisms.

Across the northern portion of the great Valley, if you glance upon the map, you can easily trace two great lines of cities dotting, like great jewels, the chain of trade and intercourse between East and West. The northern line, from Buffalo by Cleveland and Detroit, ends at Chicago; the southern line begins with Pittsburg, and extends, by Cincinnati and Louisville, to St. Louis. The nine cities of the first have increased their total population, during the last ten years, from 159,000 to 454,000; and the nine of the second line, during the same period, from

335,000 to 600,000. The most wondrous of them all, Chicago, which in 1840 had 4,800 inhabitants—which in 1830 had 70 inhabitants—had last year 125,000.

In what other way could I set before you what the Mississippi Valley now is? Mere statistics, you will say; uninteresting figures; dry bones of information. But, as I said before, it is these very figures which are, if rightly viewed, instinct with whatever is grand and marvellous. Within this brief period—for one human life, long though it may be, is brief enough compared with the age of this world—within this brief period, the Nation of the Valley has grown up with such a portentous speed and strength as reminds us of that gigantic fountain which pours suddenly a full-grown river from the unknown caverns of the lower earth: from nothing, to myriads of souls; from nothing, to millions of money; from nothing, to an infinity of strength and power, and to a high grade of culture and excellence. Thus I state the summary, by comparisons, in general terms. But it is the series of arithmetical numbers that affords the most tangible basis for thought—the firmest and clearest, and, indeed, the only valuable conceptions, upon such a point as this.

And now I have passed over two parts of this summing up. I have examined this western race, and inquired what is it by blood and by constituent parts;

and I have sought to indicate, by dint of some mathematical totals, some general idea of what it is now, in number, strength, and attainment. And it remains to essay a more dangerous task—to speak of its future. I am no prophet, either, to promise good things, or to threaten evil; nor do I pretend to any wonderful measure, even of merely human prescience. All that I venture to attempt is, to state obvious meanings of visible phenomena—of those indications which the great Master of Life has given to us on purpose that we might reason on them and conclude from them.

The Valley is to be, as it has been, a great harbor of refuge for the poor and oppressed of other lands. It is the rightful glory of our Anglo-American race to have opened welcoming arms to the refugees of every nation. No thought of selfish isolation ever entered the hearts of the men that inhabit the unparalleled region of the West. They justly felt that union and coöperation, not isolation and exclusiveness, is the principle of human progress. The Gentile Tyrian, ever under the stern and uncompromising polity of the Jewish theocracy, brought his tribute of skill and of splendid gifts to the great temple of Solomon; Ophir sent its gold, the far Indies their precious stones; and Candace, queen of Ethiopia, from the furthest ends of the earth, came on an acceptable pilgrimage to the shrine of the

Hebrews' God and the throne of the Hebrew king. All commerce, all agriculture, all art, laid their contributions upon the hallowed mount where God's home was builded of old. And thus to-day, in this vaster and immeasurably more wondrous temple—this great edifice of free civil and religious polity the strength and beauty of the wealthy Valley—shall all people and all tongues worship, and offer upon its altars their various offerings, of all the good gifts with which God has endowed them. Principally, these thronging thousands contribute of their physical strength. Canals are to be digged; railroads to be builded; all that mass of material improvements to be perfected, which is the dream of the practical statesmanship of our Union. These are needed before our land shall attain its ideal condition of a totality of natural gifts and forces, modified by human skill—ere it will yield the greatest possible amount of fruits to its people. And thus have long been pouring in the legions of a great industrial army, from Ireland, Germany, Norway, Sweden, Denmark, Holland; the men whose strong arms and laborious habits render them competent to execute precisely those masses of mere detail and drudgery so necessary to the broad schemes of the Anglo-American brain, but so distasteful to his preferences for mental labor, for organizing, for directing; for thinking, in short, that others may do. It is this long succession of immigrants which most singularly marks the wisdom of that mighty Hand which guides the fates of the Valley. The first generation furnishes laborers. But their children, half-children of the soil, and receiving the powerful impress of the invigorating new world, and of its active minds, at once rise upward and become farmers or mechanics; while the cohorts of the railroad and the scattered ranks of hired laborers are recruited from new arrivals.

Yet, again, the same over-ruling wisdom provided that this innumerable host of people, of strange manners and religion, would not find the portals of the Valley thrown open to them until the great pillars of its commonwealth—its religious and political forms—were powerfully and permanently adjusted. Not until the proper and distinctive Anglo-American forms of worship and of society were already received and vigorously in operation, did the foreign bands find room for the soles of their feet. Then, after the new people had grown large enough and strong enough for the action of the peculiar power of absorption and integration with itself which marks the Anglo-Saxon race, came the gradual influx of the strangers, pouring steadily in, fusing and disappearing within the ranks of the host already there.

Nearly four-fifths of the foreign population of our country has arrived upon our shores since 1830; and more than half of its total of three millions, since

1840 Yet how few are those who apprehend any danger to our nation or to its valuable traits or privileges, from this great transfusion of new blood! Who needs to doubt or to fear for our future? Many, at different times, have been terrified at the ruin supposed to await the land from the spread of Romanism and of its attendant civil despotisms among us. But how groundless an apprehension! When Jesuitism had the land all to itself, it was unable to keep it. Rome, unopposed, backed by the throne of France, aided by the subtlest diplomacy, the greatest generals, the wisest statesmen, long endeavored to retain her hold upon the soil—but in vain. And when she thus failed, is it for a moment to be supposed that she could succeed now? Instead of the scattered superstitious barbarians, herded into the priestly fold by the Catholic missionaries, and with but little more consciousness of why it was done than so many cattle would have had, they must now encounter a population ten thousand fold greater, intelligent, acute, trained in beliefs and—what is much more—in feelings, instincts and modes of thought and action expressly opposed or utterly foreign to them; large, broad modes of mental action which their little hierarchic formulas can neither contain nor cope with; the vivid force of that shrewd circumspect self-relfance which has been nurtured by the strong youth and toilsome adventurous manhood of the West; the unwearied, incessant, increasing flow of knowledge, of goodness, of purity, of intellectual force, supplied from so many thousands of fountains, in school-house, college, and church. Is it to be feared that such men as the Romanists will reduce the West beneath the sway of the Papacy? Shall we not rather ingulf and assimilate them, priests, churches, communicants and all? Can the Roman Bishop rule the huge and rapid waves of this great ocean of human life? It was only Christ whose word made the winds to cease and the sea to be calm;—even the apostle, essaying to pass to his Master, would have sunk for lack of faith;—and surely, surely these deceived apostles of a mistaken faith will quickly disappear beneath the swelling flood.

For my own part, I have no fear. It is true that once I spoke in the usual glowing terms, of the great battle of Armageddon that was to be fought in the Valley of the Mississippi, and of the dangers to which freedom was then to be exposed from the onslaughts and invasions of foreigners and Romanists. But study and observation have convinced me to the contrary. How frequent is the remark, even among Romanists themselves, that their church only keeps the immigrating generation! The first comers may themselves ever remain faithful and subservient sons of the church. But the attachment of their children is feeble and wavering; the grandchildren almost always lapse from their connection with it, and the fourth generation are commonly embosomed within some Protestant organization. No; Romanists will never change us. We shall assimilate them, and shall do good both to them and to ourselves in the process. The religious formulas of Europe can no more be established upon the soil of this country than could the structure of one of its mediæval despotisms be transported hither and maintained among us. Facts forbid such a belief; reason, forbids it; Faith, Hope, and Charity, all three, forbid it.

Let them come, therefore; there is room for them all, and we need them all. They will not defile or lower us; we shall purify and elevate them. They come into a purer atmosphere, upon a higher plane of life; their necessary and unavoidable movement will be upward. Even Mormonism, which occupies one of the outlying suburbs of the Valley of the Mississippi—Mormonism, one of the greatest if not the most important fact of our age and country—dark, debasing and fearful as its politics and morality may be—I believe to be a real step in advance for most of those who remove to its desert home. And it seems to me that few will fail to reach the same conclusion, who shall carefully consider whence these people come, what their characteristics and qualities are, what the new circumstances are in which they find themselves placed, and the fact that for the first time in their history or that of their ancestors, they are here brought into approximately true, healthy and legitimate relations with the earth and labor. For God's great earthly instrument for elevating man in the scale of social being is labor. Men must set out from earth, to reach heaven. He is the true son of Earth—the true Antæus; he gains new and ever greater strength by being dashed into rude forcible contact with her rugged bosom, and every rebound carries him further upward. And these Mormons, however isolated from our institutions, from the aids of our social, intellectual, religious influences, are at least starting from the right point. They are with few exceptions an industrious and even laborious people, frugal and honest and honorable within the important range of the minor practical ethics. Now God leaves none of his children alone; and thus we are in duty bound to hope and believe that in process of time old mother Earth, and their labor and industry and economy in dealing with her, will little by little lift them upward until at last they will come to the full and perfect stature of American Christian citizens. Therefore it is that I have not the least objection to have hundreds, thousands, and tens of thousands, flocking to the Great Salt Lake. Through whatever ill-favored or perilous phases, the movement must and will result in good.

Of all the various races whose blood mingles in the

Great Valley, or whose members inhabit it, one only remains hopelessly untamed, untamable, savage. The Indian alone defies the operation of the great principle of interfusion of bloods. Amidst the countless thousands of whites, or rather, just before their advancing line, he remains an isolated, solitary being. He stalks across the stage of thought or of history alone. "Indian file," we say; and it is singly, as we thus describe single physical movements, that we ever think of him, either in journeying, in character, or action. The Indian can never be civilized. He has not the faculties by which civilization lays hold upon a man to modify and to cultivate him. For we improve, through persistent patient labor, and through the affections. Were it not for the power and the habit of constant industry, were it not for the sweet fetters of love and duty to parents, family, children, friends, what would make you and me stronger or wiser, or better, or more useful—if we are so—from year to year? Scarcely would the united strength of religious obligation and of self-love avail to accomplish it without these balancing encircling forces. These supply us with the quiet incessant stimulus which holds us steadily, though with unperceived strength, to our destined line of labor. But these the solitary Indian scarcely feels at all; and, therefore, the Indian must perish. We cannot absorb him, cannot render him an integral part of our own

20

society. We drive him further westward, fight him, murder him with whisky. Our missionaries labor amongst his decreasing bands with praiseworthy perseverance, but with an utterly hopeless prospect. God's law is against him. He cannot enter into our laborious civilization, he cannot live amongst it; and he must needs disappear.

I need scarcely refer to the outlandish barbarism and self-sufficient brutality of the strange incursion of Chinamen into California. That distant State is no part nor outgrowth of the Valley of the Mississippi, except in a very indirect and distant sense; and if it were otherwise I could only say that perhaps this Chinese race has the least good and the most evil in it of any which might endeavor to unite with our own. But it is entirely improbable, and scarce possible that such a union should happen, in any measure whatever.

In thus recapitulating the admixture of races in the West, I must not omit to refer to the mingling of the eastern and southern Anglo-Americans with each other there, and with those of the northern half of the West. A quarter, almost, of the whole population of New England, has been drained out of it into new settlements. Her sons and daughters are ever moving westward, insomuch that whole villages may be found left with a strange over-proportion of elderly people in them. Over the mountains they go, teaching or trading, farming or preaching. The young maidens intermarry with the southerners or westerners, and the young men take to themselves wives of the daughters of the land. And thus are fused together the comparatively stiff and formal, though strong, practical, straightforward, acute and resolute qualities of the New Englander, with the fiery, impulsive generosity, the passionate fervor, the indolence, the semi-tropical ease, of the far South, or the broad, strong, open, hearty geniality, sometimes coarse, but always kind, of the more northern part of the West.

To speculate on future numerical totals would be lost time. There is no arithmetic of the future. Let us glance at data of a sort from which we can reason forward. Observe the material and physiological conditions for an improvable race, which are possessed by the people of the Valley.

A territory all but boundless; a climate and a soil exuberant beyond all measure, in geniality and richness; a means of internal communication unprecedented and unequalled in human history; resources for material wealth utterly incalculable; a freedom almost ideal, of thought, expression and action; a predominant hereditary blood the best in the world; a national training adapted to develop all the strongest and best powers of humanity; a gradual afflux of other races, so ordered and adjusted that the genial cheerfulness of one, the stern morality and strength of principle and shrewd practical energy of another, the gaiety and tireless industry of another, the lofty honor and daring bravery of another, shall all mingle together in the formation of one vast homogeneous race, a compound of many various human qualities—and thus form the truest representative man on earth. Look, lastly, at the various instrumentalities and institutions which human experience has elaborated or Divine wisdom has ordained, as best for communicating and increasing and diffusing knowledge, and goodness, and culture. Observe all this, and then say whether the nation of the great valley is not destined—so far as human foresight can determine—to become a controlling force in our own great commonwealth, a wise, and just, and strong, and good community, happy at home, honored by all, sanctified and blessed by God—the foremost and highest among the sons of men, the latest, noblest exposition of the magnificent symmetry and beauty and strength of a rightly cultured humanity?

No doubt the careful searcher may discern faults in the western character; eccentricity, extravagance, materialism, recklessness, insubordination. But these errors may be shown to be the necessary logical conclusions of the long series of actual premises; of the wild and dangerous training of this people, received while, as a people, yet in their early youth.

They are faults very like those of a great, overgrown boy; a creature often awkward, uncomfortable, even ridiculous, but who will speedily spread and harden into a stately and powerful man; faults of strongly growing and vigorous youth, such as will often, by a singularly small modification, become the main virtues of manhood. They need not discourage the admirer of the western character, any more than should the dust of the race-course on the garment of the victor distress his congratulating friends. It is not on this earth, it is true, that anything can be perfect, or can escape the small objections of the dilettante traveller, or come up to the rigid unpractical standard of that peculiarly ignorant man the theoretical moralist. Nor can the Great Valley nor its people. But when the circumstances are considered which have attended the growth of that people, and the results which it has achieved within these few years, the philanthropist, the statesman, the patriot will find very much greater cause to rejoice and be glad, than to lament and to fear.

So far as human foresight can discern, a future of marvellous grandeur and power awaits the Nation of the Valley. Its thronging, busy millions, masters of a wealth beyond counting, a nation well and wisely trained, pouring abroad, over all the world, by many channels, fabulous masses of rich products, and gathering in the various wealth of all the world in return, may well look forward to the day when they shall rule the destinies of all the nation—nay, it may be, of all the continent. And while it is thus the seat of a vast political dominion, it may likewise, with no less reason, aspire to stand among the nations, a beautiful and noble monument of richly-cultured intellect—of strong, deep love—of true and lovely Christian goodness. It may justly and hopefully aspire to become the first, loftiest, grandest example in all the long panorama of human history, of that grand and shapely thing which God would have every nation become: a fabric of beauty, strength and grace, far beyond any of the fanciful Utopias of philosophic schemers, or heathen or unchristian legislators; in truth and soberness, the crown and glory of the whole earth.

What dispensations the mysterious Governor of nations may have reserved for it, we know not. We must wait for, and submit to the decrees of God; even should he have determined that the whole vast Valley, like that dimly-fabled island of Atlantis, of which ancient geographers seem to speak, shall sink suddenly away, and give place to the dreary, barren fields of the ocean. Of this we know not; of such things we cannot reason. There seems to be but one single event whose form we can imagine to see within the dim shadows of the coming years; but one single occurrence of which we may speak in anticipation, and to which we need to look with any fears, either for its own ugly lineaments, or the baleful blight which it may possibly be fated to cast over the future fortunes of the multitudes in the Valley.

This is that hateful thing, whose name is to-day unfilially and impiously heard ever and anon, muttered in secret treason, or howled in the frenzy of public treason, by fools or traitors, North and South —the vile name of disunion. Let this Union be dissolved, and farewell to all those fair dreams which my feeble words have so imperfectly and briefly striven to paint. If the Union is dissolved, no human power will ever reconstruct it; farewell to these United States, and, with them, to our grand possessions of patriotic memories; to the hard-fought Revolution; to the wise counsels of Washington; the inspiring oratory of so many heaven-gifted speakers; to the warlike fame of so many glorious soldiers; to the undying wisdom of Jefferson and of Hamilton, and so many more statesmen and legislators; to all the historic treasures of the nation. For, I pray you, which of the mobs of little, feeble, squabbling States —"Sovereign States," forsooth!—would own them all? Or by what rule should a dividend of them be made? or what distribution would be consented to?

Is it indeed true that our nation cannot last one century? Is our cohesive power already destroyed?

Are we already rotten? Are our forbearance, our kindness, our brotherly love, so soon exhausted? Have we so quickly squandered our inheritance of traditions, of common blood, of common suffering and labor, of common interest, of common glory and prosperity, and must we so soon be scattered into a contemptible chaos of amorphous, disintegrated, strengthless, political atoms?

I cannot believe it. I have heard—I still hear—all the miserable outcries of the villain horde that would do this devil's work. I have not patience, nor is it necessary to recite them here. But I still have faith unshaken in the trustworthiness of the American people—in their ability, with God's help, to govern themselves. I still believe that they see and feel the unimaginable grandeur and beauty of the great and holy office which God has set them to fill—the office of demonstrating the excellency of intelligent and sanctified freedom in a nation; that they recognize and contemn the paltry selfishness of the dogs that yelp against the fair edifice of our republic; and that they will speedily send them howling to their dens, or disappointed to their graves.

There may be many perils along our path—much suffering in store for us. Perhaps the seal must be dipped in blood that is still to be set to the record of our final and assured prosperity as a nation. But even though it be thus, shall we for that turn shamefully back from the great work that is set before us to do? Shall we ignobly refuse to do the office to which God has set us apart, in the sight of all the world? I say, no. I am yet to be forced to believe that our people are so fallen backward toward a dark barbarism as to acquiesce in such an abject abnegation; and I am yet to be forced to believe that the God of our fathers has so utterly rejected us that in his hot anger he will thus cast us out and leave us a jest and a scoff among the crowned tyrants of the earth. I believe better things. I believe that he will still lead us, as he has thus far led us, along the path toward the glorious object of our natural life; I believe that better days will come; and that in the sunshine of prosperity, and our good God still leading us, we shall in future years rise still higher and more gloriously in the scale of being; that the voice of our glory and our rejoicing shall, in louder and still louder tones, announce its wondrous lesson to the nations, proclaiming liberty throughout all the land, even unto all the inhabitants thereof.

THE END.

www.ingramcontent.com/pod-product-compliance
Lightning Source LLC
LaVergne TN
LVHW021122110826
845150LV00005B/918

* 9 7 8 1 4 2 5 5 5 1 4 7 6 *